THOMAS AQUINAS

Commentary on
Aristotle's *Politics*

Thomas Aquinas

Commentary on Aristotle's *Politics*

Translated by
Richard J. Regan

Hackett Publishing Company, Inc.
Indianapolis/Cambridge

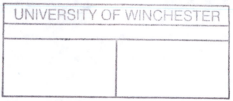
Copyright © 2007 by Hackett Publishing Company, Inc.

10 09 08 07   1 2 3 4 5 6 7

For further information, please address
  Hackett Publishing Company, Inc.
  P.O. Box 44937
  Indianapolis, IN 46244–0937

  www.hackettpublishing.com

Cover design by Listenberger Design Associates
Interior design by Elizabeth Wilson
Composition by Professional Book Compositors
Printed at Edwards Brothers, Inc.

Library of Congress Cataloging-in-Publication Data

Thomas, Aquinas, Saint, 1225?–1274.
  Commentary on Aristotle's Politics / Thomas Aquinas ; translated by Richard
J. Regan.
    p. cm.
  Includes indexes.
  ISBN-13: 978-0-87220-870-4 (cloth)
  ISBN-13: 978-0-87220-869-8 (pbk.)
  1. Aristotle. Politics.   2. Political science—Early works to 1800.
I. Regan, Richard J.   II. Title.
  JC71.A7T46 2007
  320.01'1—dc22
                                          2006031172

The paper used in this publication meets the minimum requirements of
American National Standard for Information Sciences—
Permanence of Paper for Printed Library Materials,
ANSI Z39.48–1984.

Contents

Preface

In the 13th century of the Common Era, the translation of Aristotle's *Politics* into Latin made it available to the Latin-based scholars of the West. In fact, there were two translations. The first is an incomplete translation (only Book I and most of Book II). The second is a complete translation (Books I–VIII). William of Moerbeke was the author of the second and possibly, or probably, the author of the first. Aquinas undoubtedly relied on the complete translation for his incomplete commentary (Books I, II, and III up to the end of chapter 6). It is unlikely that Aquinas relied at all on the incomplete translation and in any case could not have relied on it for the text of the final chapters of Book II and the first chapters of Book III. The second translation would not have been available to Aquinas much or at all before 1260, which is the likely date for Moerbeke's complete translation. Thus, the date for Aquinas' composition of his commentary is almost certainly after that date and probably during his second sojourn in Paris (1268–1272). I have translated the definitive Leonine edition of the *Commentary on the Politics* (Thomas Aquinas, *Opera Omnia*, vol. 48 [Rome: Dominican Friars of Santa Sabina, 1971]). That edition includes the relevant texts of the *Politics* from Moerbeke's second (complete) translation.

The relevant Latin text of Aristotle has not been easy to translate. Aristotle's style is famously elliptical, and Moerbeke's Latin, whether by design or accident, is the same. For example, the text sometimes omits main verbs, prepositions are sometimes distant from (and after) their objects, and relative clauses oddly placed. Moerbeke's rough Latin style contrasts sharply with Aquinas', and I think that Aquinas may have had almost as much difficulty reading it as I do. I do not note differences between the Latin and Greek texts of Aristotle, except when I deem them important and relevant to Aquinas' commentary. When alternate readings of the Latin text are possible, I have generally read the text so as to be in accord with Aquinas' commentary, but I footnote the other possibility when it reflects the usual reading of the Greek text. In the few cases in which I have been unable to read a text the way Aquinas does, I translate it as I read it and footnote the difference.

I have relied principally on C.D.C. Reeve's faithful translation of the Greek text (Aristotle, *Politics* [Indianapolis: Hackett Publishing Co., 1998]).

I have also consulted T.A. Sinclair's translation of the Greek text (Baltimore: Penguin, 1962). I have not commented on the text of Aristotle. The reader, however, may consult Reeve's introduction, notes, glossary, and bibliography; Trevor J. Saunders' translation and commentary (*Aristotle Politics:* Books I and II [Oxford: Clarendon, 1995]); and Richard Robinson's translation and commentary (*Aristotle Politics:* Books III and IV [Oxford: Clarendon, 1995]).

The chapter divisions of the *Politics* and cited works of Aristotle are those of Aquinas in this and his other commentaries, not the customary divisions of the text of Aristotle. (I have, however, supplied the relevant Bekker citations if the reader wishes to compare the Moerbeke translation with Aristotle's text or other translations.) The paragraphs of the text of Aristotle in each chapter are numbered sequentially and correspond to the order of Aquinas' commentary on the text. The same numbers, in bold type, mark off the corresponding divisions in the commentary. His citations of the *Politics* up to Book III, chapter 6, are incorporated into the text of the commentary in brackets. Other references to the *Politics* are footnoted.

I have attempted no commentary on Aquinas', but several general observations may be in order. First, Aquinas indicates a good, if occasionally faulty, understanding of the ancient Greek world. Second, he understands the basic arguments of Aristotle very well. Third, he clarifies and systematizes the thought of Aristotle, perhaps more than the elliptical text justifies. Aquinas sticks to explanation of the text but occasionally expands on it (e.g., on moneymaking) or qualifies it (e.g., on slavery).

This is, to my knowledge, the first English translation of all of Aquinas' commentary on the *Politics*. It also has the incidental value of making part of Moerbeke's translation of the *Politics* available and accessible to scholars.

Finally, I wish especially to thank Arthur Madigan, professor of philosophy at Boston College, for his careful reading and scholarly critique of the manuscript.

Richard J. Regan
Bronx, NY

Abbreviations

chap., chaps.	chapter, chapters
Cor.	Corinthians
Eccl.	Ecclesiastes
Gen.	Genesis
n., nn.	paragraph number, numbers
Prov.	Proverbs
Sam.	Samuel
Sir.	Sirach

Prologue

As Aristotle teaches in the *Physics*,[1] skills imitate nature. And this is because actions and effects are related as their sources are related to one another. But the source of things produced by skills is the human intellect, which is similarly derived from the divine intellect, and the divine intellect is the source of natural things. And so skillful actions necessarily imitate natural actions, and artifacts imitate things in nature. For if any teacher of a skill were to produce skillful work, the pupil learning the skill from him would need to pay attention to the teacher's activity, so that the pupil would also perform the task in the way he does. And so the human intellect, which derives its intelligible light from the divine intellect, needs to be formed by examining the things produced by nature so as to act similarly regarding the things it produces. And so Aristotle says that if skills were to produce things of nature, they would act in the same way that nature does, and conversely, if nature were to produce artifacts, it would produce them in the same way that skills do.[2]

But nature does not complete the things that belong to skills; it only prepares particular sources and offers craftsmen a model for acting in a certain way. And skills can indeed examine things of nature and use them to accomplish the skills' proper action but cannot accomplish things of nature. And so it is clear that human reason regarding things of nature is only cognitive, but human reason regarding artifacts is both cognitive and causative. And so human sciences, which concern natural things, are necessarily theoretical, while human sciences about things produced by human beings are necessarily practical, or active, by imitating nature.

And nature in its activity goes from simple things to composite things, so that what is most composite in the things produced by natural activity is complete and whole and the end of other things, as is evident in every whole in relation to its parts. And so also the practical reason of human beings goes from simple things to composite things, from incomplete things to complete things, as it were.

And since human reason can dispose both the things that human beings use and human beings themselves, who are governed by reason, it

---

1. *Physics* II, 4 (194a21–23) and 13 (199a15–16).
2. Ibid. II, 3 (199a12–15).

1

proceeds in both cases from simple things to composite things. Regarding things that human beings use, for example, human beings build ships out of timber, and houses out of stones and wood. And regarding human beings themselves, for example, human reason directs a number of human beings to form a particular association. And since there are indeed different grades and orders of these associations, the ultimate association is the political community directed to things self-sufficient for human life. And so the political community is the most perfect human association. And since the things that human beings use are ordered to human beings as the things' end, which is superior to the means, so the whole that is the political community is superior to all the other wholes that human reason can know or constitute.

Therefore, from the things I have said about political instruction that Aristotle gives in this work, we can understand four things. First, indeed, that we need such knowledge, since we need to teach everything that reason can know for the perfection of human wisdom called philosophy. Therefore, since the whole that is the political community is subject to the judgment of reason, it was necessary for a complete philosophy to give instruction about the political community, instruction called politics (i.e., political science).

Second, we can understand what kind of science this is. For we distinguish practical from theoretical sciences in that the latter are directed only to the knowledge of truth, while the former are directed to action. Therefore, politics is necessarily included in practical philosophy, since the political community is a whole, and human reason both knows it and acts regarding it. Moreover, reason does some things by making them, by action that extends to external matter, and this belongs strictly to skills called mechanical (e.g., those of craftsmen, shipbuilders, and the like). And reason does other things by action that remains in the one acting (e.g., deliberating, choosing, willing, and the like), and such things belong to moral science. Therefore, it is evident that political science, which considers the direction of human beings, is included in the sciences about human action (i.e., moral sciences) and not in the sciences about making things (i.e., mechanical skills).

Third, we can understand the worthiness and relation of politics to all the other practical sciences. For the political community is the supreme association that human reason can constitute, since all other associations are related to the political community. Moreover, all the wholes constituted by mechanical skills from things accessible to use by human beings are ordered to human beings as the things' end. Therefore, if a superior science concerns what is more excellent and complete, politics is necessarily superior and architectonic to all other practical sciences, since politics considers the ultimate and complete good regarding human affairs. And so Aristotle says in the *Ethics* that the philosophy regarding human affairs is completed in politics.[3]

Fourth, we can from the aforementioned things understand the method and order of political science. For theoretical sciences contemplating about a whole consider its parts and sources and so arrive at knowledge about it by showing the things it undergoes and the things it does. Just so, political science, considering the sources and parts of the political community, teaches knowledge about it and shows its parts, the things it undergoes, and the things it does. Moreover, political science, since it is practical, shows how individual things can be accomplished, something necessary in any practical science.

---

3 *Ethics* X, 16 (1181b14–15).

Book I

Chapter 1
Political Community

Text (1252a1–1253a38)

1.   We observe that every political community is a human association and instituted for the sake of obtaining some good, since all human beings do things for the sake of obtaining something that seems good to them. Therefore, it is clear that every human association seeks some good.

2.   And the association that is supreme and includes all other associations is the absolutely supreme good. And we call this association the political community and political society.

3.   Therefore, those who think that the statesman, the king, the household manager, and the master of slaves are the same err.

4.   For they think that associations differ only in size, not specifically. For example, they suppose that the fathers of families rule few persons, household managers more persons, and statesmen and kings still more persons, as if there were no difference between a large household and a small political community, or between political and monarchical rule. Monarchy is when one man rules, and political rule is when many rule and are ruled in turn according to the prescriptions of political science.

5.   The latter position is false. And this will be evident to those examining the position according to our usual method. For, as we need to divide other complex things into simple things, since the smallest things are parts of the whole, so also do we need to analyze the political community and its components. In such consideration, we shall also see how they differ from one another, and if we can understand anything systematic about the things mentioned. For if one has examined things as they developed in the beginning, one will consider what is best in these and other things.

6.   Therefore, we first need to unite things that cannot exist separately (e.g., a man and a woman for the purpose of reproduction). And it is not

4

by choice but by nature that human beings, like plants and other animals, seek to reproduce their kind.

7. And the ruler and the ruled are by nature united for their welfare. For those who can intellectually foresee things are by nature rulers and masters, and those who can physically do things are by nature subjects and slaves. And so the same thing benefits masters and slaves.

8. Therefore, women and slaves are by nature different. For nature, unlike the Delphic smiths who niggardly produced a single knife for all kinds of use, produces each instrument for a particular purpose. For each instrument, serving only one purpose, will then do the best work.

9. But women and slaves have the same status in foreign [non-Greek] societies.

10. This is because they have no ruler by nature. Rather, the society consists of slaves, male and female, on account of which the poets say that Greeks rightly rule over foreigners, as if foreigners [non-Greeks] and slaves are by nature the same.

11. Therefore, it was out of the two associations of men and women and of master and slaves that the first household arose. And the poet Hesiod rightly said that the first household consists of a wife and an ox for plowing, since the ox is the poor man's slave.

12. Therefore, this daily association constituted by nature is the household, whose members Charondas calls table companions, and Epimenides of Crete calls hearth companions.

13. And out of many households, the first association is the village, which is formed to satisfy more than daily needs.

14. And the village especially seems by nature to be the neighborhood of households, as sons and grandsons, whom some call members of a clan, establish their own households.

15. And so kings were the first rulers of political communities, and kings rule some peoples even now. For the most senior man rules over every household. And so also do the most senior men rule over neighborhoods because of blood relationships. And Homer says the same: "Each man lays down laws for his wives and children." (For people were dispersed and dwelt thus in ancient times.)

16. And so people say that a king even rules over all the gods, as ancient kings ruled over human beings, and indeed some kings still do. And as human beings imagine the forms of the gods to be like their own, so also do they imagine the lives of the gods to be like their own.

17. And the perfect association formed out of several villages is the political community, now complete, having a self-sufficient end, as we may properly say. Therefore, the political community was instituted for the sake of protecting life and exists to promote the good life.

18.   Therefore, every political community exists by nature, just like the first associations. For the political community is the end of the other associations, and the end is by nature. For we say that a nature belongs to each thing (e.g., human beings, horses, houses) as the thing completely comes to be.

19.   Moreover, the best in anything is its end and that for the sake of which it exists, and the end and best thing is self-sufficiency.

20.   Therefore, it is evident from these things that the political community exists by nature, and that human beings are by nature political animals. And those who live outside a political community because of their nature and not by misfortune are either wicked or superhuman, the wicked like those condemned by Homer as unsocial, lawless, and criminal. For such persons are by their nature also bent on war, being free of restraint like birds in flight.

21.   And human beings are clearly political animals more than bees and other animals living in groups are. For nature does nothing in vain, as people say, and only human beings, in contrast with other animals, use speech. Therefore, expressions of sadness and pleasure are signs and so also belong to other animals. For the nature of other animals is such as to have sense experiences of sadness and pleasure and to signify these experiences to one another. But speech indicates what is useful or harmful, and so also what is just or unjust. For, strictly speaking, it belongs to human beings alone, in contrast with other animals, to perceive good and evil, just and unjust, and the like. And communicating these perceptions produces households and political communities.

22.   And the political community has priority over the household and every individual, since the whole as such necessarily has priority over the parts. For example, take away the whole body, and neither hands nor feet will exist (except equivocally, as one might speak of the hands or feet of a statue). For such parts will have been destroyed with the body, since all things are defined by their activity and power. Therefore, we should say that things no longer such-and-such are only equivocally the same. And so it is clear that the political community by nature also has priority over the individual. For if separate individuals are not self-sufficient, they will be related to the whole in the same way as the other parts. Things incapable of participating in a political community and things in no need of it because of their self-sufficiency are not parts of it. And so those who live outside political communities are either beasts or gods.

23.   Therefore, nature impels all human beings toward such an association. And the first one to institute the political community conferred the greatest benefits. For, as human beings reaching perfection are the best of all animals, so also human beings divorced from law and justice are the

worst, since injustice with weapons is the most savage. Human beings in possession of weapons are endowed with prudence and virtue, which they can especially use for contrary things. And so human beings without true virtue are the most criminal and wildest animals and the worst offenders in sexual license and gluttony. But justice is a political matter, since right consists of the order of the political association, and right is the standard of justice.

Comment

1.   After the comments in the Prologue, therefore, we should note that Aristotle gives an introduction to Book I, in which he indicates the aim of political science, and then goes on to demonstrate what he proposes [chap. 2]. Concerning the first, he does two things. First, he shows the worthiness of the political community, which is the object of political science, from the political community's end. Second, he shows the relation of the political community to other associations [3]. Regarding the first, he aims to prove two things. The first is that the political community is directed to some good as its end. The second is that the good to which the political community is directed is the supreme human good [2].

Regarding the first, he proposes the following argument: Every association is established for the sake of some good. But every political community is an association, as we clearly see. Therefore, every political community is established for the sake of some good. Therefore, because the minor premise is obvious, he proves the major premise as follows. All human beings do whatever they do for the sake of something that seems good, whether the thing be truly good or not. But human activity establishes every association. Therefore, all associations seek (i.e., aim at) some good as the association's end.

2.   Then he shows that the good to which the political community is directed is the supreme human good, by the following argument. If every association is directed to a good, the supreme association necessarily most seeks the supreme human good. For the relative importance of means necessarily depends on the relative importance of ends. And what he adds, that the political community includes all the other associations, makes clear which association is supreme.

For an association is a whole, and wholes are ordered so that one that includes another is superior. For example, the wall of a house is a whole, but the house is a superior whole, since the wall is included in the house. And the association that includes other associations is likewise superior. But the political community clearly includes all other associations, since households and villages are included in the political community, and so the political association is the supreme association. Therefore, the political community seeks the supreme human good, since it aims at the common good, which is superior to, and more god-like than, the good of an individual, as Aristotle says at the beginning of the *Ethics*.[1]

3.   Then he relates the political community to other associations, regarding which he does three things. First, he posits the false opinion of some thinkers. Second, he shows how we can demonstrate the falsity of this opinion [5]. Third, in accord with the indicated method, he proposes the true relation of the political community to other associations [6]. Regarding the first, he does two things. First, he posits the false opinion. Second, he explains it and introduces the argument of those who propose it [4].

Regarding the first, we should note that two kinds of association are obvious, namely, the political community and the household. And the political community has two kinds of regime, namely, the political and the monarchical. A monarchical regime is one in which the ruler has complete power, and a political regime is one in which the ruler has coercive power in accord with the particular laws of the political community. And similarly, a household has two kinds of regime, namely, the managerial and the master–slave. We call the one who possesses slaves the master, and we call the one who procures or dispenses the goods of a family the manager. And so a master–slave regime is one in which a master rules over slaves, and a managerial regime is one in which one person dispenses the goods that belong to the whole family, which includes both slaves and many free persons. Therefore, some thinkers have wrongly held that these regimes are entirely the same and do not differ.

4.   Then he posits their argument, as follows. Things that differ only quantitatively do not differ specifically, since a quantitative difference does not distinguish species. But the household and the political community differ only in size, which they then demonstrated.

For if the ruled association should consist of few people, as in a small household, we call the ruler the father of a family, and his ruling power despotic. And if the ruled association should consist of many people, so as to contain both slaves and many free persons, we call the ruler the household manager. And if the ruled association should consist of still more persons (e.g., both those belonging to individual households and those belonging to a political community), then we call the regime political or monarchical. And some said that a household differed from a political community only in size, so that a big household is a small city, and a small city a big household. And what follows will make clear that this is false.

1. *Ethics* I, 2 (1094b9–10).

They similarly held that political and monarchical regimes differ only in size. For when the ruler rules absolutely and regarding everything, we call the regime monarchical. And when the ruler rules according to scientific rules (i.e., according to laws established by political science), the regime is political. That is to say, the ruler partially rules, namely, regarding things subject to his power, and is partially ruled, insofar as he is subject to the law. And they concluded from all these things that all the aforementioned regimes, some of which belong to the political community, and some to the household, do not differ specifically.

5.   Then he shows the way to demonstrate the falsity of the aforementioned opinion, saying that the assertions are false. This will be evident if one should wish to attend to the matter in the proposed way (i.e., by the skill in considering such things that he will now propose). And the way of this skill is as follows. As in other things, in order to know a whole, we need to divide composite things into simple things (i.e., undivided things that are the smallest parts of the whole). For example, in order to know words, we need to divide them into letters, and in order to know a composite natural material substance, we need to divide it into its elements. Just so, if we should consider the elements out of which the political community is composed, we shall be better enabled to see what each of the aforementioned regimes is in itself, how they differ from one another, and whether we can systematically consider the particulars of each. For in all things, we perceive that one who examines things insofar as they originate from their sources will be best able to contemplate the truth regarding the things. And as in other things, so also is this true in the things that we are considering.

And regarding these words of Aristotle, we should, in order to know complex things, consider that we need first to analyze them, namely, divide them into their elements. Afterwards, however, the synthetic process is necessary in order to judge from the elementary sources, now known, about the effects the sources cause.

6.   Then, according to the aforementioned method, he proposes the true relation of other associations to the political community, and he does two things in this regard. First, he treats of the other associations subordinate to the political community. Second, he treats of the association of the political community itself [17]. Regarding the first, he does three things. First, he explains the association of one person to another. Second, he explains the association of the household, which includes different associations of persons [11]. Third, he explains the association of the village, which includes many households [13]. Concerning the first, he does two things. First, he explains two personal associations. Second, he relates them to each other [8].

And he posits the association of man and woman as the first association of persons. And, because we need to divide the political community into its smallest parts, he says that we need to affirm that the first union is one of persons who cannot exist without each other, namely, the union of man and woman. For such union is for the sake of reproducing both men and women. And it is clear from this that they cannot survive or exist without each other.

But he shows why this union is first by what he adds: "not by choice." We should consider here that human beings have something proper to them, namely, reason, by which it belongs to them to act by deliberation and choice. And human beings also have something common to them and other things, and such is the power of reproduction. Therefore, the latter does not belong to them by their choice, that is, by their reason choosing it, but belongs to them by an aspect common to them, other animals, and even plants. For all these things have a natural appetite to leave after them other things like themselves, so that reproduction specifically preserves what cannot be preserved the same numerically.

Therefore, there is such a natural appetite even in all the other natural things capable of passing away. But because living things, namely, plants and animals, also have a special way of reproducing, namely, by themselves, he specifically mentions plants and animals. For even in plants, there are male and female powers united in the same plant, although one or the other power is more abundant in this or that plant, namely, such that we imagine a plant to be always like a male and a female at the time of intercourse.

7.   Then he lays out the second association of persons, namely, that of ruler and subjects, and this association also arises from nature for their welfare. For it is the aim of nature both to reproduce things and to preserve them. And he shows that this happens among human beings by the association of ruler and subjects. For those who by power of intellect can foresee what things are appropriate for preservation (e.g., by procuring beneficial things and repelling harmful things) are by nature rulers and masters. And those who by their physical strength can execute what the wise have mentally foreseen are by nature subjects and slaves. And it is clear from this that the same thing, namely, that the ruler rules, and that subjects are subjects, helps to preserve both. For those who, because of their wisdom, can mentally foresee things would sometimes be unable to survive, since they lack the requisite physical powers, unless they were to have slaves to execute their plans. Nor would those who abound in physical powers be able to be preserved unless the practical wisdom of another were to rule over them.

8.   Then he relates the aforementioned associations to each another. First, he relates them to each other as they actually are. Second, he refutes

an error [9]. Therefore, he first infers from what he has said that women and slaves are different by nature. For nature disposes women to beget offspring from men, but women are not physically strong, which slaves need to be. And so the two aforementioned associations differ from each other. And he assigns the reasons for the aforementioned difference in that nature does not make things the way in which the Delphian smiths made brazen (i.e., metallic) knives for the poor. For the Delphians made certain knives designed to serve many purposes (e.g., one and the same knife to cut, sharpen, and do like things). And they did this for the sake of the poor, who could not afford to have many knives. But nature does not work to direct one thing to different functions. Rather, it assigns one thing to one function. And so nature assigns women to beget offspring, not to be slaves. For all things are best done when one thing serves only one task, not many tasks.

But we should understand this when there would be an obstacle in one or the other of two tasks to which the same instrument was assigned, as, for example, if it were often necessary to perform both tasks simultaneously. On the other hand, if different tasks should be performed successively, accommodating the same instrument to accomplish several tasks raises no obstacle. And so also the tongue is compatible with two activities of nature, namely, taste and speech, as Aristotle says in the *De anima*,[2] since these two activities do not conflict with one another at the same time.

9.　　Then he refutes the contrary error. First, he explains the error. Second, he shows the reason for the error [10]. Therefore, he says first that foreigners [non-Greeks] consider women and slaves to be of the same rank, as it were, since foreigners treat women as if they were slaves.

But there can be doubt here about who are called foreigners. For some call all those who do not understand the same language foreigners. And so also the Apostle in 1 Cor. 14:11 says: "If I do not know the meaning of words, I shall be a foreigner to the speaker, and the speaker a foreigner to me." And others seem to call those who have no written language corresponding to their dialect foreigners. And so also people say that Bede introduced literary skills into the English language so that the English people would not be considered foreigners.[3] And to others, it seems that foreigners are those who are not ruled by any public laws. And all these things approach the truth in a way.

For we understand the Greek word for non-Greek [*barbaros*] to mean something foreign, and we can call human beings foreigners either

---

2. *De anima* II, 18 (420b17–18).

3. The Leonine editors have not found the source.

absolutely or in relation to someone. Those who lack reason, by which we define human beings, seem absolutely foreign to the human race, and so we call those who lack reason foreigners in an absolute sense. They lack reason either because they happen to live in a climate so intemperate that it causes most of them to be dim-witted, or because there is an evil custom in certain lands whereby human beings are rendered irrational and brutish, as it were. And it clearly comes from the power of reason that reasonable laws govern human beings, and that human beings are practiced in the art of writing. And so the fact that human beings do not establish laws, or establish unreasonable laws, and the fact that some peoples have no literary practices are signs that appropriately manifest barbarism.

But we call a human being a foreigner in relation to another when the one does not communicate with the other. And nature especially constitutes human beings to communicate with one another by speech. And so we can call those who do not understand one another's speech foreigners in relation to one another. But Aristotle is speaking here about those who are foreigners absolutely.

10.   Then he assigns the reason for the aforementioned error, saying that it is because there is no rule according to nature among foreigners. For he has said before that the ruler according to nature is one who can mentally foresee things, and the slave is one who can physically execute the things [7]. But most foreigners are physically strong and mentally weak. And so there cannot be among them a natural order of ruling and being ruled. But there is among them an association of male and female slaves (i.e., they commonly use female slaves, namely, women, and male slaves). And because there is by nature rule among those in whom reason abounds and not among foreigners, the poets say that it is fitting that Greeks, who were endowed with wisdom, rule over foreigners. That is as if to say that being a foreigner is the same as being a slave. And when the converse is true, perversion and disorder result in the world, as Solomon says in Eccl. 10:7: "I saw slaves on horses and rulers walking on foot like slaves."

11.   Then he explains the household association, which is constituted from several personal associations. And in this regard, he does three things. First, he shows of what things such an association consists. Second, he shows why it exists [12]. Third, he shows how members of this association are called [12]. Therefore, he first says that the household is constituted out of the two aforementioned personal associations, one for reproduction, and the other for well-being. For the household necessarily includes man and woman, master and slaves. And so we call this household the first such, since a household also has another personal association, namely, of fathers and sons, which the first association causes. And

so the first two associations are basic. And to show this, he introduces the words of the poet Hesiod, who said that a household has three things: the master who rules, a woman, and an ox for plowing. For an ox substitutes for a slave in a poor household, since human beings use oxen to perform tasks in the same way that they use slaves.

12.   Then he shows to what the household association is ordered. We should here consider that every human association regards some activities. And some human activities are done everyday (e.g., eating, warming oneself at the fire, and the like), but some things are not done everyday (e.g., buying and selling, waging war, and the like). But it is natural for human beings to associate with and help one another in both kinds of activity. And so he says that the household is simply an association constituted by nature for everyday life (i.e., activities that have to be performed daily). And he demonstrates this by the use of words. For example, one Charondas calls members of a household tablemates, partakers of the same food, as it were, since they share in the meal. And one Epimenides, a Cretan, calls members of a household hearth-mates, partakers of the same heat, as it were, since they are seated around the same fire.

13.   Then he explains a third association, namely, the village. And he first shows of what things this association is constituted, and why it exists. Second, he shows that this association is natural [14]. Therefore, he says first that we call the first association of many households a village, and we call a village the first association in order to distinguish it from the second association (i.e., the political community). But the village is not established for daily living, as he says that the household association is, but for needs that do not occur every day. For fellow villagers do not associate with one another in the everyday activities in which fellow members of the same household associate with one another (e.g., eating, being seated around the same fire, and the like). Rather, they associate with one another in some external activities that do not happen every day.

14.   Then he shows that the association of the village is natural. And he first demonstrates his assertion by an argument. Second, he presents certain indications [15]. Therefore, he says first that the neighborhood of households (i.e., the village) seems to be most in accord with nature. For nothing is more natural than the propagation of many animals from one, and this results in a neighborhood of households. For some call those inhabiting neighboring households clansmen, children (i.e., sons), and children of children (i.e., grandsons). In this way, we understand that a neighborhood of households arises first from the fact that sons and grandsons over several generations established separate households and dwelt close to one another. And so, since the population growth of offspring is natural, the association of the village is natural.

15.   Then he demonstrates the same conclusion by indications, and he does so first by the things that we perceive regarding human beings. Second, he does so by the things that people said about the gods [16]. Therefore, he says first that, because multiple offspring resulted in neighborhoods of households, kings originally came to rule over every political community. And some peoples still have a king, although each individual political community does not have an individual king. And this is so because those subject to a king constitute political communities and peoples.

And how this evidence corresponds to the foregoing, he shows by what he adds, namely, that the most senior man rules over every household, just as the father of a family rules over his sons. And so it comes about that the senior kinsman also ruled over the whole neighborhood established by blood relatives because of this kinship, just as kings rule over political communities. And so Homer said that each man lays down laws for his wife and sons, just as kings lay down laws in political communities. And so this kind of rule went from households and villages to political communities, since different villages are like a city divided into several parts. And so human beings of old were dispersed into villages, not gathered into one city. Therefore, it is clear that the rule of a king over a political community or a people developed from the rule of the senior man in the household or village.

16.   Then he lays out another indication through what people used to say about the gods, saying that all peoples, because of the things he mentioned, used to say that a king ruled over their gods, and that Jupiter was that king. And so some kings still rule over human beings, and kings ruled almost all the peoples of antiquity. And this was the first regime, as he will say later.[4] And as human beings liken the appearance of gods (i.e., the gods' forms) to themselves, thinking that gods are in the shape of certain human beings, so also human beings liken the lives of the gods (i.e., the gods' social intercourse) to themselves, thinking that the gods interact in the way that human beings see themselves interacting. Aristotle here refers in the customary way of the Platonists to gods as substances separate from matter but created by one supreme god, to which the pagans erroneously attributed the forms and interactions of human beings, as Aristotle says here.

17.   After Aristotle has explained the associations ordered to the political community, he here explains the very association of the political community. And he divides the exposition into three parts. First he shows what kind of association the political community is. Second, he shows that it is natural [18]. Third, he treats of the institution of the political community [23]. Regarding the first, he shows the condition of the political

---

4. *Politics* III, 15 (1286b8–11).

community in three respects. First, he shows of what things the political community is composed. For the political community is composed of many villages, just as the village is composed of many households.

Second, he says that the political community is the perfect association. And he proves this from the fact that every association of human beings collectively is directed to something necessary for life, and so the association directed to human beings having enough of such necessities will be the perfect association. And the political community is such an association. For it belongs to the nature of the political community that it contains all the things sufficient for human life as much as possible. And so it is composed of many villages, in one of which smiths practice their craft, in another of which weavers practice theirs, and so forth. And so the political community is evidently a perfect association.

Third, he shows to what the political community is ordered. For the political community was originally instituted for the sake of living, namely, that human beings adequately find the means to be able to live. But the political community's existence results in human beings living, and living well insofar as the laws of the political community direct the life of human beings to virtue.

18.   Then he shows that the association of the political community is natural, regarding which he does three things. First, he shows that the political community is natural. Second, he shows that human beings are by nature political animals [20]. Third, he shows what is prior by nature, whether the individual human being or the household or the political community [22]. Concerning the first, he gives two arguments, the first of which is as follows. The end of natural things is their nature. But the political community is the end of the aforementioned associations, and he has shown these associations to be natural. Therefore, the political community is also natural.

And he proves that the nature of natural things is their end, as follows. We say that the nature of each thing is what belongs to it when its coming-to-be is complete. For example, the nature of human beings is the nature that they possess after they have completely come to be, and the same is the case with horses and houses, although we understand the nature of a house by its form. But the disposition that something has when it has completely come to be is the end of all the things that precede its coming to be. Therefore, the end of the natural sources from which something comes to be is the thing's nature. And so the political community, since it comes to be from the aforementioned associations, which are natural, is itself natural.

19.   Then he proposes a second argument as follows. The best in each thing is the end and that for the sake of which something comes to be. But

being sufficient is the best. Therefore, being sufficient has the nature of end. And so the political community, since it is the association that is self-sufficient for human life, is itself the end of the aforementioned associations. And so it is clear that this second argument is introduced as proof of the minor premise of the first argument.

20. Then he shows that human beings are by nature political animals. And he first reaches this conclusion from the naturalness of the political community. Second, he proves it by the activity proper to human beings [21]. Regarding the first, he does two things. First, he demonstrates his assertion. Second, he eliminates a difficulty. Therefore, he first infers from the aforementioned things that the political community belongs to things that are in accord with nature. And since the political community is simply an organized group of human beings, it follows that the latter are by nature political animals.

But there could be a difficulty based on the fact that all things have the things natural to them, but not all human beings dwell in political communities. And so, in order to answer this difficulty, he then says that some human beings are not political because of misfortune (e.g., because they have been expelled from the political community) or because poverty forces them to cultivate fields or tend animals. And this is clearly not contrary to his assertion that human beings are by nature political, since other natural things are also sometimes lacking due to misfortune (e.g., when one loses a hand or is deprived of food). But human beings who are disposed to be unsocial because of their nature (e.g., by the corruption of human nature) are necessarily wicked. Or else they are superior to other human beings, namely, in that they have a nature more perfect than other human beings in general, so that they can be self-sufficient without human company. Such was the case with John the Baptist and Saint Anthony the Hermit.

He adds to this the saying of Homer, who condemned those who were solitary out of depravity. For he says that such individuals were unsocial because they were incapable of being bound by the bond of friendship, lawless because they were incapable of being bound under the rule of law, and criminal because they were incapable of being bound under the rule of reason. And those who are such by nature, being quarrelsome, as it were, and unrestrained, are at the same time necessarily disposed to be warlike. Just so, we see that solitary wild birds are predatory.

21. Then, from the proper activity of human beings, he proves that they, even more than bees or any animals living in groups, are political animals, as follows. For we say that nature does nothing in vain, since it always acts for a fixed end. And so nature, if it assigns to a thing something that is intrinsically directed to an end, gives that end to the thing. And we perceive that although some other animals have vocal power, human beings, alone among animals, have the power of speech. For although some animals utter human speech, they do not speak in the strict sense, since they do not understand what they are saying. Rather, they utter such sounds as a result of training.

And there is a difference between speech and pure vocal sound. For vocal sound signifies pain and pleasure, and so other emotions, such as anger and fear, all of which are directed to pleasure and pain, as Aristotle says in the *Ethics*.[5] And so vocal sound is given to other animals. And their nature allows them to experience sense pleasures and pains and to communicate the fact to one another by certain natural vocal sounds, as lions do by roaring, and dogs do by barking. And we substitute exclamations for such sounds. But human speech signifies useful and harmful things, and so just and unjust things, since justice and injustice consist of persons being treated justly or unjustly regarding useful and harmful things. And so speech is proper to human beings, since it is proper to them, in contrast with other animals, to have knowledge of good and evil, just and unjust, and the like, which speech can signify.

Nature gives speech to human beings, and speech is directed to human beings communicating with one another regarding the useful and the harmful, the just and the unjust, and the like. Therefore, since nature does nothing in vain, human beings by nature communicate with one another about these things. But communication about these things produces the household and the political community. Therefore, human beings are by nature domestic and political animals.

22. Then he shows from the foregoing that the political community is by nature prior to the household or an individual human being, by the following argument. The whole is necessarily prior to the parts, namely, in the rank of nature and perfection. But we should understand this regarding the matter, not the form, as the *Metaphysics* shows.[6] And he proves this as follows. When a whole human being has been destroyed, its feet and hands remain only in an equivocal sense, as we could call the hand of a statue a hand. And this is so because these parts are destroyed when the whole human being has been destroyed, and what has been destroyed does not retain the form by which we understand its definition. And so it is clear that the meaning of the word does not remain the same, and so we predicate the word equivocally.

And that the part is destroyed when the whole has been destroyed, he shows by the fact that every part is defined by its activity and the power by which it acts. For example, the definition of a foot is that it is the bodily

5. *Ethics* II, 5 (1105b21–25).

6. Aristotle, *Metaphysics* VII, 10 (1035b11–19).

member enabling a human being to walk. And so a foot that no longer has the power or activity of walking is not specifically the same as a foot that does, although we call the former a foot equivocally. And the same reasoning applies to other such parts that we call material parts, in the definition of which we posit the whole, just as we posit circle in the definition of semicircle, since a semicircle is one half of a circle. (But such is not the case with the parts of a species, which we posit in the definition of a whole, as, for example, we posit lines in the definition of a triangle.)

Therefore, the whole is clearly by nature prior to its material parts, although the parts are prior in the order of coming to be. But individual human beings are related to the whole political community like the parts of a human being to the human being. For, as hands and feet cannot exist apart from a human being, so neither is a human being self-sufficient for living apart from a political community. But if it should happen that someone is unable to participate in the society of a political community because of the individual's depravity, such a one is worse than a human being and a beast, as it were. And if someone should need nothing, being self-sufficient, as it were, and so should not be part of a political community, the individual is superior to human beings, for such a one is a kind of god, as it were. Therefore, we infer from the foregoing that the political community is by nature prior to an individual human being.

23.   Then he treats of the institution of the political community, inferring from the foregoing that all human beings have a natural drive for the association of the political community, just as they have for virtues. But as human beings acquire virtues by human activity, as he says in the *Ethics*,[7] so human endeavor establishes political communities. And the one who first established a political community brought the greatest benefits to human beings.

For human beings are the best of animals if they have the complete virtue to which nature inclines them. But human beings, if they should be without law and justice, are the worst of all animals. And he proves this as follows. The more weapons (i.e., instruments to do evil) that injustice has at its disposal, the crueler it is. And practical reason and virtue, which are intrinsically directed to good, belong to human beings by reason of their human nature. But human beings, when they are evil, use reason and virtue as weapons, so to speak, to do evil. For example, they cleverly plan various frauds, and, by abstaining from food and drink, become capable of enduring hunger and thirst so as to persevere longer in wickedness, and so forth. And so, regarding the corruption of their irascible appetite, human

---

7. *Ethics* II, 1 (1103a31–62).

beings without virtue, being cruel and without feeling, are most vicious and savage. And regarding the corruption of their concupiscible appetite, they are the worst offenders in sexual matters and gluttony.

But the political order brings human beings back to justice. And the fact that the Greeks call the order of the political community and the standard of justice by the same term, namely, right order, makes this clear. And so it is obvious that the one who established the political community kept human beings from being the worst and brought them to the condition of being the best in justice and virtues.

Chapter 2
Household and Slavery (1)

Text (1253b1–1254a17)

1.   Since it is evident of what parts the political community is composed, we need first to speak about the household, inasmuch as every political community is composed of households.

2.   And the household has parts from which it has also been established, and the complete household consists of slaves and free persons. But we should first study everything from its smallest parts, and the first, smallest parts of the household are master and slaves, husband and wife, and father and sons. Therefore, it will be necessary for us to consider what each of the three is, and what each should be. The first is despotic, the second marital, and the third reproductive, although the latter two have no exact name. And let us consider these three things that we mentioned.

3.   And there is a fourth part that seems to some to be household management and to others the most important part of it, and we should consider how it is disposed. I am speaking about the part called financial.

4.   And let us first speak about master and slave in order to see what is of necessary advantage, and if we could get to know about them better than people now suppose.

5.   For it seems to some that mastery involves a certain kind of knowledge, and that household management, mastery over slaves, and political and kingly rule are the same, as we said at the beginning. It seems to others that it is contrary to nature to be a master over slaves. For it is by law that

one person is a slave and another person free, but nature makes no such distinction. And so this rule is unjust and coercive.

6. Therefore, since property is part of the household, acquiring property is also part of household management. For one cannot live without the necessities of life. And as one will need suitable tools for specific crafts if one is to perform skillful work, so also one will need suitable instruments for household management.

7. Some instruments are nonliving things, and some living things, as, for example, the pilot of a ship needs both an inanimate rudder and a living lookout. For an assistant is used as an instrument in craftwork. So also, property is an instrument to sustain life and is of many kinds, and slaves are living property. And every assistant is an instrument superior to other instruments. For example, let us suppose that every instrument were able to perform its task at, or in anticipation of, our command, like the reputed statues of Daedalus or the tripods of Vulcan, which the poet says participate spontaneously in the contest of the gods. And let us further suppose that looms and lyres were to act automatically. Then master craftsmen would not need assistants, or masters slaves.

8. And things called tools produce things, but property is something useful for activity. For example, looms produce something else beyond their use, but we only use clothing and beds.

9. Moreover, since making and doing differ specifically, and both require instruments, the instruments need to have the same difference. And life is activity, not production. And so also slaves assist with things related to activity.

10. And we also speak of property as a part, for a part is both a part of something else and belongs absolutely to it. And property likewise belongs absolutely to its owner. And so the master is simply the master of the slave and does not belong to him. But the slave is the master's slave and completely belongs to him.

11. Therefore, these things have shown the nature and function of the slave. For any human being who belongs by nature to another and not to himself is by nature a slave. And any human being who is property or a slave belongs to another, and property is an instrument useful for activity and separate.

Comment

1. After Aristotle has laid out the introduction, in which he shows the condition and parts of the political community, he here goes on to treat of political science. First, he determines in the already indicated way the things that belong to the first parts of the political community. Second, he

determines things that belong to the political community itself [II, chap. 1]. Regarding the first, he does two things. First, he speaks about his aim. Second, he explains what he proposes [5]. Regarding the first, he does two things. First, he speaks about what things he intends to determine. Second, he indicates in what order he will do so [4]. Regarding the first, he does two things. First, he says that we should determine the things that belong to the household. Second, he enumerates the things that belong to the household [2].

Therefore, he says first that the foregoing things have made clear of what parts the political community consists. Because we need first to know the parts in order to know the whole, as he has maintained before [chap. 1, n. 5], and because every political community is composed of households as parts, we need first to speak of household management, which dispenses goods or governs the household.

2.   Then he enumerates the things that belong to the household. First, there are the things that belong to it as parts. Second, there are the things that belong to it as necessary for the parts [3]. Therefore, he says first that the parts of the household are the things out of which the household is constituted. And every household, that is, every domestic family, if it should be complete, consists of slaves and free persons. And he says *complete* because oxen take the place of slaves in households of the poor, as he has said before [chap. 1, n. 11]. And we should first consider in fewer and simpler things whatever we can consider in many things, in order to facilitate learning. Therefore, we should say that the first and smallest parts of the household are three combinations: masters and slaves, husbands and wives, and fathers and sons. And the third combination arises out of the second, and so he passes over the third. And so we should consider what each of the three is.

And so he posits names of these combinations. And he says that we call the combination of master and slave despotic (i.e., one in which the master has absolute authority). And the combination of man and woman had no name in his time, but he calls it marital, and we call it matrimonial. Similarly, the third combination of father and sons had no name, but he calls it reproductive (i.e., productive of sons).

3.   Then he posits a fourth part that pertains to the necessities of a household, saying that there is another part of household management called financial (i.e., pecuniary). And this seems to some to be the entire household management and to others the most important part of it, since dispensing household goods consists most of acquiring and preserving capital. And we should consider how this part is disposed.

4.   Then he says in what order we should deal with these things, saying that we should speak first about master and slave. This consideration will

be useful for two things. First, it will be useful in order to be able to know what is advantageous in such things, namely, for exercising mastery over slaves. Second, it avails for knowledge, so that we can thereby understand matters better than what ancient peoples thought about mastery and slavery. 5.   Then he explains the things that he has proposed and divides this consideration into two parts. In the first, he determines about the combination of master and slave. In the second, he determines about the other two combinations [chap. 10]. He divides the first part into two parts. In the first, he determines about the combination of master and slave, and in the second, he determines about another part of household management (i.e., the financial or proprietary), since the slave is a kind of property [chap. 6].

Regarding the master-slave combination, he does two things. First, he reports the opinions of certain thinkers about mastery and slavery. Second, he determines the truth about the opinions [6]. Regarding the first, he considers two opinions. One holds that mastery (i.e., absolute control) involves a kind of knowledge whereby one knows how to rule over slaves. And this opinion further holds that such mastery is the same as household management, whereby one knows how to govern a household, and political and kingly rule, whereby one knows how to rule over a political community, as he said in the introduction [chap. 1, nn. 3–4]. The second opinion holds that possessing slaves is contrary to nature, that only laws direct that some human beings be slaves, and other human beings free, and that there is by nature no difference between slaves and free persons. And so they further argued that it is unjust for some to be slaves, since it is force that brings it about that some human beings subject others to themselves as slaves.

6.   Then he determines the truth about mastery and slavery. First, he determines the nature of slavery. Second, he examines the foregoing opinions [chap. 3]. Regarding the nature of slavery, he does two things. First, he sets down some things necessary in order to know the nature of slavery. Second, he infers from the foregoing the definition of slavery [11].

Regarding the things necessary to know the nature of slavery, he posits four things. First, he proposes that property is part of the household, and that proprietary skill is part of household management. And this is so because one cannot live in a household without the necessities of life that property provides. He proves this by comparison with crafts. For we perceive that each craft needs to have suitable tools if it is to perform its task, as, for example, a smith needs a hammer if he is to make a knife. In the same way, the manager of a household needs property as an instrument for his work.

7.   Second, he proposes a division of instruments, saying that some are living things, and that others are nonliving. For example, the rudder is an

inanimate instrument of the ship's pilot, and the lookout (i.e., the sailor who guards the front part of the ship, which we call the prow) is a living instrument. For assistants in crafts have the nature of instruments, since, as master craftsmen move their tools, so also they move their assistants by their commands. And as there are two kinds of instruments in the crafts, so also property (e.g., beds or clothing) is an inanimate instrument in the household that serves to facilitate human life. Such means collectively constitute the whole property of the household, and slaves, since they are living property, are living instruments supporting the life of the household.

And living instruments, such as the assistants of a craftsman and slaves in a household, are superior to other instruments, namely, in using and moving other instruments. And we need assistants and slaves for this. For the chief craftsmen, whom we call master craftsmen, would not need assistants, nor the masters of households slaves, if each inanimate instrument were to recognize its master and be able to perform its task at his command. For example, looms would operate by themselves, and lyres play by themselves, as they say that the statue made by Daedalus moved itself by the natural disposition of its mercury. And likewise, a certain poet says that human handicraft or the art of black magic equipped tripods in a temple of Vulcan, whom the pagans called the god of fire, so that they seemed by themselves to engage almost spontaneously in a divine contest, as if fighting to serve in the ministry of the temple.

8.   Third, he proposes a second distinction of instruments. For we call the tools used in crafts productive, but property that is the instrument of a household is useful for activity. And he proves this distinction by two arguments. First, we call instruments that cause something beyond the very use of the instrument productive. And we perceive this in the tools used in crafts, as, for example, the loom that textile workers use causes something besides use of the loom, namely, the cloth. But property that is the instrument of a household provides only its utility, as, for example, clothing and beds provide only their utility. Therefore, such instruments, unlike those used in crafts, are not productive.

9.   He proposes a second argument, as follows. There are different instruments for different things. But activity and production are specifically different, since production is action that causes something in external matter (e.g., cutting and burning), but activity is action that that remains in the thing acting and belongs to the life of the thing acting, as the *Metaphysics* says.[8] And both of these kinds of action need instruments.

---

8. Aristotle, *Metaphysics* IX, 8 (1050a30–35).

Therefore, their instruments differ specifically. But life (i.e., domestic life) is not production. Therefore, the slave is an assistant and instrument of things that belong to activity, not things that belong to production.

10.   Fourth, he shows how the slave is related to the master, saying that the relation of property to its owner is the same as the relation of a part to the whole, as we say that a part belongs to the whole absolutely, not merely that it is part of the whole. For example, we do not say only that a human being's hand is part of the human being, but that the hand belongs to the human being. Similarly, we do not say only that property (e.g., clothing) is the property of a human being, but also that it belongs absolutely to that human being. And so the slave, since he is a kind of property, is not only the slave of the master but belongs absolutely to him. But the master is only master of the slave and does not belong absolutely to the slave.

11.   Then he infers the definition of a slave from the foregoing, saying that it is clear from the aforementioned things what the nature (i.e., of a slave) and his function (i.e., his duty) are, since power is related to action, and duty is the appropriate action of someone. For, inasmuch as a slave is himself something that belongs to another, as I have said [**10**], any human being who by nature belongs to another and not to himself is by nature a slave. And a human being over whom only another can rule belongs by nature to the other and not to himself. (The latter, namely, that anyone who is the property or slave of another is a human being who belongs to the other, is the converse of the preceding statement.) Moreover, it belongs to the nature of property to be useful for activity and separate.

And so we can infer the following definition: a slave is a living, separate instrument useful for activity, a human being belonging to another. And in this definition, we posit instrument as the genus and add five specific differences. By the fact that we call the instrument living, we distinguish it from inanimate instruments. By the fact that we call the instrument useful for activity, we distinguish it from a craftsman's assistant, who is a living instrument of production. By the fact that we say that the instrument belongs to another, we distinguish a slave from a free person, who sometimes serves in a household freely or for pay, not as property. By the fact that we call the instrument separate, we distinguish it from a part like the hand, which belongs to something else but is not separate. And by the fact that we call the instrument a human being, we distinguish it from irrational animals, which are separate property.

Chapter 3
Slavery (2)

Text (1254a17–1255a2)

1.   And we should next consider whether a slave is such by nature, and whether it is more fitting and just for anyone to be a slave than not to be, or hold that all slavery is contrary to nature.

2.   And it is not difficult for us to consider these things theoretically and to learn from events.

3.   For ruling and being ruled are both necessary and expedient. Some things are different from the moment of their origin, some to be ruled, others to rule, and there are many kinds of subjects and rulers. And ruling over better subjects (e.g., human beings rather than irrational animals) is always better, since better subjects do better work. And where something rules, and another thing is ruled, they perform a work.

4.   For there seems to be something ruling and another thing being ruled whenever there is a combination of many things, whether united or separate, and one common thing results.

5.   And this belongs to living things from all of nature, and there are governing principles (e.g., harmonies) in inanimate things, but such things are perhaps rather extrinsically related to our inquiry.

6.   First, living things are composed of soul and body, the former by nature ruling, and the latter by nature being ruled. But we should consider natural powers as things have them by nature[9] and not in corrupt forms. And so we should also consider those human beings who are both physically and mentally best disposed, those in whom the powers are clearly present. For the body will seem very often to rule over the soul of the diseased and the wicked, since they are disposed wrongly and contrary to nature. It is in living things, as we say, that we first consider both despotic and political rule. For example, the soul rules over the body by despotic rule, while the intellect rules over desire by political and kingly rule. And it is evident in these things that it is in accord with nature and expedient that the soul rule over the body, and that the intellect and the rational part rule over the emotional part. The contrary or even the parity of body and soul would be harmful to everything.

---

9. The Latin text of Aristotle here adds: "rather than by nature." Since this clearly contradicts the preceding text and the context, I have omitted translating it.

7. Moreover, the same is true regarding human beings and other animals. For domestic animals are by nature more worthy than wild ones. And it is better for all of them that human beings rule them, since they thereby obtain safety.

8. And the same is true about male and female, the former being by nature superior and the latter by nature inferior, and the male ruling and the female subject to the male.

9. And the same needs to be the case regarding human beings.

10. Therefore, those who differ from other human beings as much as the soul differs from the body, and human beings from irrational animals, are disposed as follows. Those whose task is to perform manual work, which is the best that can be expected of them, are by nature slaves, and it is better for them to be ruled as slaves, if one indeed also acknowledges what I have said. For the slave by nature is one who can and so does belong to another.

11. And the slave shares in reason only insofar as he takes in the meaning of words, but he does not possess understanding. For other animals serve their masters by being acted upon and do not understand by reason. The utility of slaves and that of domestic animals differ little, since both provide assistance to meet bodily needs.

12. Therefore, nature also aims to produce the bodily differences between slaves and free persons. The bodies of the former are strong for necessary manual work, and the bodies of the latter erect and useless for such activities but useful for civic life. And a free person is sometimes useful for advantage in war and sometimes for advantage in peace. But the contrary also very often happens, namely, that slaves have the bodies of free men, and free men the souls of slaves.

13. And so it is clear that if certain human beings are only physically different as much as the statues of the gods are, all will say that inferior human beings are fittingly slaves of superior human beings.

14. And if this is true about the body, it is far more justly applied to the soul. But it is not so easy to perceive the beauty of the soul as it is to perceive that of the body. Therefore, it is clear that some human beings are by nature free, and other human beings are by nature slaves, and that it is both expedient and just for the latter to be slaves.

Comment

1. After Aristotle has shown the nature and power of the slave, he proceeds here to investigate the opinions previously proposed. First, he inquires whether slavery is natural. Second, he inquires whether despotic rule is the same as political rule [chap. 5]. Regarding the first, he does three things. First, he presents a difficulty. Second, he limits it by approving

one part [2]. Third, he shows how even the other part of the difficulty has some truth [chap. 4].

Therefore, he says first that we should consider after the aforementioned things whether anyone is by nature a slave, and whether it is more worthy and just for someone to be a slave, or hold that all slavery is contrary to nature. The latter position answers the two foregoing questions. For if all slavery is contrary to nature, then no one is by nature a slave, and it will be neither just nor worthy that anyone be a slave, since what is contrary to nature is neither worthy nor just.

2.   Then he answers the proposed questions, showing two things, namely, that some human beings are by nature slaves, and that it is worthy and expedient for them to be slaves. And regarding this, he does two things. For he first proposes the way in which we should demonstrate these things, saying that it is not difficult for one to contemplate the truth and nature of the aforementioned questions, and to learn truth from things that happen.

3.   Second, he demonstrates his position in the two foregoing ways. And he does so first from events, and second theoretically [4]. Regarding events, he proposes four things. First, ruling and being ruled concern both the many things that come about necessarily or by force, and the many things that promote the welfare of human beings. And this belongs to the second question, since what is expedient for someone seems to be worthy and just for such a one.

Second, we perceive that there is a distinction regarding human beings from their very birth, such that some are fit to be subjects and others fit to rule. And this belongs to the first question, since what one has immediately at birth seems to be natural.

Third, there are many kinds of subjects and rulers. For example, men rule over women in one way, masters over slaves in another way, and kings over kingdoms in a third way. And this also belongs to the second question, since we distinguish the natural powers in things according to the diversity of the things.

Fourth, ruling over better subjects is always better. For example, ruling over human beings is better than ruling over irrational animals. And he proves this by the following argument. Every kind of ruling and being ruled is directed to some work, since one subject to a ruler obeys him in some work. But the work done by better things is better. Therefore, the kind of ruling is also better. And this fourth point belongs to the first question, since things inherent by nature are better insofar as they belong to better things.

4.   Then he demonstrates his position by an argument. First, he proposes an argument to show that some for whom it is expeditious to be slaves are by nature such. Second, he shows who are such persons [10].

Regarding the first, he proposes the following argument. In anything constituted of many things, there is something ruling by nature and something subject by nature, and this is expedient. But a human society is constituted of many things. Therefore, it is natural and expedient that someone rule and another be ruled. And the foregoing, in which he has shown that human beings are by nature political animals, and so that it is natural that a society be constituted of many human beings, demonstrated the minor premise of the argument. And so, prescinding from the minor premise, he proves the major premise.

And then he does three things in the argument. First, he posits the major. Second, he proves it [5]. Third, he draws the conclusion [9]. Therefore, he says first that there is something ruling and something ruled in everything constituted out of many things so as to make one common thing. This is true whether the many things are united, as bodily members are united to constitute the whole body, or the many things are separate, as many soldiers constitute one army. And this is natural and expedient, as he will show by particular examples.

5. Then he proves his position in four ways. First, he shows it in inanimate things. Second, he shows it in the parts of human beings [6]. Third, he shows it in the genus of animal [7]. Fourth, he shows it in the different sexes [8]. Therefore, he says first that we find the truth of the foregoing proposition in living things, not as if it is peculiar to them, but because it is common to all of nature, since there is a rule even in things that do not share in life (e.g., harmonies). And we can understand this in two ways. We can understand it in one way regarding musical harmony, since harmonious sounds always have one that predominates, one by which we judge the whole harmony. We can also understand it about the harmony of elements in a mixed material substance, in which one of the elements always predominates. But he passes over such a kind of rule because it is extrinsic to his concern.

6. Then he demonstrates his proposition in the parts of human beings, saying that the primary composition in living things consists of soul and body. And we call this composition primary by reason of its importance, since it is composed of a living thing's chief parts, not by reason of the order of the living thing's coming to be. And one of these parts, namely, the soul, is by nature the ruling part, and the other part, namely, the body, is by nature the ruled part.

But one could say that this is not natural, since it does not exist in all things. And so, in order to refute this, he adds that, in order to judge what is natural, we need to consider things disposed according to nature and not corrupted things, since the latter fall short of nature. And so, in order to judge what part in human beings by nature rules, we need to consider a human being who is well disposed in both soul and body, and the soul clearly rules the body in such a human being. But in diseased human beings and those wrongly disposed, the body very often rules the soul, since such human beings prefer bodily convenience to what is fitting for the soul. And this happens because these human beings are disposed wrongly and contrary to nature.

And he then shows that the ruling power in the parts of an animal is like external ruling power. For, regarding the human animal, we can consider two kinds of rules in relation its parts, namely, the despotic kind by which masters rule over slaves, and the political kind by which the ruler of the political community rules over free persons. For we find among the parts of human beings that the soul rules over the body, and this is by a despotic rule in which the slave can in no way resist the master, since the slave as such belongs absolutely to the master, as he has said before [chap. 2, n. 11]. And we perceive that bodily members such as hands and feet immediately execute their functions at the soul's bidding and without any resistance. We also find that the intellect, or reason, rules over the will, although by a political and kingly rule, one over free persons, and so the latter can resist in particular things. And the will likewise sometimes does not follow reason. And the reason for this difference is that only the soul can move the body, and so the latter is completely subject to the former, but the senses as well as reason can move the will, and so the latter is not totally subject to reason.

And in both regimes, it is clear that the subjection is by nature and expedient. For it is natural and expedient for the body that the soul rule over it, and likewise for the emotional part (i.e., the will subject to emotions) that the intellect, or reason, rule over it. And it would be harmful for both regimes if the part that should be ruled were to be equal or contrary to the part that should rule. For the body would be destroyed unless it were subject to the soul, and desire would be inordinate unless it were subject to reason.

7.   Then he proves the same thing in the genus of animal, saying that human beings and other animals are similarly so related that it is natural and expedient for the former to rule over the latter. For we perceive that domestic animals, over whom human beings rule, are by nature more worthy than wild animals, as domestic animals share in a way in the rule of reason. But it is also better for all animals that human beings rule over them, since the animals in many cases then obtain physical safety that they could not obtain by themselves. For example, this is evident when human beings provide them with abundant food and medical help.

8.   Then he proves the same thing regarding the different sexes, saying that the male is also related to the female in the same way: that the male is

by nature superior, that the female is by nature inferior, that the male
rules, and that the female is subject to the male. And we should note that
the first two examples concern the individual whole, and the other two
concern the universal whole that is the genus or species. And so it is clear
that the aforementioned proposition applies to both.

9.   Then he infers what he has proposed, namely, that it is the same regarding human beings as it is regarding the foregoing, namely, that it is
natural and expedient that some human beings rule and that others be
subjects.

10.   Then he shows who are by nature rulers, and who are by nature subjects. First, he shows of what sort they are regarding the soul. Second, he
shows of what sort they are regarding the body [12]. Regarding the first,
he does two things. First, he shows of what sort natural rulers and subjects are regarding the soul. Second, he posits the relation between human
beings who are by nature slaves, and irrational animals, who are also by
nature slaves [11]. Therefore, he says first that the soul by nature rules
over the body, and human beings by nature over irrational animals.
Therefore, all human beings who differ from others as much as the soul
does from the body, and as human beings do from irrational animals, are,
because of the eminence of reason in them and the deficiency in others,
by nature masters of the others. In this regard, Solomon also says in
Prov. 11:29: "The stupid will serve the wise."

And those human beings whose chief function is to perform manual
tasks are disposed in this way, namely, as irrational animals are to human
beings, or as the body is to the soul. And performing manual tasks is the
best work that they can do, since they can execute the latter but not the
works of reason. And they are by nature slaves over whom it is better that
the wise rule if it is proper to credit the aforementioned arguments, since
slaves share in the rule of reason in this regard. And it is clear that they are
by nature slaves. For those who are by nature fit to belong to others,
namely, insofar as they can be governed only by the reason of another and
not by their own reason, whereby human beings are masters of themselves, are by nature slaves. Therefore, they by nature belong to others as
slaves, as it were.

11.   Then he compares natural human slaves to irrational animals, saying
that the former share in reason only insofar as they have the understanding of reason when others teach them, but not so far as to have the understanding of reason on their own. But other animals do not serve human
beings as if they receive an understanding of reason from human beings.
That is to say, other animals remember the good and bad things that
human beings have done to them, and fear or love impels them to serve
those human beings. And so natural slaves and irrational animals serve

human beings in different ways, natural slaves by the use of reason, and irrational animals by emotional reaction. But the advantage, or the benefit, that each kind of service confers differs little, since slaves and domestic animals offer us help for the same things, namely, our physical needs. For one who is a slave by nature, because he lacks sufficient reason, cannot help us in deliberation or any work of reason. Nevertheless, a slave, because he has reason, can serve in physical tasks in more ways than an irrational animal can.

12. Then he shows of what sort slaves are regarding the body. And first he proposes his aim. Second, he proves what he has proposed [13]. Therefore, he says first that nature intends (i.e., has a drive or inclination) to differentiate between the bodies of free persons and those of slaves. This is so that the bodies of slaves are strong for carrying out necessary tasks suitable for them, namely, digging up fields, and performing like services. But the bodies of free persons should be erect (i.e., well disposed by nature) and useless for the servile works necessary to support their tender constitution but useful for the civic life in which free persons engage. And those with bodily members useful for civic life are disposed sometimes for advantage in war and sometimes for advantage in peace, namely, have bodily members fit for combat and other military activities in time of war and for performing other civic tasks in time of peace.

And nature, although it has an inclination to cause the aforementioned difference in body, nonetheless sometimes falls short in this. Just so, in all things that come to be and pass away, nature achieves its effect for the most part but falls short in relatively few cases. Therefore, when nature falls short in this respect, the contrary to what he has said very often happens, namely, that those with the souls of free persons have the bodies of slaves, or the converse.

And we should consider the conclusion Aristotle draws from the foregoing, in which he treated of the disposition of the soul, that, since the body is by nature for the sake of the soul, nature aims to form a body suitable for it. And so nature aims to give the bodies of free persons to those who have the souls of free persons, and similarly regarding slaves. And this is always true regarding internal bodily dispositions, since one cannot have a well-disposed soul if the organs of imagination and other sensory powers are ill disposed. But there can be disharmony regarding shape, weight, and other external dispositions, as he here says.

13. Then he proves what he had said. First, he proves it regarding the body. Second, he proves it regarding the soul [14]. Therefore, he says first that nature clearly aims to cause different bodies for slaves and free persons. Let us suppose that some human beings differ so much only regarding their bodies that they seem to surpass others as much as if they were statues of the gods. (Just so, we are generally accustomed to say that some seem to be like angels when we see them to be well shaped.) Then all will say that those who lack such fine bodily form are worthy to serve those who excel, as the saying goes: "The appearance of Priam is worthy to command."[10] And since this is clear regarding the greatest difference, we should also understand the same regarding the aim of nature if there were not so much difference.

14. He proves the same regarding the soul, saying that if it is true regarding the body that the deficient are fit to serve the more excellent, the more excellent the soul is than the body, the far more just it is that we determine the same regarding the soul. But we cannot so easily recognize the excellence of the soul's beauty as we can the beauty of the body. And so we judge more generally regarding the body than the soul that some human beings are fit to rule.

And he concludes by summarizing the two conclusions aimed at in this chapter, namely, that some human beings are by nature slaves, and others by nature free, and that it is expedient for those who are by nature slaves to be slaves, and just that they are.

Chapter 4
Slavery (3)

Text (1255a3–b15)

1.   But is not difficult to see that those who say the contrary are in a way right, since one speaks of slavery and slave in two ways, and some are slaves and in slavery by law. For the law declares that war captives belong to the victors.

2.   Many jurists, like a rhetorician, write that such a law consists of unjust things, as if it would be harsh to say that one forcibly overpowered by another who can use force and has greater might will be the other's slave and subject. And so it seems to some, but otherwise to others, and even among the wise.

---

10. Cf. Porphyry, *Isagoge* 4, 1.

3.   And the reason for this difficulty, and what causes opinions to vary, is because virtue gaining the upper hand can in some way most allow the use of force, and the victor always abounds in some goodness. And so it seems that there can be no use of force without a virtue.

4.   But it seems that the dispute is only about justice. For it is on this account that it seems to some that justice is benevolence, and to others that justice is that one who is superior rules. For, if we should set aside these arguments, the contrary arguments that it is unfitting that those superior in virtue should rule and be masters seem to have no validity or probability.

5.   And some, considering the question as fully as possible in relation to particular justice, since law is particular justice, hold that slavery resulting from war is just. But they do not say that it is completely just.

6.   For the cause for waging war may not be just. And one will in no way say that someone unsuitable to be a slave is properly such. And if the cause of waging war is unjust, it will happen that those who seem to be of the best lineage become slaves, and the descendents of slaves if the captives happen to be sold.

7.   And so they want to call war captives foreigners, not slaves.

8.   And when they say this, they look only at what a slave is by nature. And this is what we said at the beginning. For we need to say that some are always slaves, and some never.

9.   And the same is also true about noble birth. For they consider themselves wellborn both among themselves and abroad, but foreigners [non-Greeks] wellborn only in their native land. This is as if it is one thing to be absolutely wellborn and free, and another to be conditionally such, as the elegy of Theodectes says: "Who will deign to consign as a slave one born of divine ancestors on both sides?"

10.   And with this, they may be saying only that goodness and badness determine the difference between a slave and a free person, and one wellborn and one base-born. For they deem it fitting that, as human beings beget human beings, and irrational animals irrational animals, so also goodness begets goodness. And nature very often aims to do this but cannot.

11.   Therefore, it is clear that there is some reason for this difficulty, one view that some persons are not slaves by nature nor others free by nature, and the other view that it is expedient and just, as determined in particular cases, for one person to be a slave and another person a master. And it is fitting that some things are ruled, and other things rule, with which ruling power nature endows them. So also it is fitting for some to be masters, and if the master does his work badly, it is disadvantageous for both master and slave. For the same thing is advantageous for the part and the whole, and for the body and the soul. And the slave is a part of his master,

as if a living but separate part of his body. And so also it is advantageous that there be a friendship between master and slave if they are by nature suitable for it. But the contrary is true for those who are slaves by the law of war and by force.

Comment

1.   After Aristotle has shown that some are by nature slaves, for whom being such is expeditious and just, he here shows that even the contrary opinion is partially true. And regarding this, he does two things. First, he posits a way of slavery in which some deny that slavery is natural or just. Second, he presents a difficulty about this and answers it [2]. Therefore, he says first that it is not difficult to see that those who argue contrary to the things he has determined, namely, by asserting that no slavery is natural or just, in a way speak rightly. For we speak of slavery and slaves in two ways. One way regards natural suitability, as he has said before [chap. 3]. But there is also a kind of slave or servitude by human law. For law declares that war captives are slaves of the victors, and almost all peoples observe it, and so also we call it a common law of peoples.

2.   Then he presents the difficulty about such legal slavery. And regarding this, he does three things. First, he posits different opinions. Second, he assigns reasons for the diversity [3]. Third, he answers the difficulty [5]. Therefore, he says first that many jurists wrote that the justice of the aforementioned law belongs in the list of unjust things. And he introduces one called Rhetorician,[11] to whom it seemed harsh if one overpowered by force should be the slave and subject of one who could impose force and is superior only because he is more powerful. And so legal slavery seems to some in this way, namely, to be unjust, but contrariwise to others. And this difference of opinion exists both among common people and the wise.

3.   Then he assigns the reason for the aforementioned difference of opinion. And he first proposes something that is obvious. Second, he considers the matter about which there is a doubt [4]. Therefore, he first gives the reason for the aforementioned difficulty and the resulting different opinions of the wise. He says that the use of force can be most compatible with virtue in a particular way (i.e., wisdom, constancy, bodily courage, or any another way) if the virtue gains the upper hand (i.e., unless the contrary should happen by mischance). And so it is clear that the victor always abounds in some goodness unless it should happen otherwise by mischance. And so it seems that force is never without any virtue on the part of the one using force, and this is self-evident.

---

11. Aquinas regards the rhetorician in the text of Aristotle as a proper name.

4. Then he shows what remains in dispute, saying that the only remaining doubt is whether it is just that the victor should rule because he excels in some virtue. And so there are different opinions about this. For some say that the justice of the aforementioned law is by reason of benevolence (i.e., something introduced in favor of victors to motivate soldiers to wage war bravely). But it seems to others that the matter has an aspect of justice, that those who show superiority by military victory should rule, as Solomon says in Prov. 12:24: "The hands of the strong will rule, and the hands of the lazy will serve by compulsion." And so they say this because, if we should set aside such arguments about the actions, it seems at first glance that the counterarguments that those superior in the virtue proper to victors should not rule or be masters have no convincing force. Nor do they even have any probability, as things generally seem to people.

5. Then he answers the aforementioned difficulty. First, he shows how slavery is just. Second, he shows how it is expedient [11]. Regarding the first, he does two things. First, he gives the answer. Second, he proves it [6]. Therefore, he says first that, in order to determine the truth about the difficulty totally and fully, we should say that some consider the matter in relation to particular justice (i.e., justice in one respect, namely, as law can prescribe it in human affairs) and hold that the slavery resulting from war is just. But they do not say that slavery is altogether (i.e., absolutely) just. Therefore, he agrees with the second opinion and explains it, showing that it was speaking of relative justice, the justice of human law, not absolute justice. For we call what is just by nature absolute justice, and we call what is related to the human advantage at which law aims relative justice. For all laws are instituted for the benefit of human beings.

Therefore, since it is not just by nature that all war captives are slaves, since it often happens that the foolish vanquish the wise, he says that this is not absolutely just but is advantageous for human life. For it is beneficial for the captives, since the victors thereby preserve them, so that the subjects at least survive, and so also we call them slaves from their condition of servitude. And this is also beneficial for the victors, since soldiers are thereby motivated to fight more bravely. And in order to prevent the wicked deeds of many, it is advantageous for human society that soldiers should be brave.

And if human law could have determined efficaciously who were spiritually superior, it, following nature, would without doubt have ordained that such persons be masters. But since this could not be done, law took another sign of preeminence, namely, the victory resulting from an excellence of virtue. And so law established that victors are the masters of captives. And so he says that this is just in one respect, as law could be established, but not just absolutely. But this should be observed even regarding a spiritually virtuous person, since, inasmuch as the common good is superior to the particular good of an individual, we should not impair what belongs to the common good even though it is not good for a private person.

6.   Then he makes clear the foregoing answer. And he does so first by arguments. Second, he does so by what people generally say [7]. Regarding the first, he gives two arguments. The first is as follows. What results from an unjust cause is not absolutely just. But the cause of wars may be unjust (e.g., when someone has no just cause for going to war). Therefore, the slavery resulting from such war is not absolutely just.

He gives a second argument as follows. It happens in war that one unworthy to be a slave is taken captive. But no one can say that one who is unworthy to be a slave is justly a slave. Therefore, we cannot say that the slavery resulting from war is absolutely just. And he proves the minor premise. If anyone were to say that someone unworthy to be a slave is justly a slave, those of the most noble stock would sometimes become slaves if they were captured in war, and if they were sold, their children would then be slaves born of slaves. And this seems inappropriate.

7.   Then he proves his position by the things that people generally say. First, he cites the things that people generally say about slavery. Second, he cites the things that people generally say about freedom [9]. Regarding the first, he does two things. First, he lays out what people generally say. Second, he shows how to understand what they say [8]. Therefore, he says first that, because of the need to avoid the aforementioned inappropriateness, people want to say that only foreigners, not noble human beings, become slaves when captured in war.

8.   Then he shows how to understand what people say. And he says that they seem to speak only about natural slavery in the case of foreigners because of the foreigners' mental deficiency and not in the case of noble war captives. This is because, as he has said before [chap. 3, n. 3], some from the moment of their birth are necessarily by nature slaves, and others are not.

9.   Then he posits the things that people say about freedom. First, he cites what they say. Second, he shows how we should understand this [10]. Therefore, he says first that people speak in the same way about good birth (i.e., freedom), since the wellborn are neither slaves nor former slaves. For they say that noble human beings are wellborn not only among themselves (i.e., when they live in their own homeland and under their own sovereignty) but also everywhere on earth. But foreigners [non-Greeks], who are by nature slaves because of deficient reason, are free only in their own homeland, because of the deficiency of rulers. This is as if some should be unqualifiedly free or wellborn, namely, those who are

spiritually well disposed, and others, such as foreigners [non-Greeks], are free in one respect. And to confirm the foregoing, he introduces the words of the poet Theodectes, who in his elegy (i.e., treatise on miseries) said: "Who will think it proper that one descended on both sides," namely, the paternal and maternal, "from the most noble and divine ancestors is consigned to slavery?" (Theodectes was following the error of the pagans, who called great rulers gods.)

10. Then he shows how we should understand what people say. And he says that they seem to say only that spiritual virtue determines freedom and slavery, nobility and baseness, so that the spiritually virtuous are free and noble, but the wicked are slaves and base. Just so, the Lord says in 1 Sam. 2:30: "Those who contemn me will be base." And this is so because human beings deem it fitting that, as human beings beget human beings, and irrational animals irrational animals, so good human beings beget good human beings. And so the honor of nobility came about when the children of the good are honored as being like their ancestors in goodness.

And nature truly aims to do this, since it comes from the good composition and nature of the body that some are more or less inclined to virtuous or wicked deeds (e.g., some are by nature irascible, and others gentle). And children, for the most part, inherit their bodily nature from their fathers. The same is true of other bodily dispositions (e.g., beauty, courage, and the like). But this sometimes fails to happen because of an impediment. And so good parents very often beget good sons, but nature, because of an impediment, cannot always do this. And so wickedly disposed sons sometimes come from parents well disposed toward virtue, just as ugly sons come from handsome parents, and short sons from tall parents.

And sons may also differ from parents in goodness or wickedness not only because of natural bodily disposition but also because of an aspect that does not necessarily result from a natural inclination. And so human beings who are similar to their parents in natural disposition may also, because of a different education and upbringing, be dissimilar even in morals. Therefore, if the children of good parents are good, they will be both reputedly and really good. But if the sons of good parents are wicked, they will be reputedly noble but actually base. And the converse is true about the sons of wicked parents.

11. Then he shows how it is expedient or inexpedient for some to be slaves, summarily concluding from the foregoing that the difficulty previously posed has some plausibility. And so there is in some cases a distinction between freedom and slavery by law, not by nature. But in other cases, there is a distinction between the two by nature, and it is advantageous in

such cases for one person to be a slave and another to be his master. And this is also just. And he proves this because it is advantageous that each be a subject or a ruler insofar as each has the natural suitability. And so also it is advantageous for those who have the natural suitability to be masters over slaves. But if the masters rule badly and contrary to natural suitability, it is disadvantageous for both masters and slaves. And he proves this by the fact that we perceive that the same thing, namely, that the part is included in the whole, is advantageous for the part and the whole. Likewise, the same thing, namely, the soul ruling over the body, is advantageous for the body and the soul. And he shows that the slave is related to his master as the body is to the soul, as he has said before [chap. 3, nn. 6 and 10], but also as a part of his master, as if he were a living instrument that is a separated part of his master's body. For this separateness distinguishes the slave from the master's other parts, as he has said [chap. 2, n. 11].

And so it is clear from the foregoing that it is advantageous for slaves and masters fit to be such by nature that one be the master, and the other the slave. And so there can be friendship between them, since the association of both in what is advantageous for each is the essence of friendship. But those who are not related to each another as master and slave by nature but by law and force are disposed in the contrary way. For they do not have friendship with each another, nor is it advantageous for them that one be the master, and the other be his slave.

Chapter 5
Slavery (4)

Text (1255b16–40)

1.   And it is clear from these things that despotic and political rule differ. Nor are all ruling powers the same, as some say, since one belongs by nature to free persons and the other by nature to slaves.

2.   And household rule is by nature monarchical, since one person rules every household, but political rule is a regime of free and equal persons.

3.   Therefore, we call someone a master because he is such, not because of his knowledge. And we similarly call persons slave or free because they are such, not because of their knowledge.

4. But there will be both a master's and a slave's knowledge. The latter is the kind that a certain person in Syracuse taught. He taught youngsters household tasks for a fee. And this instruction will concern many things, such as cooking and other like kinds of service. For there are different tasks for different things, some more esteemed and others more necessary. And as the proverb says, some slaves are superior to other slaves, and some masters to other masters. Therefore, all kinds of a slave's knowledge are such.

5. And a master's knowledge consists of knowing how to use slaves, since one is a master in using slaves, not in possessing them.

6. But the knowledge of how to use slaves has no great importance or esteem, since masters need to command things that slaves should know how to do. Therefore, for any masters who have the means to avoid this evil, an administrator takes on such duties, and the masters engage in civic life and philosophy.

7. And knowledge of how to acquire slaves (e.g., in just wars or hunting) differs from both of the other forms of knowledge. Therefore, we have in this way determined about slaves and masters.

Comment

1. After Aristotle has inquired about the truth of the opinion that holds that slavery is not natural, he proceeds here to inquire about the other opinion, which holds that despotic rule is the same as political rule, and that it involves a certain kind of knowledge. First, he excludes the former. Second, he excludes the latter [3]. Regarding the first, he does two things. First, he shows that despotic rule (i.e., the rule of masters over slaves) is not the same as political rule. Second, he shows that household rule is not the same as political rule [2]. Therefore, he says first that the aforementioned things can make clear that the opinion of those who said that despotic rule (i.e., the rule of masters over slaves), political rule, and any rule are the same is false. For political rule is rule over persons free by nature, and despotic rule is rule over slaves. And he has said before that regimes differ in subjects and rulers, so that a regime of superior subjects is a superior regime [chap. 3, n. 3]. Therefore, despotic rule and political rule are different regimes, and political rule is more excellent.

2. Then he shows the difference between political rule and household rule. And household rule includes despotic rule, since despotic rule is rule over slaves, and household rule governs all who dwell in a household, some of whom are slaves, and others free. Therefore, household rule differs from political rule in that the former is monarchical (i.e., the rule of one person), since one head of the family rules over the entire household.

But political rule is the rule of free and equal persons. And so rulers and subjects, because of their equality, exchange roles, and many persons are also constituted rulers in the same or different offices.

But this difference does not seem proper. First, it seems improper because not every household rule seems to be monarchical. Rather, household rule seems to be monarchical only when the father rules a household, and to be aristocratic when husband and wife rule, and to be timocratic or political when brothers in a household rule, as the *Ethics* says.[12] Second, it seems improper because monarchy is one kind of regime, as he will say later [III, chap. 6, n. 3]. And we should say in response to the first point that Aristotle is speaking here about household rule in its best and enduring condition. But brothers rule in a household only until they divide their inheritance, and then each rules over a separate household. And a wife rules in a household in one respect, not absolutely, since she is also subject to her husband. But if it should happen otherwise, there is a disorder and corruption of the household. And we should say in response to the second point that he is speaking here about a particular regime, polity, as we distinguish political rule from kingly rule, as he has maintained before [chap. 1, n. 3].

3.   Then he disproves the aforementioned opinion regarding its claim that despotic rule is a form of knowledge. And he shows first that it is not knowledge. Second, he shows that it has a connected knowledge [4]. Therefore, he says first that we do not call some persons masters because of their form of knowledge, namely, because they know how to rule, but because nature or law so disposes them to rule, and that we should say the same about slaves and free persons. Rather, despotic rule is the reason why we call someone a master. Therefore, despotic rule is not a form of knowledge.

4.   Then he shows that despotic rule has a connected form of knowledge. And regarding this, he does two things. First, he states his aim, saying that there is a master's knowledge (i.e., knowing how to rule) and a slave's knowledge. Second, he further explains the knowledge of each, first a slave's [4] and then a master's [5]. Therefore, he says first that a slave's knowledge is the kind that a certain citizen of Syracuse taught. He charged fees and taught youngsters household tasks (i.e., how to perform the tasks that maids and other slaves customarily performed). And this knowledge extends to more than preparing food and performing such services. But we note that these tasks differ in two respects, namely,

---

12. Aristotle, *Ethics* VIII, 10 (1160b22–1161a16).

esteem and necessity. For some tasks are more esteemed but less necessary (e.g., the task of preparing fine foods), and some tasks are more necessary but less esteemed (e.g., making bread). And so also the proverb developed that not all slaves are equal, and one is better than another, as one master is better than another. Therefore, since such tasks belong to slaves, all such forms of knowledge belong to slaves. And so, in distinction from these, we speak of liberal skills, which we assign to the activities of free persons.

5.   Then he makes clear of what a master's knowledge consists. And regarding this, he does three things. First, he makes clear what he proposes. Second, he shows the condition of a master's knowledge [6]. Third, he treats of the knowledge of something related [7]. Therefore, he says first that we call the knowledge by which one knows how to use slaves well, not how to acquire them, a master's knowledge. And he proves this because we call persons masters (i.e., masters over slaves) in that such persons use slaves rather than possess (i.e., acquire) them.

6.   Then he shows the condition of this knowledge, saying that it is not of great importance or esteem. First, he proves this by an argument, namely, that a master's knowledge consists of one knowing how to use slaves by commanding them, and this is nothing important. For the things that the slave needs to know how to do, and the things that the master needs to command, are the same. And so it is clear that such knowledge is of no great moment. Second, he shows the same by human custom. For people do not consider such knowledge to be of any moment. And so masters who can free themselves from suffering this evil (i.e., being burdened with the care of their slaves) are free and have time for the civic, political, or philosophical life. And they commit the care of their slaves to an administrator.

7.   Then, because he had said that a master's knowledge does not consist of knowing how to acquire slaves, he adds that another form of knowledge does, and that such knowledge differs from a master's or a slave's. This knowledge is of many kinds, and he gives two examples. With one kind, human beings acquire other human beings as slaves, and the knowledge concerns how to wage just wars, in which law makes captives slaves. (But if the war were unjust, the acquisition of slaves would be unjust and so not in accord with such knowledge.) And there is another knowledge whereby human beings acquire animals as slaves, and the knowledge concerns hunting.

And he summarily concludes that he has determined this much about masters and slaves.

Chapter 6
Property

Text (1256a1–b39)

1.   We shall completely consider all kinds of acquiring property and moneymaking in our usual way, since we have said that even slaves are part of one's property.

2.   Therefore, one will first ask whether making money is the same as household management or a part of it or subordinate to it, and if it is subordinate, whether it is like wool combs for weaving cloth or like bronze for making statues. For the combs and the bronze are not subordinate in the same way. Rather, combs are tools for weaving, and bronze material for statutes. And I am speaking of the presupposed material out of which the work is done (e.g., wool for the weaver and bronze for the sculptor).

3.   Therefore, household management is obviously not the same as moneymaking, since it belongs to the latter to acquire things, and to the former to use them. For what other activity than household management makes use of things concerning the household?

4.   But it is debatable whether a different kind of thing is a part of household management.

5.   That is to say, if it belongs to moneymaking to see from what sources money and property will be acquired. And there are many kinds of acquiring property and many kinds of wealth. And so we first ask whether farming is part of moneymaking or a different kind of thing, and in general about the care and acquisition of foods.

6.   Moreover, there are many kinds of food and so also many ways of life of both animals and human beings, since it is impossible to live without food. Therefore, different kinds of foods support different ways of life in animals. For some animals live in herds, and others in isolation, and both ways are advantageous in providing food for the animals. Therefore, some are carnivorous, some vegetarian, and some will eat both meat and vegetation. And so nature has determined ways of life for their ease and choice. And since different animals by nature take pleasure in different foods, not the same food, the ways of life of carnivorous and vegetarian animals differ.

7.   And the same is true of human beings, since their ways of life differ in many respects. For example, shepherds are the least industrious, since

they take their food from domestic animals without toil. But since sheep needed to migrate in order to graze, shepherds also needed to accompany them, as if the shepherds were engaged in mobile farming. Other human beings live off spoils in various ways: some by robbery; some, who live near a lake, a marsh, a river, or the sea, by fishing; and some off birds or wild animals. But most human beings live off the land and cultivated produce. Therefore, there are almost as many ways of life. Shepherds, raiders, fishers, and hunters have increase of food spontaneously from nature, not from barter or commerce. And some, by combining these ways (e.g., shepherding with raiding, and farming with hunting), live comfortably, supplementing the most deficient way of life with what it lacks, in order to make it self-sufficient. Likewise, regarding other ways of life, they live in whatever way advantage impels them.

8. Therefore, nature itself seems to provide such acquisition of food to all animals at the first stage of generation and after complete generation. For, regarding the first stage, some animals (e.g., those that produce larvae or eggs) produce along with the offspring enough food to last until the offspring can acquire it for themselves. And those animals that produce live offspring have food, called milk, within them with which to feed their offspring for a time. And so it is likewise clear that we should judge, since it is also for the offspring, that plants exist for the sake of animals, and other animals for the sake of human beings. Domestic animals are for both the use and the food they provide, and most but not all wild animals are for the sake of food and other uses, such as clothes and other implements out of them. Therefore, nature, if it produces nothing incomplete or in vain, necessarily has done all these things for the sake of human beings. And so also war will by nature somehow be a way of acquiring property, since taking spoils is part of war. And it is necessary to wage it against both animals and the human beings whom nature constitutes to be subjects but who refuse, as this predatory first kind of war is by nature just, as it were.

9. Therefore, one natural kind of acquiring property is part of household management, and the acquisition needs either to exist or to be provided. And things necessary for life and useful for the political community and the household are accumulated.

10. And wealth truly seems to consist of acquiring these things, since the self-sufficiency of such property for the good life is not unlimited, as the poet Solon said it was: "There is no prefixed limit of wealth for human beings." As in other skills, there is indeed a limit. For the tools proper to any craft are limited, both in number and size. And wealth consists of many tools for the use of household managers and statesmen. Therefore, some acquisition of property belongs by nature to household managers and statesmen, and it is clear why.

Comment

1. After Aristotle has determined about masters and slaves, who are a kind of property, he determines here about property in general. And he divides this consideration into two parts. In the first, he determines about it theoretically. In the second, he determines about it practically [chap. 9]. Regarding the first, he does two things. First, he speaks about his aim. Second, he poses questions [2]. Therefore, he says first that, since he has said that slaves are a kind of property, we need to consider about property in general and about the skill of moneymaking in the same way that we dealt with slaves [chap. 2, n. 4–chap. 5, n. 7].

2. Then he poses certain questions. First, he raises them. Second, he begins to answer them [3]. And he divides the first question into two parts. The first of these asks whether skill in making money (i.e., acquiring money) is entirely the same as household management or a part of it or neither the same nor a part but subordinate to it. For it is clear that moneymaking somehow belongs to household management. And so the former needs to be related to the latter in one of these ways. But that a skill is part of another skill, and that the skill is subordinate to the other skill, are not the same thing. For we call a skill that considers part of what another skill considers, part of the other skill. For example, the skill in making knives is the skill of a smith, since knives are one kind of product made out of iron. And we call a skill that does something of service to another skill a subordinate skill. For example, the skill in smelting iron is subordinate to the skill of a smith. And money, since it serves the household, seems to be subordinate to the household rather than a part of it.

And so he raises a second question. For one skill serves another in two ways. A skill serves another in one way by preparing for it the tool with which it operates. For example, the skill that produces the comb with which one weaves wool provides the proper tool for the skill of weaving. A skill serves another skill in another way by providing for it the material on which it operates. For example, the skill that smelts bronze serves the skill that makes a statue out of the bronze, and the skill that prepares wool serves the weaver. Therefore, there is a question whether the skill in acquiring money serves household management in providing the material or is the tool for it.

3. Then he begins to answer the aforementioned questions. And he shows first that moneymaking is not the same thing as household management. Second, he inquires whether moneymaking is part of household management or subordinate to it or something extraneous to it [4]. Therefore, he first answers the first question, showing that moneymaking is not entirely the same as household management, since acquiring money belongs to moneymaking, but using money belongs to household management. For household management is the only skill to which using things useful for the household belongs. And it is also clear in other things that the skill that uses something is different from the one that produces or acquires it. For example, the skill of piloting is different from the art of shipbuilding. Therefore, household management is different from moneymaking. And this also makes clear that moneymaking is subordinate to, rather than a part of, household management, since skill in producing things always serves the skill in using them. For example, the skill that produces bridles serves military skill. And this also makes clear that moneymaking is subordinate by way of preparing means rather than material. For money and all wealth are means of household management, as he will say later [10].

4.   Then he inquires whether moneymaking is part of household management or something extraneous to it, and he divides his consideration into two parts. In the first part, he raises the question. In the second part, he considers it [5]. Therefore, he says first that, inasmuch as moneymaking is not the same as household management, which uses wealth and property in general, one can question whether moneymaking is a part of household management itself or a different kind of thing.

5.   Then he pursues the aforementioned question, showing first how moneymaking differs from other ways of acquiring property. Second, he determines the proposed question [chap. 8, n. 7]. Regarding the first, he does three things. First, he raises a question about how moneymaking differs from other ways of acquiring property. Second, he determines about other ways of acquiring property [6]. Third, he determines about moneymaking [chap. 7]. Therefore, he says first that it belongs to moneymaking to consider the sources by which money is acquired, and many other things are acquired besides money (e.g., agricultural produce and the like). And so there is a question whether farming, by which some wealth is acquired, is a part of moneymaking or another kind of skill. And because farming is directed to acquiring food, we can raise the same question about the skill that attends to acquiring food in general.

6.   Then he answers the latter question. First, he divides the acquisition of foods into many kinds. Second, he shows the kind of thing the acquisition of food is [8]. Regarding the first, he does two things. First, he shows the different foods of animals. Second, he shows the different foods of human beings [7]. Therefore, he says first that there are many kinds of food, and this results in different ways of living in both animals and human beings. For, inasmuch as it is impossible to live without food, different foods necessarily result in different ways of living in animals. For we perceive that some animals live together in groups, and others live

scattered and separate, insofar as this is helpful for acquiring food. For some animals are carnivorous (i.e., meat-eaters), some are vegetarians, and some indiscriminately eat animal meat and vegetation. And so nature distinguished their ways of life by the foods that they by nature choose, and insofar as they live in ease or conflict. For animals that eat other animals are necessarily in conflict and need to live apart, since they could not otherwise find food. But animals that eat food that can be easily found live together. And different things are desirable to different animals in each of these kinds of food. For example, not all carnivorous animals take pleasure in the same meats, nor do all vegetarian animals take pleasure in the same produce. And so also carnivorous animals may have different ways of living, and also vegetarian animals.

7.   Then he shows that there are different foods in the case of human beings and says that different foods also distinguish human ways of life in many respects. For human beings acquire food in three ways. Some acquire food without toil or from spoils, and these, namely, shepherds, are the least industrious. For food from domestic animals (e.g., sheep) is available without toil to human beings who live in leisure, except that, since flocks needed to migrate from place to place for grazing, shepherds are compelled to follow the flocks, as if the shepherds were cultivating a living and mobile field. And other human beings take their food from spoils, whether as robbers from other human beings; or as fishers, out of lakes, marshes, rivers, and other places; or as hunters of birds and wild animals, out of fields and woods. The third way of living belongs to most human beings, who live off products of the land and cultivated produce, and these have the food produced.

Therefore, these are most of the ways of human life. For besides the way of those who produce food and those who live off commerce, about which he will deal later [chaps. 7–9], there are four simple ways of life, namely, shepherding, raiding, fishing, and hunting, as what he said makes clear. But since a simple way of human life is most deficient because it lacks many things, some human beings, in order to be self-sufficient in all things, combine the aforementioned ways. And so they live pleasantly, supplying for themselves from one way what they lack from another. For example, some combine the life of shepherds and raiders, some the life of farmers and hunters, and some other ways of life, as it suits the advantage of each.

8.   Then he shows the kind of thing the aforementioned acquisition (i.e., of food) is. First, he shows that it is natural. Second, he shows that it is part of household management [9]. Third, he shows that it is limited [10]. Regarding the first, he proposes the following argument. As nature provides for animals in the first stage of their generation, so also does it after

their complete generation. And nature provides for them at the first stage of their generation, and this is evident in various animals. For some animals do not beget complete offspring. Rather, some animals (e.g., birds) produce eggs, and others (e.g., ants, bees, and the like) produce larvae in place of eggs. And such animals produce (i.e., beget along with their fetuses) as much food as can suffice for them until the offspring are completely generated. For example, it is evident in the egg, whose yolk yields food for the begotten chick from the white of the egg, and this lasts as long as the chick is within the shell. The like is true in larvae. And other animals (e.g., horses and the like) beget complete offspring, and in such animals, the animals that beget the offspring have for a time food in them with which to feed their offspring, and we call this food milk. And so it is clear that nature provides food for animals in the first stage of their generation.

And so it is clear that nature provides food for animals after they are complete. And so plants exist for the sake of other animals in order to nourish them, and other animals for the sake of human beings. Domestic animals provide food and other benefits. And most but not all wild animals provide food for human beings or assist them in other ways, since human beings acquire clothing from them (namely, from their skins) or other implements (e.g., from their horns, bones, or teeth). And so it is clear that human beings need other animals, and plants, for their life. But nature neither leaves anything incomplete nor does anything in vain. Therefore, it is clear that nature made animals and plants for the sustenance of human beings. But when a person acquires what nature made for the person, the acquisition is natural. Therefore, the acquisition by which one acquires such things as belong to the necessities of life is natural. And part of this consists of taking spoils, which one needs to do regarding animals, which are by nature subject to human beings, and regarding foreigners, who are by nature slaves, as he has said before [chap. 4, nn. 7–9], as if this should be the original naturally just war. And he said that taking spoils is a part of such acquisition of property, since farming, which acquires food from plants, is the other part.

9. Then he concludes from the foregoing that a natural kind of acquiring property, about which he has just spoken, is part of household management insofar as we call anything subordinate a part. For the natural kind of acquiring property is subordinate to both household management and the political community. And this is so because statesmen and household managers need to provide that things in reserve for the necessities of life and the benefit of both the household and the political community exist or are acquired. For neither the household nor the political community can be governed without the necessities of life.

10. Then he shows that the aforementioned acquisition of property is not unlimited, saying that true wealth consists of such things as alleviate the needs of nature. And so these things are true wealth because they take away need and make their possessors self-sufficient, namely, to have enough to live well. But there is other wealth, the acquisition of which is unlimited, as he will say later [chap. 8, nn. 1–6], and about which the poet Solon, one of the seven wise men, says that there is no predetermined limit for human beings. And so such wealth is not true wealth, since it does not satisfy the desire of human beings.

And Aristotle proves by the following argument that the wealth consisting of things necessary for life is limited. The tools of any activity are limited in number and size. For example, the skill of a smith does not have an unlimited number of hammers or one hammer of infinite size. But the aforementioned wealth is a tool of the household manager and the statesman, since they use it to govern the household or the political community, as he has said [9]. Therefore, such wealth is not infinite but has a limit.

And he summarily concludes that there is a natural acquisition of property, one that is necessary for both the household manager and the statesman. And so what he has said makes clear why.

Chapter 7
Moneymaking in Theory (1)

Text (1256b40–1257b23)

1. And there is another kind of acquisition of property that we especially and rightly call moneymaking. And it is for this reason that there seems to be no limit to wealth and acquisition of property, and many think that this acquisition of property and that just discussed are one and the same thing because of their close association. But they are neither the same nor very different. One is natural, and the other comes through practice and skill, not by nature.
2. Let us begin our consideration of this kind of acquisition thus. There is a double use of each thing. Both uses are of the thing as such, but not in the same way. One is the proper use of the thing, and the other

is not. For example, we can use shoes to protect our feet or trade them for something else. Both are uses of shoes, since trading shoes with someone who needs them in exchange for money or food uses the shoes as shoes but not according to their proper use. For shoes are not made for the sake of trading them. And the case is the same regarding other items of property.

3.   For all things can be exchanged. And barter has its origin because human beings by nature have more than enough of some things and less than enough of other things. (Thus it is also obvious that commerce does not belong to natural moneymaking.) For barter was necessary to provide self-sufficiency for human beings.

4.   Therefore, in the first association, which is the household, it is clear that there was no need of exchange. But with a more extensive association, those of the same household shared in all things, and those of separate households also shared in many other things, for which they needed to make compensatory exchanges according to their needs. Many foreign peoples still do this by barter. For they exchange some useful goods for other useful goods but nothing else (e.g., wine for wheat, giving the one and receiving the other, and the like).

5.   Therefore, such exchange is neither contrary to nature nor any form of moneymaking. For it supplies what nature designed for self-sufficiency.

6.   But this led to a way of exchange devised by reason. For the use of money was necessarily acquired when there was more foreign trade of necessary imports and surplus exports, since not all the things that peoples naturally need are easily transportable. And so people agreed to give and receive in exchanges something intrinsically useful that was useful and very advantageous for human life (e.g., iron, silver, and the like). The amounts were first determined by size and weight, and later by printing marks on the metals in order to free people from the need to measure the metals, since the printed mark indicated the amount.

7.   Therefore, after necessary exchanges resulted in money, another kind of moneymaking, commerce, arose. Therefore, it was at first perhaps done simply, and then, with experience, it became more skillful, and so also people learned whence and how to make the greatest profit out of exchange.

8.   And so it seems that moneymaking most concerns coins, and that the function of moneymakers is to be able to judge the sources out of which they will make a great deal of money. For this creates wealth and money.

9.   For people very often think that wealth consists of much money, since that is why there is moneymaking and commerce.

10.   On the other hand, money and the laws regarding it sometimes seem to be complete madness and not at all natural, since coins are worth nothing if those who use them change their value, and useless for the necessities of

life. And wealthy persons will very often lack necessary food, although it is unfitting that wealth is such that a person abounding in it dies of hunger. Just so, the famous story about Midas says that he, because of his insatiable desire, died of hunger when everything offered him as food was made of gold.

11. Therefore, those seeking wealth and moneymaking in the right way seek something else, since there is another way of making money and acquiring wealth that is in accord with nature, and this is household management. But commerce makes money through exchange of money, not in the fuller, proper way. And commerce seems to concern money, since money is the matter and the end of such exchange.

Comment

1. After Aristotle has determined about one kind of acquiring property (i.e., acquiring food and other necessities of life), he here determines about another kind of acquiring property called moneymaking. And regarding this, he does two things. First, he lays out its condition. Second, he determines about it [2]. Regarding the first, he determines three things about the second kind of acquiring property. For he first determines its name, saying that we call it moneymaking, namely, because it consists of acquiring money. Second, he says that, since there is no limit to acquiring money, it seems to human beings that, because of the second kind of acquiring property, there is no limit to the wealth and acquisition of property they may acquire. For many think that this way of acquiring property is one and the same as the first kind of acquiring property, because of their close association. Third, he lays out the relation of this kind of acquiring property to the first kind, saying that it is neither the same as, nor far different from, the first kind. And he shows that it is not the same because the first kind of acquiring property (i.e., acquiring food and other necessities of life) is natural, and the second kind (i.e., acquiring money) is not. For nature did not invent money, but experience and skill introduced it. And so he said that the two kinds are not far apart, since one can possess even the necessities of life for the sake of money, and vice versa.

2. Then he begins to determine the nature of moneymaking. And since money was invented to facilitate exchanges, he does three things regarding this. First, he shows how exchange is related to the things exchanged. Second, he determines about natural exchange [3]. Third, determines about monetary exchange [6]. Therefore, he says first that, in order to consider about moneymaking, we should begin as follows. Each thing has two uses, which are the same in that each use is of the thing as such and not incidental to another use, but differ in that one use is the

proper use of the thing, and the other is a common rather than a proper use. For example, shoes have two uses. One use is proper, namely as covering for the feet, since shoes were made for this use. The other use, namely, exchange, is not proper, since shoes were not made in order that human beings exchange them for something else. But human beings can use shoes in exchange for bread or food. And using shoes in exchange, although not a proper use of shoes, nonetheless uses them as such and not as incidental to another use, since the one who exchanges them uses them according to their worth. And as he has said about shoes, so should we understand about all other things that human beings can own.

3.   Then he determines about natural exchange, doing three things in that regard. First, he shows of what things this exchange consists. Second, he shows how it was introduced [4]. Third, he shows how it is related to nature [5]. Therefore, he says first that all things can be exchanged. And the first exchange was of things that nature bestows for the necessities of human life, since some people have more of these things and others less (e.g., some have more wine, and others more bread). And so human beings needed to exchange such things until each had what was sufficient for each. (And so it is clear that, since money is not from nature, as he has said [1], commerce [i.e., exchange of money] is not from nature.)

4.   Then he shows how this exchange of necessary things was introduced. He says that there was no need of such exchange in the first association (i.e., an individual household), since all the necessities of life belonged to the head of the household, who provided everything. But when there was a larger association, namely, a neighborhood or political community, those of the same household, among whom there could be no exchange, shared in all things, and those of separate households shared in many other things as well. Therefore, there needed to be exchanges of different things, namely, that if one were to receive from another what the other had, the latter would recompense the former with what the latter had. And many foreign peoples who do not use money still practice barter, and they exchange only things that are advantageous for life (e.g., giving and receiving wine, wheat, and the like).

5.   Then he infers from the foregoing that such exchanges are not contrary to nature, since they concern things that nature provides. And it is not a kind of moneymaking, since it is not transacted by the use of money. And he proves that it is not contrary to nature, since it supplies self-sufficiency (i.e., that human beings by such exchanges have things necessary to support human life adequately).

6.   Then he determines about monetary exchange, doing two things in that regard. First, he shows how reason invented this kind of exchange, since it is not from nature. Second, he shows that it is unlimited [chap. 8,

n. 1]. Regarding the first, he does three things. First, he determines about the original invention of monetary exchange. Second, he determines about an additional kind of monetary exchange [7]. Third, he determines about the moneymaking that concerns such exchanges [8].

Therefore, he says first that another system of exchange, invented by reason, developed out of the original exchange of mutually necessary things. For the mutual assistance of human beings by exchanges came to involve more foreign trade, namely, people began to make exchanges with remote persons as well as neighbors, importing things that they needed and exporting things of which they had a surplus. Therefore, the use of money was invented because of the need of exchange, since human beings could not easily transport natural necessities (e.g., wine, wheat, or the like) to remote parts of the world. And so, in order to make exchanges in remote parts of the world, people established mutually to give and receive something that could be easily and expeditiously transported but would of itself have utility. Metals (e.g., bronze, iron, silver, and the like) are such. For they are intrinsically useful insofar as one makes vases or other implements out of them, and yet they could be easily transported to remote places, since a small amount of them, because of their rarity, were worth a great deal of other things. Just so, human beings who have to make a long journey now carry silver or gold coins instead of bronze ones for their expenses.

Because of the aforementioned need of exchange at remote places, the value of metal was first determined only by its weight and size, as, for example, some peoples use forms of bulk silver. But later, in order to free human beings from the need to measure and weigh metal, they printed a mark to signify that the metal is of such-and-such amount. Just so, some localities use standard signs to measure wine and grain. Therefore, it is clear that coins were invented for the exchange of necessary things.

7.   Then he determines about an additional, different kind of exchange. He says that, after money resulted from the aforementioned exchange, an exchange that was necessary for acquiring necessary things from remote places, a kind of monetary exchange was introduced by which money is exchanged for money. And he calls the latter exchange commerce, namely, the occupation merchants engage in. And this was first done simply and as if by chance (e.g., some merchants in foreign lands in the course of transferring money spent more than they took in). And so something involving skill later arose by experience, namely, that human beings weigh where money was exchanged, and how they could make the greatest profit. And this belongs to commercial skill.

8.   Then he determines about moneymaking, doing two things in this regard. First, he infers from the foregoing the matter and activity of this skill. Second, he answers a question [9]. Therefore, he infers from the

foregoing that, since money began to be exchanged for money for the sake of profit in a skillful way, we call the skill regarding money moneymaking. And its activity is to be able to weigh from what sources a person could make a great deal of money. For moneymaking is directed to making a great deal of money and wealth as its end.

9.   Then he resolves a question about the foregoing. For, inasmuch as he had said that moneymaking produces wealth and money [8], one could ask whether money and wealth are altogether the same thing. Regarding this, therefore, he does three things. First, he posits the opinion of certain people. Second, he introduces arguments to the contrary [10]. Third, he infers determination of the truth of the matter [11]. Therefore, he says first that human beings very often think that wealth is nothing but a great deal of money, since all moneymaking and commerce, the end of which is to multiply wealth, is about money as its proper matter.

10.   Then he posits the contrary opinion, saying that it sometimes seems fatuous to say that none of the things in accord with nature (e.g., wheat, wine, and the like) are wealth, and that all wealth consists of money, which law introduced. And he introduces two arguments for this. The first is that, given the diverse situations of human beings, no wealth without worth or benefit for the necessities of life is true wealth. But if the situation of the human beings who use wealth is altered (e.g., if it should please a king or community that coins have no value), money is of no value and offers nothing for the necessities of life. Therefore, it is foolish to say that wealth is absolutely nothing but a great deal of money.

He posits the second argument as follows. It is unfitting to say that one who is rich needs food or dies of hunger. But it can happen very often that a human being with much money needs food and dies of hunger. Just so, the famous story says that someone called Midas, because of his insatiable desire for money, asked and begged of a god that everything offered to him be made of gold, and so he, having much gold, died of hunger when all the food offered him was converted to gold. Therefore, money is not true wealth.

11.   Then he concludes by determining the truth of the matter, saying that those who correctly understand the matter because of the aforementioned arguments, hold that wealth and money, or moneymaking, are different things. For some wealth, namely, the wealth concerning things necessary for life, is in accord with nature, as he has said [chap. 6, n. 10], and such acquisition of wealth properly belongs to household management. But the moneymaking that is commerce multiplies money only by exchanging money, not in every way. And so all such moneymaking consists of money, since money is the beginning and end of such exchange, in which money is given for money. Therefore, it is clear regarding this that

those who abound in things necessary for life are in truth richer than
those who abound in money.

Chapter 8
Moneymaking in Theory (2)

Text (1257b23–1258b8)

1.   And the wealth from that moneymaking is unlimited. The skill of
medicine aims at healing without limit, and the end of any skill is unlimited, since any skill aims to produce its end to the greatest extent. (Means
to the end, however, are not unlimited, since the end is the limit for each
skill.) So also, the end provides no limit for this kind of moneymaking,
and such wealth and acquisition of money are the end of the moneymaking. But the end of household management is not to make money, since
this is not the task of household management.
2.   Therefore, it seems that there is a necessary limit of all wealth, but I
perceive that the contrary happens in practice. For all who have money increase it without limit to provide things to use.
3.   And the reason is that the two kinds of moneymaking are similar,
since each kind uses the same thing. Both kinds use acquisition of money
but not in the same way. For one kind of moneymaking, there is another
end, and for the other kind, increasing money is itself the end. Therefore,
it seems to some that the latter is a function of household management,
and they persist in thinking that they should maintain and increase their
amount of money ever more.
4.   And the reason for such a disposition is eagerness for life itself rather
than the good life. Therefore, since this desire is unlimited, they also desire without limit whatever conduces to it. And those who aim at the good
life also add what conduces to physical pleasures. And so, since this also
seems to consist of acquiring property, their every care concerns the acquisition of money.
5.   And the second kind of moneymaking comes about because of this,
since, the enjoyment of pleasure being excessive, people seek things that
conduce to excessive pleasure.

6.   And if they could not acquire this by moneymaking, they would strive for it by another means, using all of their faculties in ways contrary to nature. For example, it belongs to courage to develop boldness, not to make money. And it belongs to military skill to produce victory, and medical skill to produce health, not to make money. But all these people engage in moneymaking as if this should be their end, and everything should be advantageous for that end. Therefore, we have discussed about unnecessary moneymaking, both what it is, and why we feel need of it, and necessary moneymaking, which differs from the other. And household management is in accord with nature, which concerns food and is limited.

7.   And the answer to what they questioned at the outset, whether moneymaking belongs to household managers and statesmen, is also clear. It doesn't as such, but money needs to be at hand for them to use. For just as political science does not make human beings but takes them from nature and uses them, so also nature needs to provide food, whether from the land, sea, or anything else. And it belongs to the household managers to decide how to distribute the products from these sources. For it does not belong to the weaver to make the wool. Rather, it belongs to him to use the wool and also to know what kind is useful and suitable, or too small and unsuitable.

8.   For one may well ask why moneymaking is part of household management, and medical skill is not, although it is as necessary that members of the household be healthy as it is to provide for their life or any other necessary thing. The answer is because it belongs to the household manager and ruler to see even to health but not in the same way as it belongs to the doctor. So also it belongs to the household manager to see about money but not in the same way as it belongs to a subordinate skill.

9.   But it is most necessary, as I have said before, that nature provides the wealth. For example, it is a function of nature to provide food for offspring, since the residue from what is produced is food for all of the offspring. Therefore, moneymaking from crops and animals is in accord with nature for all human beings.

10.   There are two kinds of moneymaking, as we have said: one, commerce; the other, household management. The second kind is necessary and praiseworthy. The first consists of exchange and is justly despised, since it is from one to another, not by nature. Charging a fee for loans is most reasonably odious, since the acquisition of money is from money itself, and not about what we have acquired. For money was invented to facilitate exchange of goods. But interest makes money itself greater. And so also we derive its name, since offspring are like their progenitors, and interest is money generated by money. Therefore, this acquisition of money is most contrary to nature.

Comment

1. After Aristotle has shown how law introduced the moneymaking kind of exchange, he shows here how such acquisition of money is unlimited. And regarding this, he does two things. First, he shows what he proposes. Second, he assigns the reason for the foregoing things [3]. Regarding the first, he does two things. First he shows what he proposes. Second, he resolves a difficulty arising from this [2].

Therefore, he says first that the wealth acquired by this kind of moneymaking, namely, commerce, all of which concerns money, is unlimited, and he proves this by the following argument. In any skill, the desire of the end is unlimited, and the desire of means to the end is limited by the rule and measure of the end. For example, medical skill aims at health without limit when it brings about health as much as possible. But it administers medicine in the measure that is useful for health, not as much as possible. And the same is true in other skills. And the reason for this is because the end as such is desirable, and what is intrinsically such, if it should be greater, will be more such. For example, if something white blinds vision, something whiter blinds vision more. But money is the end of commerce, since the aim of commerce is to acquire money, and only a means of household management to its end (i.e., household governance). Therefore, moneymaking seeks unlimited money, but household management seeks a limited amount of money.

2. Then he resolves a difficulty arising from the foregoing. And regarding this, he does two things. First, he raises a question. Second, he answers it [3]. Therefore, he says first that it seems, because of the aforementioned argument, that there needs to be a limit of wealth in household management. But if one should consider what happens in practice, the contrary seems to be true, since all household managers, wanting to have money for things useful for living, increase money without limit.

3. Then he resolves the foregoing difficulty, saying that the reason for the aforementioned difference seems to be the close relationship of the two kinds of moneymaking. That is to say, there is a close relationship between the moneymaking that serves household management, which seeks money for the exchange of necessary things, and commerce, which seeks money for its own sake. For the activity of both kinds of moneymaking is the same, namely, the acquisition of money, but not in the same way. In household moneymaking, the acquisition of money is directed to another end, namely, governance of the household, but in commercial moneymaking, namely, commerce, increasing money is the end. And so, since commerce is closely related to household management, it seems to some household managers that what belongs to merchants, namely, to be zealous to maintain and increase money without limit, is their duty.

4.   Then he assigns the reason for what he had said, that household managers sometimes persist in increasing money without limit. And because some abuses result from the reason he assigns, he divides this section into three parts by the three abuses that he posits [4, 5, and 6]. Therefore, he says first that the reason for this disposition, namely, that household managers seek to increase money without limit, is because human beings are eager to live howsoever, not to live well, which is to live virtuously. For, if they were to strive to live virtuously, they would be content with things sufficient to sustain nature. But since they omit this effort and want to live according to their own will, each of them strives to acquire things with which to satisfy the individual's desire. And because the desire of human beings has no limit, they desire without limit things whereby they can satisfy their desire.

There are also others who are anxious to live well but add to living well what belongs to physical pleasures, since they say that human beings enjoy the good life only by living immersed in such pleasures. And so they seek things whereby they can enjoy physical pleasures. And since it seems to human beings that abundant wealth can bring this about, their every care seems to be to acquire a great deal of money. And we should consider that he assigns the reason why things belong to the household manager from the aim of human life, since the household manager has the good life of its members as his goal. Therefore, the first abuse is that human beings strive to acquire money without limit because they do not have the right endeavor for the good life.

5.   Then he posits the second abuse. For household managers are anxious about acquiring money. Therefore, another kind of moneymaking, namely, commerce, is added to the care of the household besides the care that is proper to household management, namely, the acquisition of things necessary for life. But since they strive excessively to enjoy physical pleasures, they seek things that can conduce to such excess, namely, abundant wealth. And so the second abuse is that unnatural and unnecessary moneymaking is included in household management.

6.   Third, he posits the third abuse, saying that, since human beings sometimes lack enough financial skill to be able to acquire things to satisfy their excessive desire for physical pleasures, they strive to acquire money in other ways. And they abuse their faculties (i.e., their virtues, skills, or position) in ways contrary to their nature. For example, courage is a virtue, and its proper function is to make human beings bold for attacking and withstanding, not to accumulate money. And so, if one uses courage to accumulate wealth, one does not use it in accord with nature. So also,

military skill is for the sake of victory, and medical skill for the sake of health, but neither skill is for the sake of money. But some use military and medical skills to acquire money and so make both into instruments to make money (i.e., to acquire money), subordinating such skills to money as the end to which all other things need to be directed. And so Eccl. 10:19 says: "All things yield to money."

Therefore, he summarily infers from the foregoing what he said about unnecessary moneymaking, namely, the moneymaking that acquires money without limit as its end. And money is also the reason why human beings need it, namely, because of their unlimited desire. He also spoke about necessary moneymaking, namely, the moneymaking that is different from the foregoing kind. For necessary moneymaking acquires money up to a limit because of another end, namely, to provide for the necessities of life. And household management, properly speaking, concerns things in accord with nature (e.g., things pertaining to food), and this moneymaking is limited, unlike the first kind of moneymaking. Or one can understand that necessary moneymaking differs from unnecessary moneymaking. Necessary moneymaking is household management, and no other things are exchanged.

7.   He had previously raised the question whether moneymaking is a part of household management or subordinate to it, and he distinguished moneymaking from other acquisition of property [chap. 6, nn. 4 and 5]. Now he answers the question. And regarding this, he does two things. First, he shows that moneymaking is subordinate to household management. Second, he shows how one kind of moneymaking is praiseworthy and another kind contemptible [10]. Regarding the first, he does three things. First, he answers the previously posed question. Second, he raises another difficulty [8]. Third, he makes clear something he previously said [9]. Therefore, he says first that the foregoing can now show the answer to the initial question, whether moneymaking belongs to household managers and statesmen or is altogether extraneous. And the truth is that moneymaking is not the same as household management, as he has said before [chap. 6, n. 3], but subordinate to it, since one needs money in order to govern the household.

And he proves this by the fact that there need to be in the household and the political community both human beings and the things necessary for them. But political science does not produce human beings. Rather, it receives them as produced by nature and then uses them. Therefore, likewise, nature, not political science or household management, produces food, whether from the land (e.g., crops) or from the sea (e.g., fish) or from anything else. Therefore, producing or acquiring such food is not the proper and immediate task of political science or household management. Rather, their proper task is to distribute those things in the household as circumstances require. Just so, we perceive that it belongs to the weaver to use wool and to know which wool is suitable for his task, and which wool is bad and unsuitable, not to make the wool. Therefore, both nature, which produces human beings and food, and the moneymaking that acquires things serve household management, just as both nature, which produces wool, and the buying that acquires it serve the weaver's skill.

8. Then he raises a question as follows. Since members of the household need health, as they need things necessary for life, such as food and clothing, why is medical skill not, like moneymaking, part of household management? And he answers that it belongs to the household manager and the ruler of a political community to consider about health in one way, namely, by using the advice of doctors for the health of their subjects. But it belongs to the doctor, not to household managers or rulers, in another way, namely, by considering what things preserve or restore health. Likewise, it also belongs to the household manager to consider about money in one way, namely, by using money already acquired and the services of those who acquire it. But it does not belong to the household manager to consider whence and how money can be acquired. Rather, the latter belong to a subordinate skill, namely, moneymaking.

9. Then he shows what he had said before [chap. 6, n. 8], namely, that nature produces necessary things. And he says, as he has said before [7], that the things that household management and political science use need especially to preexist from nature, from which subordinate skills also receive them. And he proves this by the fact that it is the function of nature to give food to what nature generates. For we perceive that the residue of generation from what was produced is food for the thing generated. For example, it is clear that animals are generated from menstrual blood, and nature converts what is left over from this material into milk and prepares food for the offspring. And so, since human beings are constituted out of things from nature, other things from nature are food for them. And so there is a natural kind of moneymaking (i.e., one that acquires food or money for food from natural things, namely, produce and animals). But it is not in accord with nature that one acquires money from money itself and not from natural things.

10. Then, with the two kinds of moneymaking stipulated, he shows which kind is praiseworthy, and which kind contemptible. And he says that we call one kind commerce, namely, the one that acquires money out of money and for the sake of money, and the other kind is household management, namely, the one that acquires money from natural things (e.g., crops and animals), as he has said [9]. The second kind is necessary for

human life and so also praiseworthy. But the first, namely, commerce, is transformed from what is a necessity of nature to what desire demands, as he has said [5], and so rightly despised. For such moneymaking is contrary to nature, since it is neither from natural things nor directed to satisfy the needs of nature. Rather, it derives from the transfer of money from one to another, namely, insofar as human beings make money from money.

And although the moneymaking that is commerce is justly despised, there is another kind of acquiring money that is most reasonably despised and odious.[13] And this moneymaking is lending money for a fee (i.e., charging a fee, as those who profit excessively by lending money do). For this acquisition of money is made from money itself, not in the original way established for acquiring money, since money was created to facilitate transfer of goods (i.e., exchanging them), as he said before [chap. 7, n. 6].

And there is another kind of moneymaking, interest (called *tokos* in Greek), whereby money increases itself. And so the Greeks called it *tokos*, since that means offspring. For we perceive that things generated by nature are like the things generating them. And so there is a kind of generation when money increases from money. And so also such acquisition of money is the most contrary to nature, since it is according to nature that money is acquired from natural things, not from money. Therefore, one kind of moneymaking is praiseworthy, and three kinds contemptible, as he has said.

Chapter 9
Moneymaking in Practice

Text (1258b9–1259a36)

1.   And since we have sufficiently determined about the theory of moneymaking, we need to proceed to consider the practice. For all such things enjoy free theoretical consideration but need practical experience.
2.   Useful kinds of moneymaking about acquiring property require expertise: which kind is the most valuable, and where and how to acquire it

---

13. In this and the next paragraph, Aquinas distinguishes two forms of interest: (1) charging a fixed fee, possibly pawnbroking; (2) charging a rate of interest.

(e.g., the acquisition of what kind of horse or cattle or sheep, and similarly what kind of other animals). For one needs to be knowledgeable about animals relative to one another: which are the most valuable, and which ones in what places, since some are plentiful in some places, and others in other places. Second, one needs to be knowledgeable about the cultivation of land, some cleared for crops and some planted with fruit trees. Third, one needs to be knowledgeable about beekeeping and rearing other animals, such as fishes and fowl, from which one can obtain support. Therefore, these kinds of moneymaking are primary and most appropriate.

3. Commerce is the most important means of exchange and has three parts: shipping commercial goods, transporting them over land, and assisting merchants. And these things differ from one another, since some things are more secure and other things more profitable. The second means of exchange is lending money at interest. The third means is working for pay as lowly skilled and unskilled hired hands. (The unskilled workers are useful only for the body.) The fourth kind of moneymaking is in between the natural and the unnatural, since it partakes of both nature and exchange. This includes acquiring unproductive but useful things extracted from the earth or produced by it (e.g., logging and all kinds of mining). And there are many kinds of mining, since many kinds of metals are extracted from the earth.

4. And I have now spoken about each of these things in a general way. And to speak in detail and more assiduously about these things might be useful for carrying out the activities, but to spend more time on them would be burdensome.

5. And the most skillful activities are those in which there is the least luck. And the lowest skilled activities are those in which the body is most defiled. And the most slavish activities are those in which the body is most used. And the most ignoble activities are those in which the least excellence is required.

6. And since some authors have written about these things (e.g., Chares of Paros and Apollodorus of Lemnos about the cultivation of land, both land cleared for crops and land planted with fruit trees). And likewise, others have written about other things, and those engaged in such things may consider these works.

7. Moreover, scattered accounts about how some succeeded in making money need to be collected, since all these things are useful for those who esteem moneymaking.

8. For example, there is what Thales of Miletus did. This concerned a way of making money attributed it to him because of his wisdom, but it may be something universal. According to the story, when people reproached

him for being poor, saying that his philosophy was useless, he concluded from studying the stars that there would be a rich olive harvest. While it was still winter, he raised a little capital and paid deposits to all of the olive growers in Miletus and Chios. This cost him very little, as there were no competitors. And when the harvest time came, there was a sudden and large demand for olives, and he charged whatever he wished. Since he had made a great deal of money, he demonstrated that it is easy for philosophers to become rich if they wish, but that is not what they strive for. Therefore, according to the story, Thales demonstrated his wisdom in this way.

9.   But, as we have said, there is something universal that is involved in such moneymaking, namely, securing a monopoly for oneself if one could. Therefore, some cities needing money also become wealthy in this way, since they create a monopoly over the commodities they sell.

10.   A certain Sicilian, with money deposited with him, simultaneously bought all the iron from the iron foundries. And after this, when buyers came at market time, he was the only seller. He did not raise the price excessively but still made 100 talents on an investment of 50. Therefore, when Dionysius heard this, he commanded the man to leave Syracuse and take the money with him, as if the man had discovered a way to wealth unsuitable for Dionysius' own affairs.

11.   And Thales and the Sicilian had the same insight. Both strove to create a monopoly for themselves. And this information about commerce is useful for statesmen to know. For many political communities have need to acquire money and such wealth as much or more than households do. Therefore, some statesmen are also politically active only for this.

Comment

1.   After Aristotle has taught knowledge about the origin of moneymaking and its properties and parts, he here determines things that belong to its use. And he speaks first of his aim. Second, he asserts what he proposes [2]. Therefore, he says first that, since we have adequately determined about moneymaking in the things that belong to knowing its nature, we need briefly and in passing to posit the things that belong to its use, namely, how we should use it. For all such things belonging to human actions enjoy free (i.e., unhindered) consideration, since it is easy to consider them in general. But one needs to have experience about them in order to be able to make perfect use of them.

2.   Then he determines things that belong to the use of moneymaking. And regarding this, he does two things. First, he distinguishes the kinds of moneymaking. Second, he posits some useful examples of moneymaking [6]. Regarding the first, he does two things. First, he assigns the

kinds of moneymaking necessary for human life. Second, he assigns the unnecessary kinds [3]. And he has said before that the moneymaking, whereby human beings acquire money from things that nature provides for the necessities of life, is necessary [chap. 8, nn. 8–9]. And he posits two parts of such moneymaking. The first is the moneymaking whereby human beings can acquire money by buying and selling such things.

And regarding this part, he says that these kinds of moneymaking are useful (i.e., useful examples), and so human beings should be knowledgeable about such goods that they acquire: which of them are the most valuable, where they are sold at the highest price, and how they are sold (e.g., when and under what other conditions). And he explains what acquirable goods he is speaking about. For example, there is the acquisition of horses, cattle, birds, and other animals. And one who wishes to make profit from these things needs to know which of these are the most valuable, and where they are. For some are plentiful in some places, and others in other places, namely, so that one buys where they are plentiful and sells where they are valuable.

And the second part of such acquisition is to acquire a supply of goods to sell from cultivation of the land, whether the land is cleared, that is, without trees (e.g., fields in which wheat is sown), or planted (e.g., vineyards, gardens, and olive groves). For human beings acquire abundance of wheat, wine, and the like through such cultivation. And human beings also need to be knowledgeable about beekeeping and rearing other animals, both those of the sea, namely, fish, and those of the air, namely, fowl, from whatever things one may acquire support for human life. For one can acquire money from their abundance. Therefore, these are clearly the primary and most proper kinds of moneymaking and called such because one then acquires money from natural things, for the sake of which money was first invented.

3.   Then he distinguishes the kinds of moneymaking of exchange. And he has said before that the moneymaking of exchange is the moneymaking by which money is acquired from other things than those necessary for life [chap. 7, nn. 7–8]. And he calls it the moneymaking of exchange because moneymaking is transferred from necessary to unnecessary things. And regarding the first, he does three things. First, he distinguishes the parts of such moneymaking. Second, he excuses himself from a more diligent consideration of these parts [4]. Third, he clarifies some things that he had said [5].

Regarding the first, he posits four kinds of such moneymaking. The first and most important is commercial, since merchants especially acquire money. And he distinguishes three parts of commerce. The first part is shipping, namely, the trade that merchants engage in overseas. And we call the second kind transporting (i.e., transporting freight), namely, engaging in trade by transporting goods overland on wagons or beasts of burden. And we call the third kind assisting merchants (e.g., when one does not transport the goods by sea or land but assists merchants by sharing money or goods with them). And these kinds differ in relation to one another, since some are more secure (e.g., trade by land) and others more profitable but more dangerous (e.g., trade by sea).

And the second chief kind of moneymaking by such exchange is charging for lending money, namely, moneymaking that acquires money by interest.

And the third kind of such moneymaking is by wage earning (e.g., by hired hands). There is a difference in this, since some hiring is for lowly skills, that is, those that defile the body (e.g., the skill of cooks and such servants). And other hiring is for unskilled work, which is useful only for the body, and also in which only the body is useful (e.g., those who are hired for money to plow fields or do anything else of that sort).

And the fourth kind of moneymaking is in between moneymaking by exchange and the original kind (i.e., the necessary kind), namely, acquiring profit from mining stones and metals from the earth. And this moneymaking has something in common with the other two. For it has something in common with the original kind, since money is made from the earth and things produced by the earth, as agriculture concerns things produced by the earth. And it is one with moneymaking by exchange in that such metals do not generate any produce belonging to the necessities of life, as fields and animals do. But such things are useful for other things (e.g., building houses or making tools). And this fourth kind includes specifically different kinds of metals, such as gold, silver, iron, and the like.

4.   Then he excuses himself from a complete determination of these things, saying that he has already spoken generally about these kinds of moneymaking. But it would be useful for the activities of those wanting to acquire money to determine more diligently in detail about particular moneymaking activities. Nonetheless, it is burdensome for those attending to more important things to delay long over such things.

5.   Then he explains some things that he previously said about lowly skilled and unskilled activities. And he says that those activities are the most skillful in which luck is least involved, since we say that luck causes what happens beyond the foresight of reason, of which skill consists. And so activities subject to a good deal of luck involve little skill (e.g., fishing with hooks, and the like). And conversely, activities whose effects are little subject to luck are the most skillful (e.g., the work of carpenters and other craftsmen). And those activities that most defile the body (e.g., the work

of dyers, dishwashers, and such like) involve the lowest skills (i.e., abject but useful skills). And those activities in which the greater part of their exercise concerns the body and little regards reason (e.g., the work of porters, messengers, and the like) are the most slavish. And those are the most ignoble of all for which the least excellence, whether of the soul or the body, is required, as is clear in some of the aforementioned things.

6. Then he proposes useful proofs relative to the foregoing kinds of moneymaking. First, he teaches us to consider such proofs from literature. Second, he teaches us from examples [7]. Therefore, he says first that some wise men have written about the foregoing. For example, a certain Chares of Paros and Apollodorus of Lemnos wrote about the cultivation of land, both that cleared for crops and that planted for fruit, as Palladius also did with the Romans. And others wrote about various other kinds of moneymaking. Therefore, all who have responsibility should more fully consider the foregoing things from these authors' writings.

7. Then he proposes proof by considering examples. First, he lays out his aim. Second, he gives examples [8]. Therefore, he says first that one should consider both the writings of those who devised skills about the aforementioned kinds of moneymaking, and whether any scattered examples about people acquiring great money are recounted in various stories. For these examples will be useful for those who strive to acquire money.

8. Then he gives two examples [8 and 10]. Regarding the first, he does two things. First, he proposes the example. Second, he shows for what it is useful [9]. Therefore, one should know about the first example that Thales of Miletus was one of the seven wise men and the first to begin to study about natural philosophy. (The other six were occupied about human affairs.) And what he did has some useful consideration for acquiring money, although it was ascribed to his wisdom, not desire for money. But we can understand a universal pattern about acquiring money from what he did. When people reproached him for being poor and said that his philosophy was thus useless for him, he studied the stars, of which he was expert, and concluded that, contrary to custom, there would be an abundance of olives the following year. For there was also an abundance of olives the year before, and olives are most often in short supply after a year of abundance. Therefore, while there was still an abundance of olives in winter, he paid a little money in two cities, namely, Miletus and Chios, as deposits for the harvest of the next year, which people expected to be small. Therefore, when the harvest time of olives came, and many simultaneously and suddenly sought to buy olives, he charged as much as he wanted to. And so he collected much money and showed that it is easy for philosophers to become rich if they wish to do so, but they do not strive for this. And Thales demonstrated his wisdom in this way.

9.   Then Aristotle shows why such an example is useful for moneymaking, saying that it is very useful for acquiring money if one could set up a monopoly (i.e., a single seller's market), namely, that only one seller sells some things in the city. [Here follows a digression on the different meanings of *polis,* the Greek word for *city,* when the vowels are changed, and traces *monopoly* to one of these meanings.] And since this contributes greatly to acquiring money, so some cities, needing money, establish a monopoly, namely, are the only ones who sell salt or the like.

10.   Then he posits the second example. First, he describes what was done. Second, he shows that it comes back to the same thing as the first example. Therefore, he says first that a certain man in Sicily, who had money on deposit with him, simultaneously bought all the iron from the foundries in which it was cast. And so, when merchants came to buy it, he was the only seller, but, in order to sell it more quickly, he did not charge a very excessive price. Nonetheless, he made 100 talents from an investment of 50. And Dionysius, the tyrant of Syracuse, thinking the man very enriched, commanded him to leave Syracuse but permitted him to take his money with him. For tyrants think that it is unsuitable for them that some citizens greatly enrich themselves, as he will say later.[14]

11.   Then he shows that that example comes back to the same thing as the first, since both the Sicilian and the philosopher Thales perceived the same thing, namely, that they exercised a monopoly. And it is also useful that statesmen consider that many cities, like households, need to acquire money, and the city still more, inasmuch as it needs more things. And so some statesmen seem to aim chiefly to multiply money in the public treasury.

Chapter 10
Family

Text (1259a37–1260a36)

1.   And so there were three parts of household management. One is despotic, about which I have spoken before. One is paternal. And the third

---

14. *Politics* V, 11 (1313b18–19).

is marital. For there is also rule over both wife and children as free persons but in different ways. The rule over a wife is political, and the rule over children kingly. For the male is by nature more fit to rule than the female unless something contrary to nature should be somehow evident, and the elder and mature than the younger and immature.

2.   Therefore, in political kinds of rule, the roles of ruler and subject are for the most part interchanged. For political regimes by their nature aim at equality and no difference between citizens. But if one person should rule, and another should be a subject, the regimes seek distinctions in outward appearance, mode of address, and honors, as Amasis spoke of the mode of address about a foot washbasin. And the male is always related to the female in this way.

3.   And there is kingly rule over children. For the begetter is the ruler by reason of love and age, and this is a kind of kingly rule. And this is why Homer rightly addressed Zeus as "father of human beings and the gods," calling the king over them "father" of all of them. For a king needs to be different by nature but the same in kind. And this is the condition of the elder to the younger, and of the begetter to the begotten.

4.   Therefore, it is clear that the care of the household concerns human beings more than material property, the virtue of human beings more than the possessions we call wealth, and free persons more than slaves.

5.   First, therefore, one will ask about slaves whether they have any other, more honorable virtue (e.g., moderation, courage, justice, and other like habits) than they have as tools or servants. Or do they have none beyond bodily service? For there is doubt about the answers to both questions. For if there is such virtue, what is the difference between slaves and free persons? And if there is not, this is inappropriate, since they are human beings and share in reason.

6.   And there is almost the same question about wives and children, whether they have virtues, whether wives should be moderate, brave, and just, and whether children should be moderate. And so we should consider in general about subjects and rulers by nature whether they have the same or different virtue. For if both need to share in noble character, why will it be necessary that one always rule, and another always be a subject? For it is impossible for them to differ by more and less, since being a subject and being a ruler differ specifically, not to a degree. And if the one needs to have virtues, and the other does not, this is astounding. For if the ruler will not be self-controlled and just, how will he rule well? And if subjects lack virtue, how will they be good subjects? For one who lacks self-control and is cowardly will not perform his duties.

7.   Therefore, it is clear that both need to share in virtue, but there are differences between them, as there are also among those by nature subjects.

And this will be immediately illustrated regarding the soul. For in it, something by nature rules, and something else is by nature subject, and we say that the powers of these things (e.g., the rational and the irrational powers) are different. Therefore, it is clear that there is also the same relationship in other things. Therefore, many things rule and are ruled by nature. For example, free persons rule over slaves in one way, males over females in another way, and men over children in still another way. And parts of the soul are present in all of them but in different ways. For slaves completely lack deliberation, females have it but weakly, and children have it only imperfectly. Therefore, we should think that the same is necessarily true regarding moral virtues, that all need to share in these moral virtues to the degree the virtues are necessary for each to perform the task proper to each, not in the same way. Therefore, a ruler needs to have complete moral virtue, since his task is absolutely that of master builder, and reason is the master builder. And each of the others needs to have as much moral virtue as the ruler conveys to them. And so it is clear that moral virtue belongs to all of the aforementioned, and that the moderation, courage, and justice of men and women are not the same, as Socrates thought. But the courage of men is in ruling, and the courage of women is in serving. And the relationship is the same regarding the other moral virtues.

8.   This is clear, and the more so if we consider the matter in greater detail, since those who speak in general terms about having a good soul, acting virtuously or rightly, or such like deceive themselves. For those who, like Gorgias, enumerate the virtues speak far better than those who determine virtue in general terms. Therefore, one needs to hold in every case what the poet said about women, that silence is to their credit, although not always to men's. And since a child is not mature, it is clear that his virtue belongs to him in relation to his end and his tutor, not in relation to himself. So also is the virtue of slaves relative to their masters, and we have held that slaves are useful for necessary things. Therefore, it is clear that the slave needs little virtue, only enough so as not to fail to do his work because of intemperance or cowardice.

Comment

1.   After Aristotle has determined about the association of master and slave, with the addition of a general treatment about acquiring property, he here determines about the other two domestic associations that he had posited before [chap. 2, n. 2], namely, of husband and wife, and of father and sons. And he divides it into two parts. In the first, he determines some things about such associations. In the second, he excuses himself from a

more diligent consideration of the associations [chap. 11, n. 4]. Regarding the first, he does two things. First, he determines about the afore-mentioned associations, relating them to other forms of rule. Second, he raises a general question about all those forms of rule [5]. Regarding the first, he does three things. First, he posits a relation of the aforementioned associations to other forms of rule. Second, he clarifies the afore-mentioned relation [2]. Third, he shows that care of household manage-ment is most engaged about such associations [4]. Therefore, he says first that he has said before that there are three parts of household management (i.e., governance of the household) regarding the three aforementioned associations [chap. 2, n. 2]. He has already spoken about one of them, namely, the despotic, which belongs to master and slave [chap. 2, n. 4–chap. 5, n. 7]. And so it remains to speak about the second (i.e., the paternal, which belongs to father and children) and the third (i.e., the marital, which belongs to husband and wife).

And he says three things about these associations. First, he says that there is an order of preference, or ruling power, in each of these associa-tions. For husbands rule over wives, and fathers over children, as free per-sons, not as slaves. And these two kinds of rule differ from despotic rule in the latter respect. Second, he says that these two associations are not of the same type. Rather, husbands rule over wives by a political form of rule (i.e., as one chosen to rule is in charge of a political community), but fa-thers are in charge of sons by a kingly form of rule. And this is so because fathers have full power over sons, just as a king does in his kingdom, but husbands have power over wives only insofar as the law of marriage re-quires, not full power regarding all things. Just so, the ruler of a political community has power over citizens according to the community's laws. Third, he shows that these two forms of rule are in accord with nature, since what is preeminent in nature always rules, as he has maintained be-fore [chap. 3, nn. 2–3]. But the male is by nature preeminent over the fe-male, unless something happens contrary to nature (e.g., in the case of effeminate men). And fathers are likewise by nature preeminent over sons, as those older over those younger, and the mature over the immature. Therefore, the male rules over the female, and fathers over sons.

2. Then he clarifies the aforementioned relations: first, the relation of marital rule to political rule; second, the relation of paternal rule to kingly rule [3]. Therefore, he shows first the relation of marital rule to political rule regarding the difference between the two. For persons ruling and persons being ruled exchange roles in political regimes, since those who hold public office one year are subjects in another. And this is so because it is proper that there be such rule among those who are equal by nature and differ by nature in no way. But during the time one person rules, and

others are subjects, human ingenuity added differences. These regard external appearance, which consists of distinctive external marks, modes of address, since officeholders have titles, and human beings address them differently than before, and honors, namely, in that citizens show signs of respect to those in office that they did not previously show. Just so, the poet Amasis spoke about a foot washbasin as follows. The washbasin, if such distinctive marks were circumscribed on it, and two other gifts were bestowed on it, would not seem to differ from the ruler of a political community. Therefore, it is clear that political rule alternates from person to person, but this does not happen in the rule of husband over wife, since the male does not later become a female, nor the female a male. Rather, they always remain the same.

3.   Then he relates the paternal form of rule to the kingly by their likeness. And he says that the rule of father over children (i.e., sons) is kingly. For in this form of rule, we note two things, namely, that the father who begets rules over his sons because of love, since he by nature loves them, and also because of age, having the natural privilege of age over them, as it were. And in this regard, it is a kind (i.e., likeness) of kingly rule. And so Homer called Zeus (i.e., the supreme god) "father of human beings and the gods" (i.e., king of them all, both human beings and the higher substances that he called gods). For the king who rules forever and has full power in all things necessarily differs by nature from his subjects in the magnitude of his goodness. And yet the king is necessarily one in kind with his subjects, at least regarding the human kind of king, and it will be better if he also belongs to the same clan. And this is also the relation of the elder to the younger, and of the begetter to the begotten, namely, that the elder and begetter have the natural privilege of age. And so the king necessarily differs by nature from others. For were he not to be better in natural goodness, it would not be just that he always rule with full power over those equal to him, as Aristotle will say later.[15] Therefore, a natural difference distinguishes kingly rule from political rule, which is by nature between equals. And love distinguishes kingly rule from that of a tyrant, who rules for his own convenience, not because of love that he has for his subjects.

4.   Then Aristotle infers that the chief aim of the household manager concerns these two associations more than other things. For the household manager strives about human beings more than the acquisition of inanimate things (e.g., wheat, wine, and such like). And he should strive for the virtue by which human beings live well more than the virtue by

---

15. Ibid. III, 16 (1287b41–1288a2).

which one acquires and increases property well, which is the meaning of the word *wealth*. And he should likewise be zealous for the virtue of free persons more than the virtue of slaves. And we can assign the reason for this. For the chief aim of each thing concerns its end, and one seeks inanimate things for the sake of human beings, as the things' end, and slaves for the sake of free persons to serve them.

5.   Then, since he had mentioned the virtue of free persons and slaves, he raises a question about this. And regarding it, he does three things. First, he raises the question. Second, he answers it [7]. Third, he poses a further question based on that answer. Regarding the first, he does two things. First, he raises a question about master and slave. Second, he raises a question about other kinds of rule [6]. Therefore, he says first that there can be a difficulty about slaves. For it is clear that a slave should have an instrumental and subservient virtue, namely, a virtue by which the slave knows and can follow the master's command and serve him, as he has said before that there are servile kinds of knowledge [chap. 5, n. 4]. But there is a question whether there are, beyond those virtues, other, more worthy virtues proper to a slave (e.g., the moral virtues of moderation, courage, justice, and the like), or no virtue other than the virtue pertaining to manual labor belongs to a slave. And he says that there seems to be a difficulty on each side of the question. On the one hand, if having such virtues belongs to slaves as well as free persons, slaves will not seem to differ from free persons in any way. On the other hand, it seems improper if slaves, although they are human beings sharing in reason, should not have the virtues by which human beings live according to reason.

6.   Then he raises the same question regarding other kinds of rule, saying that one can also ask the same thing about wives and children as about slaves, namely, whether or not wives and children need to be self-restrained, brave, and just. And one can also raise the question generally regarding every kind of rule, namely, whether or not the ruler and subject have the same virtue. And he poses an objection to each side of the question. On the one hand, if both ruler and subject need to share in noble character (i.e., moral goodness), there will be no reason why one person should be a subject, and another always rule (i.e., throughout his life). (But it would be different if they ruled and were ruled successively, as happens in political rule.) Nor can we say that the virtue of the ruler and that of the subject differ by more and less, since more and less do not distinguish species. Rather, ruling and being a subject differ specifically. And so it does not seem sufficient to explain the difference between ruler and subject that one person has more virtue than another. On the other hand, if we should say that one person needs to have virtue, and that another does not, something inappropriate also follows. If the ruler will not be

self-controlled and just, he will not be able to rule well. And if the subject should not have those virtues, he will not be able to be a good subject, since he will often fail to do his duty because of lack of self-restraint or because of cowardice, and so will not be a good subject.

7.   Then he answers the question under consideration. First, he proposes the answer in general. Second, he proposes the answer in particular [8]. Therefore, he first infers from the arguments introduced for one side that both the ruler and the subject need to share in virtue, since, otherwise, the former would not rule well, and the latter would not be a good subject. But there is a difference between the kinds of virtue in each, and he shows this by things that are by nature subject to other things. And he gives an example regarding parts of the soul, one of which is by nature ruled, namely, the irrational part, the irascible and concupiscible powers. And we hold that each part has a virtue but a different kind of virtue, since the virtue of the rational part is prudence, and the virtue of the irrational part includes moderation, courage, and like virtues. And so it is clear that other things that rule and are ruled by nature are also related in the same way. And since nature is different in different things, so there are by nature different things that rule and are ruled. For example, a free person rules over his slaves in one way, and the male over the female, and the man over his children, in other ways, as he has also maintained before [1–3]. And the aforementioned parts of the soul are present in all of these. And so also the virtues of these parts are present in all of the foregoing, but in different ways.

And he first shows this as regards the rational part of the soul, to which deliberation belongs. For the slave as such does not deliberate about his actions. And the reason for this is that we deliberate about things in our power, but the slave's activities are in the power of his master, not in his own power. And so the slave does not have the free power of deliberating. But the female, since she is free, has the power of deliberating, although her deliberation is weak. And the reason for this is that her reason, because of the tenderness of her nature, weakly adheres to decisions and is quickly drawn away from them because of particular emotions (e.g., desire, anger, fear, or such like). And children have deliberation but not fully developed deliberation. And the reason for this is that they do have the complete use of reason, so that they can discern the particular things that one should pay attention to in deliberations. And so they are disposed in a different way to what belongs to reason.

And we should likewise consider the matter regarding moral virtues, since all human beings partake of them, but not in the same way. Rather, each one partakes of them as much as necessary for one's own task. And so the one who rules, whether over the political community, slaves, wife, or sons, needs to have complete moral virtue, since his task is absolutely the work of a master builder (i.e., a chief craftsman). For, as the chief craftsman directs and commands his assistants who do manual work, so the ruler directs his subjects. And so he has the duty of reason, which is related as the chief craftsman to the inferior parts of the soul. And so the ruler needs to have complete reason, but each of the others who are subjects has as much reason and virtue as the ruler conveys to them (i.e., they need to have as much as suffices to follow the direction of the ruler by fulfilling his commands). And so it is clear that some moral virtue, namely, for example, moderation, courage, and justice, belongs to all of the aforementioned subjects.

But the same virtue does not belong to men and women and other subjects, as Socrates thought. Rather, the courage of men is to command, namely, that no fear cause them to fail to order what should be done, but women and any subjects need to have subservient courage, namely, that they do not fail to do their duty out of fear. So also courage in the commander of the army and that of soldiers are different. And we should say the same about all the other virtues that concern ruling in the ruler and serving in subjects. And this makes clear that these virtues do not differ by more or less but in some respect by reason.

8. Then he shows in greater detail what he previously said, saying that what he said will be clearer to those who wish to consider the matter in greater detail. For those who wish to speak about human actions only in general deceive themselves, since they cannot fully arrive at the truth. For example, if individuals were to be satisfied to know that virtue rightly disposes the soul or is the way in which human beings act rightly, or some such thing, and to wish to know nothing more about virtue, they would deceive themselves. They would have incomplete and useless knowledge about virtue. For those who enumerate virtues in particular, as Gorgias did, speak far better than those who speak only in general. And the reason for this is that acts concern individual things. And so we need to consider in detail things belonging to acts.

And so, as a certain poet said about women something that belongs particularly to their virtue, so also should we think regarding all things. For it belongs to the character and worthiness of women to be silent, since it proceeds from the modesty due them. But silence does not belong to the character of men. Rather, it belongs to their character that they speak when it is fitting. And so also St. Paul in 1 Cor. 14:34–5 warns women to be silent in the churches and ask their husbands at home if they wish to learn anything. But since the child is not mature, his virtue is not in relation to himself (i.e., not ruled by his own understanding) but disposed as suitable for his proper end and obeying his tutor, namely, his teacher. And so the wise man in Sir. 30:11 says: "Do not give power to your son in his youth, and do not regard his thoughts." Likewise, the virtue of the slave is in relation to his master. For Aristotle has said before that the slave is useful for the necessities of life [chap. 2]. And so the slave needs only a little virtue, enough not to fail to perform his duties because of inordinate desire or cowardice.

Chapter 11
Craftsmen

Text (1260a36–b24)

1.   And if what I said about slaves is true, someone will now ask whether craftsmen will need to have virtue, since they very often fail to perform their tasks because of lack of self-control.
2.   But there is a very big difference between the two situations. For the slave shares in the life of the household, but the craftsman is more remotely associated with it and contributes virtue insofar as he contributes service. For a common artisan has a kind of servitude, and a slave is one of the things such by nature, but neither a shoemaker nor any other craftsman is.
3.   Therefore, it is clear that the master should cause such virtue for his slaves but not as master instruct them about their tasks. Therefore, they speak wrongly who deprive slaves of reason and say that masters should only issue commands, since one should admonish slaves more than children. But we have determined about these things in this way.
4.   And about the virtue of husbands and wives, the virtue of children and fathers, their moral discourse, what is right and wrong, and how one should pursue good and avoid evil, we need to consider in regard to things that concern regimes.
5.   For every household is a part of the political community, and these things belong to the household, and we need to perceive the virtue of the part in relation to the virtue of the whole of which it is a part. Therefore, it is necessary to educate both women and children regarding the regime, if it makes a difference for the political community that children and women are virtuous. And it necessarily does. For women represent a half of the free persons, and children become stewards of the regime.

6.   Therefore, since we have determined about these things, we should speak about the rest in other places. Putting aside this discussion, as if now finished, let us make a fresh start and first consider about the opinions of others on the best regime.

Comment

1.   Having answered the previous question, he here poses another question, which arises from the answer to the previous question. And regarding the new question, he does three things. First, he poses the question. Second, he answers it [2]. Third, he draws a corollary from the answer [3]. Therefore, there is a question about what he said before [chap. 10, nn. 5–8]. For if it is true that slaves should have some virtue, lest they fail to perform their tasks because of lack of self-control or out of cowardice, a like argument would seem to demonstrate that craftsmen need to have some virtue in order to be good craftsmen. For it very often happens that they make something defective in their work because of lack of self-control or other vices (e.g., negligently slacking off when they attend to other things).

2.   Then he answers the question under discussion, saying that there is a big difference between slaves and craftsmen. And he proves this by two arguments. The first is because the slave shares in the life of the household in something (i.e., the human intercourse of the household as a slave). For he has said before that the slave is an instrument in things that belong to activity (i.e., human intercourse) [chap. 2, n. 9]. And so, since moral virtues perfect human beings in human intercourse, slaves need to share in some moral virtue in order to be good. But the craftsman is more remote from human intercourse, since the activity of a craftsman, as such, concerns artifacts, which we call things made, and not things done in human intercourse. And so we call someone a good craftsman (e.g., a good blacksmith) because he knows how to, and can, make good knives, even if he should use his skill wickedly or negligently. But he contributes as much virtue in his work as he performs service for human intercourse. For example, we see that some artisans, such as common artisans (i.e., hired hands like cooks), have a fixed service when they are assigned to and perform certain particular tasks. And they need moral virtue in this respect in order to be good in their work.

And he proposes a second argument. The slave is one of the things from nature, and he has proved before that some human beings are by nature slaves [chap. 3]. But no shoemaker or any craftsman is such by nature. Rather, reason invented all skills. But virtue is related to things in us from nature, since we have a natural inclination to virtue, as he said in the

Ethics.[16] And so it is clear that one needs moral virtue in order to be a good slave, but not in order to be a good craftsman.

3.   Then he draws a corollary from what he has said. For he has said why the slave needs virtue [chap. 10, nn. 5–8]. And human beings, who have an inclination to virtue, need to acquire it through the zeal of the one who governs them. For example, lawmakers should make citizens virtuous, as he says in the *Ethics.*[17] And so it is clear that the master should cause the virtue that his slave should have in order to be good, by teaching him how he should act, by punishing him if he acts wrongly, and by rewarding him if he acts rightly. But we should not say that it belongs to the master to have mastery (i.e., a masterly knowledge that instructs his slave in servile tasks, for example, how to cook or do some such things). But the master should teach the slave how to be self-controlled, humble, patient, and such like. And so those who say that masters should use only commands with slaves, not reason, do not speak correctly. For we should admonish slaves more than young sons, since young sons are not yet capable of being admonished. And we have thus determined about these things.

4.   Then he excuses himself from a more diligent determination about the two associations. And regarding this, he does three things. First, he explains his excuse. Second, he assigns the reason for what he has said [5]. Third, he connects the aforementioned things to the things to be spoken of [6]. Therefore, he says first that, regarding things that we ought to say about regimes (i.e., political communities), we need to treat of the virtue of husband and wife, the virtue of father and sons, their communication or intercourse, what is good or bad in this, and how to procure what is good and avoid what is evil. And so we cannot at present here determine these matters before we speak about regimes.

5.   Then he assigns two arguments why we need to determine the aforementioned things about regimes. The first is because we should consider the disposition of the part in relation to the whole of which it is a part (e.g., the disposition of the foundation of a house in relation to the house). But the household is part of the political community, to which the two associations, namely, of father and sons, and of husband and wife, primarily belong. And so we need to consider in relation to regimes how children and wives should be educated.

He proposes a second argument. For we should consider in the case of regimes things whose disposition makes a difference regarding the goodness of the political community. But such things consist of the instruction

---

16. *Ethics* II, 1 (1103a23–26).
17. Ibid. (1103b2–6).

of children and women, how instruction is good for both, since women make up half of the population of free persons in the political community, and boys become men, who need to be stewards of the community. Therefore, we should determine about the instruction of children and wives in regimes.

6. Then he connects what he has said to what he is to say, saying that he has determined about the foregoing, and that he needs to speak in other places (i.e., next) of the rest, which belong to regimes. Therefore, we should at present put aside the discussion belonging to household administration, as if now finished, and make a fresh start by considering the opinions of others on the best regime.

And then the first book ends.

Book II

Chapter 1
Political Unity

Text (1260b27–1261b15)

1.   We wish to consider about the political community that is best for having all things whereby human beings can live as much as possible as they choose. Therefore, we need to consider the different regimes that certain cities said to be well ruled by laws use, and also whether there are other regimes that some thinkers said and perceived to be well disposed. And we do this in order that what is rightly disposed and useful may be apparent.

2.   And let no one think that seeking something more besides such regimes is simply cleverness on our part. Rather, let him understand that we adopt this method because none of the existing regimes are rightly disposed.

3.   First, we should begin with what nature gives us as the source of theorizing. For it is necessary that all citizens share in everything, nothing, or only some things.

4.   Therefore, it is clearly impossible that they share in nothing. For the political community is a sharing, and citizens need to share, first of all, in the territory of the political community. For there is one territory, and it belongs to one political community. And citizens are members of that community.

5.   But is it better that citizens in a well constituted city share in everything that can be shared, or better for them to share in only some things? For example, citizens may share in children, wives, and property with one another, as Plato says in the *Republic*. For Socrates there says that children, wives, and property should be common. Therefore, we ask whether it is better to do as we now do or to follow the legal system prescribed in the *Republic*.

6.   And so the proposal that the wives should be common to all raises many different difficulties. It does not seem evident from Socrates' arguments

why he says that this system should be legally established. Moreover, the proposal is impossible as regards the end that he says in the dialogue should belong to the political community. And he has determined nothing about how to apportion the wives.

7.   And I say that it is best that every political community be as united as possible, since Socrates presupposes this.

8.   But it is clear that a political community that becomes progressively more and more unified will cease to be a political community. For the political community by nature consists of many people. And the more unified it is, the more it will become a household, and the household become a human being. For we shall surely say that a household is more unified than a political community, and an individual human being more unified than a household. Therefore, if one could do this, one should not, since it would destroy the political community. And a political community is composed of both many human beings and different kinds of human beings, since a political community is not made of like human beings. For there is a difference between a military alliance and a political community. The former is quantitatively beneficial, even if it should provide the same kind of assistance. For a military alliance is by nature suitable to provide military assistance like a greater weight pulling a lesser weight. And there is also a difference between a political community and a clan, as when the people have not been separated into villages but are like the Arcadians. But it is necessary to constitute something unified out of different kinds of things. Therefore, equal reciprocity between the different parts preserves political communities, as I have said before in the *Ethics*, since this is necessary even regarding those who are free and equal.

9.   And it is impossible that all rule simultaneously. Rather, they need to do so by annual succession or some other rotation or time period. And so it happens in this way that all share in the ruling power, as if shoemakers and carpenters were to change places and not always be shoemakers or carpenters. And since it is better that things concerning the political community also be so disposed, it is clear how it is better that the same persons always rule, if possible. But among those in which this is by nature impossible, since all are equal by nature, and it is also at the same time just that all share in the ruling power, whether the rule is good or bad, this imitates the ideal, namely, in that equals in turn yield office and are like they were at the beginning. For some rule, and others are subjects, as if having become different persons. And those ruling differ in the same way, since different people occupy different offices. Therefore, it is clear from all these things that it is not fit by nature that the political community should be so united, as some say, and that the so-called greatest good in political communities destroys them, although the good of each thing preserves it.

10.   And it is clear in another way that excessive quest for unity of the political community is not better. For the household is more self-sufficient than an individual human being, and the political community than a household. And the political community aims to come about when it becomes a self-sufficient association of many people. Therefore, if greater self-sufficiency is preferable to lesser self-sufficiency, lesser unity is also preferable to greater unity.

Comment

1.   After Aristotle has determined in Book I about things belonging to the household, which are elements of the political community, he begins here to determine about the political community itself by the method he touched on at the end of that book [I, chap. 11, n. 6] and at the end of the *Ethics*.[1] First, he lays out what others have said about the political association. Second, he begins to determine about those things in his own opinion at the beginning of Book III [III, chap. 1]. Regarding the first, he does two things. First, he speaks about what his aim is. Second, he carries out his aim [3]. Regarding the first, he does two things. First, he lays out his aim. Second, he makes an apology for it [2].

   Therefore, he says first that his chief aim is to consider about the political association in order to know what mode of political intercourse is the best, how to have all the things by which human beings can live to the greatest extent as they choose. To pursue this, we need to consider regimes (i.e., constitutions) of political communities that others have discussed. Some of these regimes are those that particular cities use and people praise regarding the fact that their laws govern them well, and some those that certain philosophers and wise persons have discussed and seem to be well-disposed. And so we need to consider this in order to clarify what is right and useful in the social intercourse and regime of the political community. For comparing many regimes can make clearer what is best and most useful.

   And we should note that he says that it belongs to the best regime that human beings live to the greatest extent as they choose (i.e., as they will). This is because the will of human beings chiefly concerns the end of human life, to which end the whole political intercourse is directed. And so, as human beings think in different ways about the end of human life, so they think in different ways about the intercourse of the political community. For those who hold that pleasures, power, or honors are the end of

---

1. *Ethics* X, 16 (1180b28–1181b24).

human life consider the best disposed political community one in which human beings can live pleasurably, acquire much money, gain great honors, or rule over many. But those who posit the end of the present life in the goodness that is the reward of virtue consider the best disposed political community to be one in which human beings can live most peacefully and in accord with virtue. And so it is absolutely true that the best disposition of the political community, in everybody's opinion, is one in which human beings can live as they choose.

We should likewise note that he says that he will consider about political regimes regarded as well governed and about the constitutions of political communities discussed by wise persons, constitutions that seem to be well-disposed. He will do so because, in order to discover truth, it is much more profitable to consider probable things than obviously false things.

2.   Then he makes an apology for his aim. He says that for someone to look for something about political regimes beyond things that others have spoken of need not be taken to proceed from an intention to make clever arguments (i.e., to show the person's wisdom). Rather, such a one will use this skill because things that others have said seem not to be well considered.

3.   Then he carries out his aim by pursuing what others have said about the constitution of a political community. First, he proposes the different constitutions that various thinkers have discussed. Second, he shows who and what sort were the ones who concerned themselves about such things [chap. 17]. The first part is divided into two parts by the difference that he touched on in the foregoing. For he lays out in the first part the constitutions of political communities that various wise persons have discussed. In the second part, he lays out the political constitutions observed in certain well-functioning political communities [chap. 13]. The first is divided into three parts. First, he posits the constitution of a political community that Socrates or his disciple Plato, who brings Socrates into his dialogues, discussed. In the second, he lays out the constitution of a political community discussed by someone called Phaleas [chap. 8]. In the third, he lays out the constitution of Hippodamus [chap. 10]. Regarding the first, he does two things. First, he thoroughly treats of a constitution that Plato called the most useful for a political community. Second, he pursues examination of Plato's directions regarding other things [chap. 6]. Regarding the first, he does two things. First, he raises a question. Second, he pursues it [6]. Regarding the first, he does three things. First, he poses a three-part question. Second, he excludes one part [4]. Third, he inquires about the other two parts [5].

Therefore, he says first that we should begin this consideration from what happens by the nature of the political community. For, inasmuch as the political community is an association, we need first to consider whether all citizens should share in everything, nothing, or only some things.

4.   Then he excludes one part, since it is impossible to say that citizens share in nothing. And he proves this in two ways. First, the political community consists of a sharing. And so it would be contrary to the nature of the political community if citizens were to share in nothing. Second, it is obvious that all citizens need to share at least in the territory of the political community, since one and the same territory belongs to one and the same political community. But we call those who are associates in the same political community fellow citizens. And so they necessarily share in the territory of the political community.

5.   Then he leaves the other two parts in doubt, namely, whether it is better that the political community to be rightly integrated share in whatever any persons may share, or share in only some of such things. For there are some things in which there cannot be any sharing (e.g., all things belonging to the person, such as bodily members). But citizens may share with one another in sons, wives, and property, as Plato's *Republic* teaches.[2] For Socrates said there that the best political community should be one in which all citizens have common property and common wives, namely, that all men have sexual intercourse with all women indiscriminately. And so children are common, since the fathers of the children would be uncertain. And Socrates touches on this in the *Timaeus*.[3] Therefore, we should inquire whether it is better to establish political life as it now exists or by the law that Socrates described in the *Republic*.

6.   Then he inquires about the aforementioned question. And he shows first the unsuitability of the aforementioned position about common wives and property. Second, he shows the position's insufficiency [chap. 5]. Regarding the first, he does three things. First, he argues against the law of Socrates regarding common wives and sons. Second, he argues against the law of Socrates regarding common property [chap. 4, nn, 1–7]. Third, he argues generally against the law of Socrates regarding both [chap. 4, nn. 8–10]. Regarding the first, he does two things. First, he proposes things that can indicate the unsuitability of the position of Socrates on common wives. Second, he pursues those things [7]. Regarding the first, he posits four things. The first is that the law of common wives has many other difficulties besides the unsuitable ones mentioned next.[4] The

---

2. *Republic* V.

3. *Timeaus* 17C–19B.

4. Aquinas reads "other" for "different" in the first sentence of 6 and so constructs an additional category.

second is that the reason why Socrates said that law should establish this system does not seem to be reasonable. The third is that such a law could not achieve the end, namely, the benefit of a political community that Socrates intended. The fourth is that Socrates inadequately explained his position. For, inasmuch as common things can be applied to individuals only by a fixed way of allotment, he, although instituting common wives, did not explain the way in which they would be allotted to individual men for sexual intercourse.

7.   Then he pursues three of the things that he has said, since the fourth, about insufficiency, is intrinsically clear. For he shows first that the reason assigned by Socrates for this law is unreasonable. Second, he shows that the political community cannot by such a law gain the end that Socrates intended [chap. 2]. Third, he shows that this law has many difficulties [chap. 3]. Regarding the first, he does two things. First, he lays out the reason assigned by Socrates for the law. Second, he argues against it [8]. Therefore, he says first that Socrates supposed as a principle, as it were, that it was best that the political community should be as unified as possible. And so he wanted all things, even sons and wives, to be common, so that citizens were united with one another to the greatest extent.

8.   Then he gives three arguments against the aforementioned reason. Regarding the first, he says that it is clear that the unity of the political community could become so much greater than it should be that it would not remain a political community. For he has just said that the political community by nature consists of many people, and multiplicity is contrary to unity. And so also, if the political community were more unified than it should be, it would then no longer be a political community. Rather, the political community would become a household, and if this household were in turn more unified than it should be, the household would be reduced to a single human being. For no one doubts that a household is more one thing than a political community, or that a human being is more one thing than a household. And so even if one could make as much unity in the whole political community as there is in a household, one should not do so, since the political community would then be destroyed.

But one could say that Socrates understood a kind of unity that excludes dissimilarity, not a multitude, of persons. Therefore, Aristotle adds that the political community should be composed not only of many human beings but also of different kinds of human beings (i.e., of human beings of different conditions). For the political community is not composed of human beings completely alike in their conditions. And he shows this in three ways.

First, he shows that the political community differs from many soldiers assembled to fight together, since an army is useful by reason of its numerical size alone, even if all the troops are of the same type. For such a multitude forms a unit to provide assistance. As a greater number of human beings may pull a greater weigh when they wish to do so, so also a greater number of like soldiers helps more for victory.

Second, he shows that a political community, in being composed of different kinds of human beings, differs from a clan in which the members do not dwell in separate cities or villages but in which each member dwells separately by himself, as with the Arcadians.[5] And Arcadia is a province in Greece in which each person lives alone. And so all of them are in a way equal and like.

Third, he shows the same thing by the fact that the things out of which it is necessary to make a complete thing differ in kind. And so we find that every complete whole in things of nature is composed of parts different in kind (e.g., human beings of flesh, bones, and nerves). But every whole composed of parts of the same kind (e.g., air, water, and other purely material substances) is incomplete in the way of nature. And so it is clear that a political community, since it is a complete whole, needs to consist of parts dissimilar in kind.

And so he said in the *Ethics* that an equal reciprocity (i.e., a proportionally equal return to each one for what one has done) preserves a political community,[6] since there needs to be such reciprocity among those who are free and equal. For if there were no return to someone for what one has done, there would be a form of slavery, as he said in the same place.[7] And in things exactly equal, this return, which he here calls reciprocity, is done by exact equality, so that each receives as much gain as each contributed, and each suffers as much loss as each caused. But in things proportionally, not exactly, equal, proportional equality will also be observed. For example, the less important the one who caused an injury is, the proportionally greater the punishment he should receive, since striking a person of higher dignity is more blameworthy than striking a person of lower dignity. Therefore, since it belongs to the nature of a political community to be composed of dissimilar human beings, it is clearly not true that the political community should be unified to the greatest extent, as Socrates thought. For if the dissimilarity of citizens should be taken away,

---

5. Aquinas misread the text of Aristotle, who is referring to the fact that the Arcadians had a confederation, not that they live as solitaries.

6. *Ethics* V, 8 (1132b33).

7. Ibid. (1132b34).

there will no longer be a political community. And this diversity seems most to be taken away when property, wives, and sons become common.

9.   He gives a second argument, also introducing this argument in order to show that there has to be difference between citizens. Some necessarily rule, and others are necessarily subjects, since it is impossible that all rule at the same time. Rather, if all should rule, this has to be in turn, whether so that each rules for a year or some other fixed time (e.g., a month or a day), or by any other arrangement (e.g., the rulers are chosen by lot). And in this way of ruling in turn, it happens that all rule at different times. Just so, if the same human beings in a political community were not always shoemakers or carpenters but such in turn, then all citizens would become shoemakers and carpenters.

But he adds that it is better that the political community be so disposed, if possible, that the same persons always rule. For he says that this is possible when some men in a political community are found to be far more excellent than others, and it will be best that they always rule the political community. But when this is not possible because all citizens are almost equal by natural diligence and virtue, it is then just that all share in ruling, whether the ruling be good or evil. For it is just that equals in the political community share in the common benefits and burdens. Therefore, it would be just, if it were possible, that all rule at the same time. But since this is not possible, it serves to approximate such justice that equals in turn yield to one another, just as they were alike at the beginning, since honorable rank, when some of them rule, and others are subjects, made them dissimilar and different in one respect. And so also there is a difference among those who rule at the same time when different citizens in the political community exercise different powers or offices. And so it is clear that a difference between rulers and subjects is necessary for a political community, whether absolutely or for a period of time.

Therefore, it is clear from the foregoing that the political community is not by nature so unified, as some say, that all citizens are alike. And what they call the greatest good in political communities, namely, the greatest unity, destroys the political community. And so greater unity cannot be the good of the political community, since what is good for each thing preserves it.

10.   He gives a third argument, and it proceeds from the foregoing in another way. For the first argument was taken from the dissimilar parts out of which the political community is necessarily composed, but the third argument is taken from the end of the political community, which is to provide for an adequate human life. And he says that he can show in another way that it is not better that human beings seek to unite a political community too much, since such unity takes away from the adequacy of

human life. For a household or entire family is clearly more sufficient for human life than an individual human being. And a political community is more sufficient than a household, since a political community should exist whenever an association of many people is self-sufficient for human life. Therefore, if something less unified is more self-sufficient (e.g., a household than an individual human being, and a political community than a household), then it is clearly more desirable that the political community should be less rather than more unified regarding the diversity of citizens. For the more diversified human beings of the political community are, the more self-sufficient it will be. And so it is clear that what Socrates said about the best political community being the most unified is false.

Chapter 2
Common Wives, Sons, and Property

Text (1261b16–1262a24)

1.   But if it is not best that the political association be unified to the greatest extent, the fact that all persons simultaneously call things mine and not mine does not seem to demonstrate this. (Socrates thinks that this is a sign that the political community is completely unified.) For the word *all* has two senses. Therefore, if it means each one individually, it will perhaps be closer to what Socrates wants to accomplish. For each one calls the same man his son, the same woman his wife, and speaks similarly about property and each thing concerning him. But those who have common wives and children will not then speak like that. Rather, all collectively, not each one individually, will call the wives, children, and property theirs. And it is clear, therefore, that it is misleading to say *all* persons, since words like *all*, *both*, *odd*, and *even* lead to contentious syllogisms even in public speeches because of their double meaning. Therefore, it is in one sense desirable but impossible that all say the same thing, and it is in the other sense completely unsuitable to do so.
2.   Moreover, regarding common things, the statement has another defect, since what is common to many receives the least care. For people take the most care of their own things and less care of common things, only as much as they affect an individual. For things with many different owners are more neglected, as if someone else has the responsibility. For example,

in household service, many slaves often perform work worse than fewer do. And 1,000 sons are attributed to each citizen, but they do not belong to each one individually, and each son is likewise the possible son of an uncertain father. Therefore, all citizens will neglect the sons.

3.   Moreover, each will say *mine* of any citizen acting well or ill, however many there may be by nature (e.g., my son or another's). That is to say, he will speak in this way about each of 1,000 or however many sons in the political community. But this is questionable, since it is unclear who begat a son, or whether the son begotten survived. Is it really better that each of 2,000 or 10,000 people call the same thing *mine*, or better that we use the word *mine* as we now do in political communities? For one person now calls his son the same person that another calls his brother, and another his cousin. Or one calls someone by another relationship, whether of blood or by marriage and its responsibility, primarily one's own marriage and secondarily that of one's relatives. Moreover, people call others kinsmen or clansmen. For it is better to be a real cousin than a son in the sense used by Socrates.

4.   Moreover, it is impossible for people to avoid suspecting that certain persons are their brothers, children, fathers, or mothers. For people necessarily accept evidence about one another from the likeness of children to parents. And some who write about foreign lands indeed say that this happens. For example, certain people of upper Libya have common wives but distinguish their own children by the children's likeness to them. And there are also some females even of other animals (e.g., horses and cattle) that by nature produce offspring that resemble their sires, like the mare in Pharsalus that the people called the honest mare.

Comment

1.   Aristotle has argued against the reason that Socrates assigned for legislating about common wives and children, showing that it is not best that the political community be unified to the greatest extent. Here Aristotle begins to show that a political community does not gain the greatest unity by the foregoing law, proposing four arguments to support this. Regarding the first, he says that the fact that all say at the same time, "This is mine," and "This is not mine," does not seem to demonstrate that a political community is most unified. (This is to assume, for the sake of argument, that it would be best for the political community to be most unified.) For if all things should be common, no one could say, "This is mine," except about what another were also to say, "This is mine." And Socrates thought that that this is a sign that a political community is completely unified. For he perceived that conflicts arise in a political community from the fact that

one person takes care of his own property, and another person takes care of his own property. And so human beings are moved to strive for different things, since each one says of different things: "This is mine." But if all were to say about one and the same thing, "This is mine," all would strive for the same thing, and so, as Socrates supposed, the political community would be unified to the greatest extent.

But this is not the case. For when you say, "All say: 'This is mine'," the proposition has a double meaning, since the word *all* can be interpreted distributively or collectively. If distributively, the sense would be that each one individually could say about such-and-such a thing: "This is mine." And then what Socrates said would perhaps be true, since each one would love one and the same person as his own son, and likewise one and the same woman as his wife. And the same is also true about means of subsistence (i.e., property). But those who enjoy common wives and children will not say, "This is mine," in that sense. Rather, all will say this collectively, as if possessing one and the same common thing, but in such a way that no one as an individual will say: "This is mine." And the same is also true if property should be common, since it will belong to no one individually as his own.

Therefore, it is clear that Socrates uses a sophistical syllogism when he goes on to say that the statement "All say: 'This is mine'" is a sign of complete unity. For the terms *all persons* and *each thing*, because of their double meanings even in public speeches (i.e., public debates), make the syllogisms contentious (i.e., sophistical). For example, if one should say regarding two sets of three things that both are even, this is true if we should understand the statement collectively, since the two sets of three in combination are even. But if we should understand the statement distributively, both sets are odd. And so we should say that it would be good in one sense that all say about the same thing that it is theirs, namely, insofar as *all* is interpreted distributively. But this is impossible, since it implies contradiction. For by the very fact that it belongs to this person, it does not belong to another. And if we should understand *all* collectively, not distributively, this will be unsuitable (i.e., unfitting for a political community).

2. He gives a second argument and thereby shows that the saying of Socrates is not only unbeneficial for the political community but also causes the greatest harm to it. For we perceive very little care is taken of what is the common property of many, since all take the greatest care of their own property. But human beings take even less care of common property than as much as belongs to each one, so that all collectively take less care than they would if the property were to belong to only one person. For when one person thinks that another will do some work, all neglect doing it. For example, it happens in the work of servants that many sometimes do worse work when one servant expects that another person will do it. And it follows from the law of Socrates that each citizen would have 1,000 or more sons and so will take less care of each than if he were to have only one. And if we should add that these 1,000 sons belong to each citizen, but each is the possible son of an uncertain father, citizens will take far less care of the sons. And so all citizens will then likewise neglect care of the children, and this will be most detrimental to the political community.

3. He gives a third argument, saying that in this way (i.e., according to the position of Socrates), each citizen will say, "This is mine," something according to nature (e.g., "This is my son" or "This is another's son"), of each citizen acting well or ill, however many. And the citizen will speak in this way about each of 1,000 or however many sons in the political community. And the citizen will not say this as if he knows for certain that this individual is his son or another's. For if wives should be common, with many men having intercourse with the same woman, it cannot be clear from which one the son may have been begotten, since many men do not beget the son. And since many sons die, it is also uncertain whose son may have survived.

Therefore, we should consider whether it is better that one in this way calls anyone of 2,000 or 10,000 men the same thing (i.e., his son or cousin), or better that one calls a youth his own, as people now do in political communities. For we perceive that some citizens call one and the same youth their son that others call their cousin or by some other relationship, whether we consider the relationship by blood or marriage. Or citizens call the youth theirs because they initially had responsibility for him (e.g., as his guardian or teacher) or for things that belong to him.[8] And although a citizen calls one person his son or cousin, he will call another person his first cousin or clansman. People call the children of two brothers first cousins, and those belonging to the same clan (e.g., those from the same group in a political community) clansmen. Therefore, it is clear that many citizens say about one and the same person, "He is mine," by both the law of Socrates and the custom currently observed in political societies.

And it seems to be preeminent by the law of Socrates that many citizens will call a particular person their son. On the other hand, it is preeminent by custom that different citizens will individually, not collectively, call one and the same person their cousin, son, brother, or any such thing. And it is

---

8. Aquinas reads the responsibility mentioned in the text of Aristotle as distinct from the marriage relationship.

far better and more effective for exercising friendship and responsibility that one esteem someone as one's own cousin than that one esteem him as a common son in the way Socrates supposed. This is because, as Aristotle said [2], human beings love more, and take better care of, their own things than they do common things. And so it is clear that the law of Socrates brings harm rather than benefit to the political community.

4.   Aristotle gives a fourth argument, saying that Socrates thought that citizens, by sharing sons and wives, would regard them as common and avoid calling anyone their own son or brother. But he cannot avoid some from suspecting that certain persons are their brothers, sons, fathers, or mothers, and this is because of the resemblance that we often find between sons and fathers or mothers. And so certain writers about foreign lands (i.e., how the world is inhabited) recount that some peoples in upper Libya have common wives but distinguish children by the latter's likeness to their parents. Thus each male accepts as his son the one that looks like him. And we perceive that the same thing happens in the case of females of other animals (e.g., mares and cows), which have from nature the power to produce male offspring resembling their sires. For example, it is reported about a certain mare that the people in Pharsalus called it the honest mare because she produced colts resembling their sires.

And so it is clear that Socrates, by the law that he says should be enacted regarding common wives and children, also cannot bring it about that there are no private attachments between human beings.

Chapter 3
Common Wives and Sons

Text (1262a24–1262b36)

1.   Moreover it is also not easy for those establishing this community to avoid some evils (e.g., assaults, voluntary and involuntary homicides, brawls, and insults). None of these things is proper against fathers, mothers or close relatives, just as none against remote persons are, and these things necessarily happen more often if people do not know their relationship than if they do. And the latter can make customary expiations for it, but the former cannot make any.

2.   And it is also improper that Socrates, while making sons common, prohibits sexual intercourse by lovers but does not prohibit acts of love or other sexual practices between fathers with sons, which is the most indecent thing, or between brothers, since even the love alone is. And it is also unfitting to prohibit sexual intercourse by lovers only because of the very powerful pleasure in it and to think it makes no difference that the lovers are fathers and sons, or brothers.

3.   And it seems more beneficial that the farmers have common wives and children than that the guardians do. For there will be less intimacy when wives and children are common. But subjects should be such, in order to promote obedience and prevent rebellion.

4.   And on the whole, the contrary of things that rightly established laws produce necessarily results from such a law, and it is for this reason that Socrates thought it necessary to establish things in his way regarding wives and children. For we indeed think that friendship is the greatest good for political communities, since citizens then cause the least civil disturbance. Socrates most praises the unity of the political community, and this also seems, as Socrates says, the product of friendship. (And we know from the *Symposium* that Aristophanes says that lovers, because of their overabundant love, desire to become a natural unit and one thing instead of two. In this case, therefore, one or both necessarily perish.) But friendship necessarily becomes diminished in a political community when wives and children are shared, and fathers or sons rarely call sons or fathers "mine." For a little sweetness mixed into a large amount of water makes the mixture imperceptible. Just so, it also happens that there is very little need in such a regime to cultivate the mutual intimacy signified by these terms, whether of sons for fathers, fathers for sons, or brothers for each another. For something one's own and something loved are the two things that most cause human beings to love and take diligent care. And neither of these can exist for those who are politically organized in this way.

5.   And regarding the transfer of children from the farmers and craftsmen to the guardians, and vice versa, there is great confusion about how this will be done. Moreover, those giving and transferring children necessarily know which ones they give and to whom they give them.

6.   Moreover, in these things, the aforementioned evils (e.g., assaults, illicit acts of love, homicides) would necessarily happen more often. For those given by the guardians to the other citizens no longer call the guardians their brothers, children, fathers, or mothers, nor do those given by the other citizens to the guardians any longer call the other citizens such, since they are afraid of committing such offenses because of kinship. Therefore, we have in this way concluded our discussion about sharing wives and children.

Comment

1. Aristotle has shown that the reason that Socrates assigned for his law, namely, that it would be best for the political community to be united to the greatest extent, was unreasonable, and that sharing wives and sons does not produce the greatest unity. Here Aristotle wants to show the many evils and unsuitability that result from such a law, giving six arguments. Regarding the first, he says that it is not easy for those who establish this sharing of wives and sons to avoid the evils and the unsuitability that he will mention. First, the system cannot happen without assaults and homicides happening in the political community. These things are sometimes involuntary (e.g., when one does them accidentally) and sometimes voluntary (e.g., when one does them out of hate or anger), and there will also be brawls, insults, or verbal taunts. And it is far more unfitting that one does all of these things to parents or other close relatives than to strangers and remote people, since the more nature inclines one to love another, the more unfitting it is to harm the other. And one far more does such harm or injury to those whom one does not know for certain to be one's sons than to those whom one knows for certain to be such.

One can also consider with this that the relationship has been absolved, as may sometimes be the case because it is remote, or even when blood relatives are disowned because of some offense.[9] But those who do not know of the relationship cannot think that the relationship has been absolved. And so it is clear that such evils in political communities will be more unfitting if we suppose that wives and sons are shared, namely, because the evils may often be done to relatives.

2. He gives a second argument, taking it from the improper things that result from lustful desires, as he took the first argument from the improper things that result from anger or hate. Therefore, we should consider that all people considered it improper and unworthy that sons have sexual intercourse with their mothers, or fathers with their daughters.[10] And this would necessarily happen if we were to suppose common sons, since it would happen that a son would have sexual relations with his mother as with any other woman. And it would likewise happen that a father would have sexual relations with his daughter as with any other woman. Therefore, Socrates, anticipating this impropriety, wished to

---

9. Aristotle is referring to expiatory rites to atone for crimes against kinsmen. Aquinas reads the ablutions mentioned to mean absolving circumstances.

10. Aquinas, without explanation, substitutes cases of incest for the cases of homosexuality cited by Aristotle.

avoid it by a law, namely, one in which the rulers of the political community prohibited sexual intercourse between sons and mothers when the mothers were necessarily known, at least by the rulers who received the sons to be brought up. And likewise, the same rulers would prohibit sexual intercourse between fathers and daughters when there could be any suspicion that the woman was the man's daughter.

Aristotle attacks this law of Socrates in two ways. First, he says that this law seems to be inadequate. For Socrates prohibited only sexual intercourse between sons and mothers and not all lustful love, since he did not indicate to a son that a particular woman was the son's mother nor prohibit other lustful practices (e.g., embraces and kisses). And it is most improper that such practices between relatives exist, since even lustful love between them is improper. Second, Aristotle argues against such a law because of the reason that Socrates assigns for it. For Socrates said that sexual intercourse between mothers and sons was to be prohibited for no other reason than to avoid the very strong pleasure that would arise from the natural love between mothers and sons, which would be added to the lustful love. And he wished to avoid the strong pleasure in sexual intercourse lest human beings be too enticed to lack of self-restraint. Therefore, Aristotle says that it is improper to say that one should abstain from sexual intercourse with one's mother only for this reason and not simply because the woman is one's mother. And the argument is the same about other relatives, since relatives owe respectful honor to one another because of their blood relationship, and lustful sexual intercourse takes away that honor.

3.   He gives a third argument, saying that the law of Socrates about sharing wives and sons is more beneficial for the farmers and others of the lower classes than for the guardians of the political community (i.e., its rulers and other important men who take care of its common affairs). This is because the sons of farmers will be raised up, and the sons of important men lowered, if all citizens should be brought to a common denominator. And so there will then be less friendship between important and ordinary people. For friendship is preserved between them insofar as farmers and such like are subject to rulers, since proportional equality preserves friendship, as the *Ethics* says.[11] And the status of subjects is preserved in people of the lower classes obeying their rulers and not being rebellious. But the latter will happen if subjects are equal to more important people in sons and wives. And so it is clear that the law of Socrates prevents the friendship in the political community that should exist between rulers and subjects.

---

11. *Ethics* IX, 1 (1263b34).

4. He gives a fourth argument, saying that such a law produces altogether the contrary of what good lawmakers strive for and is contrary to why Socrates thought the law should be established. For people generally think that friendship is the greatest good in political communities, since citizens will not rebel if there should be friendship among citizens. And all lawgivers strive for the political community to be free of civil disturbances. And so all good lawmakers strive for friendship among all citizens. Socrates also said that unity was the best thing in the political community. And the unity of human beings with one another is the effect of friendship, as it generally seems to all people, and as Socrates also said. And so also Aristophanes said in the *Symposium* that mutual lovers desire to become one natural thing. And since this is impossible, they desire to become as much one as possible.

Therefore, in the case of which Aristophanes is speaking, it would follow that either both lovers would be destroyed when they became one thing, or one of them, converted into the other, as it were, would be destroyed. But because of such sharing of wives and sons in the political community, friendship is consequently diminished. And friendship will have very little weight for the love that a father expresses when he calls someone his son, since he at the same time calls many others in the political community his sons, or that a son expresses when he calls someone his father, since he at the same time calls many others his father. For we perceive that if one should mix a little sweetness into a large quantity of water, the mixture becomes imperceptible. For example, if a little honey is poured into a large quantity of water, one does not taste any of the sweetness of the honey. Intimacy arises in the political community from the words one uses when one calls a particular person one's father, son, or brother. And so people will care little about such intimacy if anyone older should call anyone younger his son, or, conversely, anyone younger should call anyone older his father, or all of the same age should call themselves brothers.

And the reason for this is because there are two things that most make human beings take diligent care of others and most love them. One is that something is their own individual thing, and so human beings take more care of their own things than common things, as he has maintained before [chap. 2, n. 2]. The other is the special love that one has for someone, and this love is for someone that one particularly loves rather than for one among many. For example, we perceive that even parents love only sons more than they would if they should have many sons, as if love would be diminished by sharing it for many sons. Therefore, it is clear that if there should be such an organization of the political community as Socrates established by law, the friendship of citizens for one another would be diminished. And this is contrary to the aim of lawmakers.

5. He gives a fifth argument, saying that the system of Socrates required transfer of sons, namely, that those born of certain mothers would be given to others to bring up, so that no one would know his own son. And it is not obvious how this could be done, namely, that the sons of farmers and artisans were transferred to the nobles (i.e., the guardians of the political community), or the converse. For such transfers would bring great confusion to citizens. And on the other hand, conjecture about one's own sons could not be altogether eliminated, since those who gave and exchanged children would necessarily know from whom they received them, and to whom they gave them. And so the law of Socrates would not result in what was intended and would also bring about great confusion.

6. Aristotle gives a sixth argument, saying that, because of this transfer of children, things that he mentioned before, namely, assaults, lustful acts of love, and homicides among relatives, would especially happen regarding such children. For we perceive that children who are currently given into the custody and upbringing of others do not refer to their relatives with as much affection as they would if they should grow up with the relatives. And so they do not greatly fear committing any of the offenses against relatives. Therefore, far more would they not fear committing any such offenses if they were not to know their own relatives.

And he concludes in a final epilogue that he has determined in this way about the sharing of wives and sons that Socrates wanted to introduce.

Chapter 4
Common Property

Text (1262b37–1263b29)

1. Related to these things is the consideration of property. How should one make arrangements for it in the best regime? Should property be common or not? And one will consider this matter apart from what the law about wives and children established. I am asking whether, if there should be separate households in the way in which they currently are, it would be better that all property and its use be common. For example, should the fields be private, but the crops stored and dispensed communally, as some peoples do? Or, conversely, should the land be common and cultivated in common, but the crops divided for private use, as they say some foreigners do? Or should both fields and crops be common?

2.   It will be another and easier way if persons other than citizens cultivate the land, and property arrangements will cause many evils if citizens work the land for themselves. For when the produce derived and the work contributed are not equal, there will necessarily be recriminations against those who receive much and work little by those who receive less and work more.

3.   And living together and sharing in all human things is very difficult, but especially so in such things. Companions traveling in a group show this, since most of them quarrel about drink and fight with one another over little things.

4.   Moreover, we are most offended with those servants of whom we have the most need for menial tasks. Therefore, common property has these and other such difficulties.

5.   And the present arrangement, embellished with good customs and a system of just laws, will be far different, since it will have what is good from both (i.e., property being both common and private). For property needs to be common in one respect but completely one's own. Separate care of property will not cause quarrels. Rather, it will increase production as each attends to what belongs to each. And there will be common use because of the virtue of citizens, as the proverb says: "Friends share everything in common." And this system is possible, since it already exists in outline, or could exist, in some political communities, especially rightly disposed ones. For each one has his own property and uses it for his friends, as common to all. For example, in Sparta, citizens use one another's slaves as if the citizens' own, and one another's horses and dogs if they should need them for journeys in the fields through the region. Therefore, it is clearly better for property to be private but to make its use common, and it is the proper task of the lawmaker to decide how citizens do such things.

6.   Moreover, how indescribably pleasurable it is to think that some property is one's very own, since each one loves himself, and this is natural. Selfishness is condemned, and rightly so, but this is not genuine love of self but more love of self than is proper. Just so, we condemn only those who love money excessively, since all love to call each thing their own.

7.   And it is most pleasurable to give and help friends, strangers, or others, and one does this with one's own property. Thus unsuitable things happen to all who try to unify the political community too much.

8.   And in addition to this, they clearly eliminate the practice of two virtues: self-restraint regarding women, since it is a good deed to abstain from sexual intercourse with the wife of another because of self-restraint; and generosity regarding one's property. For the generosity of a person

will not be manifest, and no one will perform even one generous act, since the practice of generosity consists of the use of property.

9.   Therefore, Socrates' legislation will seem attractive and humane. For people hearing it receive it with joy, thinking that there will be a wonderful friendship of everybody with everybody, and contrariwise when one blames the evils currently existing in regimes on the fact that property is not common. The things I refer to are disputes over contracts and judgments based on false testimony, and fawning over the rich. But these things arise out of wickedness, not from the lack of sharing. For we perceive that those possessing and sharing all things dispute more than those possessing property separately. But we see few people quarreling about common property compared to the many possessing property separately.

10.   Moreover, it is fair to speak both of how many evils those sharing all things do not suffer, and of how many goods they do not acquire. And such a life seems to be altogether impossible.

Comment

1.   After Aristotle has argued against the law of Socrates regarding common wives and children, he here argues against that law regarding common property. And regarding this, he does two things. First, he lays out his aim. Second, he shows what he proposes [2]. Regarding the first, he does three things. First, he connects his aim to the preceding things, saying that a related thing (i.e., a consequence) is the consideration of property, whether those who should be engaged in the best political life should have common or private property.

Second, he shows that we should consider this question separately from the foregoing question about common wives, saying that that we should do so even if nothing were established about common sons and wives. That is, assuming that sons and wives are not common, and that each man individually has his own wife and sons, as is now customary, we should then consider whether it would be better that property and its use are common to all than that each one has his own property, as is now customary.

Third, he distinguishes the ways in which citizens can share in possessing property. And he lays out three ways. The first is that each citizen owns his own field, but all the crops are handed over to the common treasury and distributed to all. And some peoples observed this way. The second way is that, conversely, the land is common and cultivated in common, but the crops are divided among citizens for each citizen's individual use. And some foreigners observed this way. The third way is that both the fields and the crops are common, and Socrates said that law should establish this system.

2. Then Aristotle shows what is true about the question under discussion. First, he argues against the law of Socrates about common property, showing that such a law would result in evils. Second, he shows what good things the law takes away [5]. Regarding the first, he gives three arguments. The first is that if property were common to all citizens, one of two things would necessarily be the case, namely, that some foreigners or some citizens would cultivate the fields. And if others were to cultivate the fields, there would be a difficulty, since it would be difficult to recruit so many foreign farmers. But this way would be easier than if some citizens were to do the work, since the latter would cause many evils. For it would be impossible that all citizens would cultivate the fields, since the more important citizens would need to attend to more important business, and the less important citizens to farming. And yet it would be necessary that the more important citizens, who did less work in the field, would receive more of the crops. And then the distribution of the crops would not correspond proportionally to the activities or labor involved in the farming. And so recriminations and disputes would necessarily arise when the less important citizens, who did more work, complained that the more important citizens, who were doing little work, received much, while they, who were doing more work, conversely, received less. And so it is clear that this law would result in discord rather than the united political community that Socrates wanted.

3. He gives a second argument, saying that it is very difficult for many human beings to live together and share in any human goods, especially wealth. For we perceive that those who share in some wealth have many disputes with one another. This is clearly the case of those who travel together, since they often disagree with one another in settling accounts of expenses on food and drink, and sometimes fight with one another over little things and offend one another in word or deed. And so it is clear that if all citizens were to hold all property in common, there would be many disputes among them.

4. He gives a third argument, saying that the household servants of whom their masters have much need for menial tasks most offend the masters. And this is due to their common interaction in daily life, since those who do not often interact together do not often have disputes with one another. And so it is clear from this that sharing among human beings often causes discord. And he finally infers that the foregoing and other like evils would result from common property in a political community.

5. Then he shows what good things the aforementioned law would take away, and he gives three arguments. Regarding the first, he says that if political communities should be organized as they currently are, namely, with property allotted individually to citizens, and good customs and just laws so ordain, there will be a big difference in the abundant goodness and benefit regarding what Socrates mentioned. For there is some good in both things, namely, establishing property as private and establishing it as common. And if property should be private, and customs and just laws should ordain that citizens share their goods with one another, there will be such a way of enjoying the good life that derives from both, namely, common and private property.

Property indeed needs to be absolutely private regarding ownership but common in one respect. For the result of property being private is that its management is individual, with each citizen taking care of his own property. And two good things result from this. One is that each citizen concerns himself about his own property and not that of another. And when each does that, there are not the disputes among human beings that are usual when many have care of the same thing, and it seems to one that it should be done in one way, and to another that it should be done in another way. The second good is that each citizen, being more attentive and solicitous about property as his own, will increase it more. And there will in this way be private property but property common regarding use because of the virtue of citizens, who will be generous and benevolent toward one another. Just so, the proverb says: "Friends share everything in common."

And lest this seem impossible to anyone, he adds that it is the law in some well-regulated political communities that some things are ipso facto common regarding use. And some things become common by the will of their owners, namely, when each citizen, having his own property, sets aside some of his goods for the benefit of his friends, and his friends use some of his goods for themselves, as if the goods were common. For example, this was so in the city of Sparta, in which one citizen could use the slave of another for his own service, as if the slave were his own. Likewise, Spartans could use the horses and dogs of others as if their own if they needed to go to fields, albeit fields in the same area. And so it is clear that it is far better that property is owned privately but is common in a respect regarding its use. But how the use of private property can be common belongs to the providence of the good lawmaker.

6. He gives a second argument, saying that one cannot easily describe how much more pleasurable it is to consider that things belong to oneself. For this pleasure comes from the fact that human beings love themselves, since this is why they want good things for themselves. Nor is it vanity to love oneself. Rather, it is natural. Sometimes one is rightly censured because one loves oneself. But when we say this as censure, it is to censure loving oneself more than one should, not absolutely. Just so, we censure lovers of money, although all love money in some way, since we censure lovers of money insofar as they love money more than they should. And the law of Socrates takes away this pleasure, which concerns having one's own property.

7.   Aristotle gives a third argument, saying that it is very pleasurable that human beings give or bring help to friends, strangers, or any others. But one can do this because one has one's own property. And so the law of Socrates taking away private ownership of property also takes this good away. And he at the end infers that these unsuitable things happen to those who wish to unify the political community too much by introducing common property, wives, and sons.

8.   Then he objects to both positions, namely, common wives and common property, at the same time, also introducing three arguments in this regard. One is that those who wish to unify the political community too much evidently destroy the practice of two virtues, namely, self-restraint and generosity. For abstaining from sexual intercourse with the wife of another is a practice of self-restraint insofar as that virtue concerns women, and there will be no room for this if all wives should be common. Likewise, introducing common property takes away the practice of generosity, since it could not be clear about anyone whether he is generous. Nor could anyone perform an act of generosity, since no one has individual property, in the use of which the practice of generosity consists. The rich man distributes and gives his own things, but one giving common things is not very generous.

9.   He gives a second argument, saying that the aforementioned law of Socrates seems to be superficially good and humane (i.e., something fostering friendship among human beings or something lovable by them). And there are two reasons for this. One is because of the good that one expects to come from such a law. For when one hears that all things are common among citizens, one receives this with joy, thinking that this will result in a wonderful friendship of everybody with everybody. The second is because of the evils that one thinks this law takes away. For people condemn the evils now prevalent in political communities (e.g., disputes between human beings over contracts and judgments based on false testimonies, and that the poor fawn over the rich). They condemn these evils as if all these things happen because property is not common.

But if one should rightly consider the matter, people do these things out of human wickedness, not because property is not common. For we perceive that those who possess things in common dispute with one another far more than those who have private property. But fewer disputes arise out of common property because those who have property in common are few in relation to those who have separate property. Nonetheless, if all were to have property in common, there would be far more disputes.

10.   He gives a third argument, saying that people should consider not only how many evils those with common property and wives do not suffer, but also of how many goods they are deprived. For the lawmaker should tolerate some evils in order not to be deprived of greater goods. And the law of Socrates deprives people of so many goods that such a way of life seems to be impossible, as the unsuitable things just laid out make clear.

Chapter 5
The First Regime of Socrates

Text (1263b29–1264b25)

1. We need to think that the error of Socrates lies in his false presupposition. For the household and the political community need to be in some way united but not completely. For a political community may be so united that it will cease to be one, or if it barely survives, it will be a worse one. This is as if one should equate harmony with one note, or rhythm with one beat. But as we said before, many human beings need to be unified and make a community by means of education. And it is odd that one who will introduce a system of education and thinks that it will make a political community virtuous, thinks that such things as common wives, sons, and property, not customs, philosophy, or laws, provide direction. For example, the lawmakers in Sparta and Crete ordained customs and laws regarding property for common meals.

2. And we should not ignore the fact that we need to consider the long time and many years in which the idea of common property was undiscovered but would have been if such things were well disposed. For almost all such things have been discovered, although not undertaken, and those who know about them do not use them. And this will be most clear if one should see such a regime actually established. For one could not make a political community without dividing and separating things, some for common meals, and some for clans and tribes. And so also the law of Socrates will establish nothing else except that the guardians do not cultivate the fields, which the Spartans also currently try to do.

3. But Socrates did not say, nor is it easy to say, what will be the way in which citizens share in the whole regime. Almost the entire population of the political community consists of a body of diverse citizens, but he has previously determined nothing about them. And farmers necessarily have either common or private property, and common or individual wives and

children. For if all things are common to all citizens in the same way, how will farmers differ from the guardians? Or how will the farmers benefit by supporting the rule of the guardians? Or why do they as subjects endure it? Perhaps the farmers discern the utility of something like the system of the Cretans, who allow slaves other things but deny them physical training and bearing arms. But if they have private property, as in other political communities, what will be the kind of community? For there are inevitably two political communities in one, and these are contrary to each other, since they make some the guardians, as wardens, and farmers, artisans, and the like the citizens.

4.   And there will be the accusations, disputes, and all the other evil things he says exist in other political communities. But Socrates says that they will not need many regulatory laws (e.g., laws regarding the town, trade, and the like) because of education, which he provides only for the guardians.

5.   Moreover, he makes farmers owners of the property but makes them pay taxes. But the farmers are far more likely to be burdensome and crafty than serfs and slaves of certain peoples.

6.   But whether these things are likewise necessary or not, he has not yet determined anything, nor about related questions concerning their regime, education, and kind of laws. And it is neither easy nor unimportant to discover what kind of citizen some of the people are to be in order to preserve the association of the guardians.

7.   But if he will make the farmers' wives common and their property private, or if both their wives and their property are common, who will manage the property, as the husbands are managing things in the fields? And it is improper to compare this with wild animals to show that women should deal with the same things as men, since wild beasts are not concerned with household management.

8.   And how Socrates establishes rulers is also dangerous, since he makes them always the same people. And this causes rebellion even with those of little worth, although easily with spirited and warlike men. And he clearly needs to make the same people rulers, since gold from a god is always mixed into the same kind of soul, not sometimes into different kinds of soul. And he says that, as soon as people are begotten, the god mixes gold into some, silver into others, and bronze and iron into those who will be artisans and farmers.

9.   Moreover, although he takes happiness away from the guardians, he says that the lawmaker should make the whole political community happy. But the whole political community cannot be happy without most, all, or some parts being happy, since the happiness of the whole political community does not belong to the same things that the evenness of an even

number does. For there can be a whole even number without either of two parts of it being even, but this is impossible with happiness. And if the guardians are not happy, who else will be? Certainly not the skilled artisans or the many common artisans. Therefore, the regime of which Socrates spoke has these objections and others no less serious.

Comment

1. After Aristotle has argued against the law of Socrates by showing that it is unsuitable, he here argues against it by showing that it is inadequate. Regarding this, he does two things. First, he shows that it lacked a sufficient reason. Second, he shows that the proposal was insufficient [3]. Regarding the first, he does two things. First, he shows that the reason is insufficient because of a false presupposition. Second, he shows that the reason is insufficient because of the lack of the experience required in establishing laws [2].

Therefore, he says first that we need to think that the reason why Socrates deviated from the truth about the law regarding common property, sons, and wives is because he assumed a false presupposition. That is to say, he presupposed that the greatest good of political communities was the greatest unity. But this presupposition is not quite correct, since, although a unity is necessary for the political community and the household, as Aristotle has said [chap. 1, nn. 7–10], unity in every respect is not. And so the unity of a political community can become so great that there will no longer be a political community (e.g., if everybody belongs to the same craft and dwells in the same household). And the unity can become so great that there will be almost no political community. And so the political community is then worse, since the more each thing approaches ceasing to be, the worse off it is, as would be the case if one should abolish separation of the offices necessary for the well-being of the political community. And he gives an example. If one should make a one-note chorus (i.e., all singing in one note), there will now be no harmony (i.e., blending of notes), and he likens the political community consisting of different things to this. Likewise, rhythm (i.e., a formal arrangement like that of a triangle) would be destroyed if one were to want to make only one musical beat. And so unity can become so great that the political community is destroyed.

But it is necessary, as he has said before [chap. 1, n. 8], that there are many different parts in a political community, and that the political community is united and a community because of education by rightly established laws. But if one who was about to introduce education to unite the political community should think that the law about common sons and wives makes the political community good, it is unfitting that he should think that he can do so by such associations. Rather he can do so by good customs and laws, and philosophy (i.e., wisdom about such things). Just so, he has said before [chap. 4, n. 5] that Spartans made their individual property common as to use. And the lawmaker in Crete also made some things common to support public common meals for citizens at certain times to foster greater intimacy among them.

2.   Then he shows that the insufficiency of the reason is due to lack of experience. And he says that in order to establish laws rightly, one should not ignore that one should consider the matter in the light of history, so that experience makes clear whether such laws or decrees are well disposed. For we should consider that almost all conceptually possible things concerning human intercourse have been discovered in the course of history. But some of these things have not been undertaken (i.e., some of these things never came to be legally established up to the present time), since their unsuitability was immediately apparent. And other things have been established but abandoned when human beings recognized that the things were not useful.

And this becomes most evident if one should in the light of experience look at such an organization of the political community as Socrates proposed. For there can be a political community only by dividing and separating things (e.g., distributing common goods for various common meals, and for different clans or tribes [i.e., associations of the city or countryside]). It is altogether necessary that common goods regarding property are distributed. Therefore, the establishment of such a law about common property ensures only that the guardians (i.e., those who always dwell in the city) do not have care of the farming, as they have no fields of their own. But even if there should be no common fields, it can be established that others cultivate the fields, as the Spartans try to do.

3.   Then he shows the unsuitability of the law of Socrates regarding what it proposed. Regarding this, he does two things. First, he shows the inadequacy of the aforementioned law regarding the things of which it consists. Second, he shows the law's inadequacy regarding some consequences [6]. Regarding the first, he introduces three arguments. The first shows the inadequacy of the aforementioned law regarding the fact that it could not adequately distinguish the people making up the political community. And he says that the law of Socrates seemed to ensure only that the guardians did not cultivate the fields, the fields not being their own. But Socrates also failed to say what was the way of the whole political life to be established by his law for those sharing in the life (i.e., possessing all things in common). Nor, if the law is observed, can anyone else say. For the people of a political community need to be a people of different

persons of different classes. And Socrates determined nothing about how there can be this difference.

For we need to say that property, sons, and wives are common to farmers, as with other citizens, or that the farmers, unlike other citizens, individually have their own sons, property, and wives. In the second way, this may account for the farmers' difference from other citizens both because of their ownership of property and because of their parentage. But there is no difference that can distinguish farmers from guardians (i.e., those who dwell in common in the city) if all the aforementioned things are common in the same way as with all the other citizens. Nor could we assign what reward those who bear the burden of governance in ruling the political community get,[12] and so they will work in vain. (Rulers currently have the advantage that more property is allotted to them, and their sons are ennobled.) Nor, likewise, could we assign how those allowed to rule support that power to rule (i.e., because of what previous condition of theirs they are raised to the ruling power). For we now customarily raise those nobler by birth or more excellent in wealth to the ruling power. And excellence in virtue is not always so clear that we can thereby sufficiently find human beings to be raised to positions of power.

But someone could say that those who observed the law of Socrates would undertake to observe something like what the Cretans do. The Cretans allow slaves to do farming and other such productive tasks and prohibit only physical training (i.e., bodily exercises) and bearing arms to them. Accordingly, it would be unnecessary to distinguish between farmers and guardians, since those so engaged in farming and the other tasks will be slaves, not citizens. But if such things in the political community that Socrates intends to establish will be organized as in other political communities, namely, that some citizens are farmers and craftsmen, there will not seem to be one community. This is because there will necessarily be two contrary political communities, as it were, in one political community. On the one hand, there will be the guardians, who watch over the political community and do nothing else. On the other hand, there will be the farmers and craftsmen doing their work. And these two groups are necessarily contraries, since some do the work, but others do no work and receive more of the crops, as he has also said before [chap. 4, n. 2]. But if property should not be common, disputes will not arise, since each one will take care that his own fields are cultivated, whether by others or

---

12. In this number, Aquinas raises questions about the rewards and qualifications of rulers in the law of Socrates, but Aristotle here questions the benefits of the guardians for the farmers.

himself. And when less important citizens serve more important citizens
and receive some profit from them, there will be a sharing between them.

4.   Aristotle gives a second argument, saying that, in a political community having all things common, as Socrates proposed, there will be many
recriminations and disputes and all the other evils that Socrates says now
exist in political communities. For citizens will dispute with one another
about unequal work, unequal reward, and many other things, although
Socrates thought that there would be no such evils in a political community in which all things were common. And so Socrates said that the political community because of a way of education did not need many laws. It
needed only a few laws, namely, those concerning settlement of the town,
business of the courts, commercial matters, and other like things, without
the arrangement of which the political community cannot exist. But he
also assigned such legal education only to the guardians (i.e., the wardens
of the political community) and not to the farmers, who dwelt outside the
city of the guardians. And so it is clear that the law of Socrates was inadequate, since it could not wipe out the evils that he sought to take away.

5.   Aristotle gives a third argument, saying that Socrates by his law committed the whole disposition of property to the farmers, to whom he said
it should be committed to provide the produce of the fields to the citizens
who are free to engage in other things. And so Socrates thought that farmers, because of this power, would become accommodating and humbly
serve other citizens. But entirely the opposite would happen. For it is far
more likely that farmers, because they had all property in their power,
would be burdensome to other citizens and find crafty ways to defraud
them than that the farmers would humbly serve the others. And so it is
clear that the law of Socrates about common wives and property was inadequate, since it could not accomplish what it attempted.

6.   Then Aristotle shows the inadequacy of the law of Socrates regarding
other consequences. First, he shows this in general. Second, he shows it in
particular [7]. Therefore, he says first that the things that Socrates proposed about common wives and property are either necessary or unnecessary for the political community. But whichever way, Socrates determined
nothing about related things (i.e., consequences), namely, what sort of
arrangement of political life there ought to be, what sort of education, and
what sort of laws are proper to those who have all things in common in
this way. For it is not easy to find such people, and those who can serve the
aforementioned political community need to differ much from others.
And so some special laws and a special education would need to instruct
them.

7.   Then Aristotle shows the inadequacy of the law of Socrates in particular. First, he shows this regarding wives. Second, he shows it regarding

rulers [8]. Third, he shows it regarding the general happiness of the political community [9]. Regarding the wives, he touches on two points. First, an adequate arrangement about wives is impossible if they should be common to guardians and farmers, whether property should be private and individual to each, or common to all.[13] If property should be common, the farmers need to manage it. And if property should belong to the guardians, who else will manage it except the farmers? And how will the husbands of the women dwelling in the city be able to manage things in the fields? For the men will not be able at the same time to have sexual intercourse with wives living in the city and to cultivate the fields.

Second, he says regarding wives that Socrates said that women ought to deal with the same things as men, namely, till the fields, wage war, and do the like other things that men do. And Socrates took an analogy (i.e., a comparison) from wild animals, among which the females do the same things as the males. But Aristotle says that this comparison is unsuitable. It is dissimilar because wild animals do not share at all in household life, in which life women have their own tasks, and need to attend to them and always abstain from political affairs.

8.   Then he shows the inadequacy regarding the rulers, saying that it is not safe for the political community that its rulers are established in the way that Socrates did. For Socrates directed that the rulers always remain the same. And this causes rebellion even with human beings of little worth but much more with spirited and warlike men, who cannot easily let themselves always be subjects, and others always rule. And Aristotle adds the reason why Socrates established that there were always the same rulers. For Socrates said that there is gold in some mines, silver in others, and iron or bronze in others. Just so, he said that God has implanted gold, as it were, in the souls of some human beings, who abound in wisdom and virtue, and they rightly rule. There is silver in others, who belong to the second class. And there is bronze or iron, as it were, in others, who are imperfect in wisdom and virtue, and such men, according to him, should be farmers and artisans. And it is clear that this condition does not change, so that gold would sometimes be put into one kind of human being and sometimes into another kind. Rather, gold is always put into the same kind of human being, and so it follows that the same ones always rule.

9.   Then Aristotle shows the inadequacy regarding the general happiness of the community. For Socrates said that the lawmaker should consider

---

13. Aristotle is concerned about problems of property management for farmers, who would have farms be in the country and common wives in the city. Aquinas, however, makes the wives common to both the guardians and the farmers.

what makes the whole political community happy regarding both virtuous deeds and external goods. But Socrates by his law removed happiness from individual citizens, since he wished that they not have anything as their own, whether property, wives, or sons, things that belong to happiness as useful means, as Aristotle says in the *Ethics*.[14] And the whole political community cannot be happy unless all or most parts of it enjoy happiness, since the happiness of the political community is not like the evenness of an even number, or such like. For the parts of an even number are sometimes odd numbers, as, for example, two groups of three are parts of a group of six. Moreover, if the guardians of a political community are not happy, who else will be, so that the happiness of the political community could be grounded in the latter? For we cannot say that farmers and common artisans (i.e., hired hands), who are the lowest classes in the political community, are happy, since happiness, which is the best thing in the political community, cannot be preserved in the community's lowest part.

And in a final summary, he concludes that the political life of the political community about which Socrates spoke has the aforementioned objections and some others of no less importance than those already mentioned.

Chapter 6
The Second Regime of Socrates (1)

Text (1264b26–1265b26)

1.   Plato also says almost the same thing in his later work, the *Laws*. Therefore, it is best to consider a few things about that regime here. For Socrates has completely determined about few things in the *Republic*— how having common wives, children, and property is necessary, and the organization of the regime.

2.   The mass population is divided into two parts: one, farmers; the other, warriors. And a third group is formed out of the warriors, and this part deliberates and rules over the political community. But Socrates determined nothing about whether farmers and artisans have some or no

---

14. *Ethics* I, 13 (1099a31–b7).

share in the governance, or whether they should bear arms and fight alongside the warriors. And he thinks that wives should fight alongside, and share in the same education as, the guardians. And he filled in other things with extraneous discussions.

3. And there needs to be a certain kind of education for the guardians.

4. Most of the *Laws* consist of actual laws, and he said little about regime. And wishing to make a society more in common with our political communities, he gradually returned to the earlier regime. Aside from common wives and property, he gives the same other things to both regimes (e.g., the same kind of education, the same life free of necessary tasks, the same common meals).

5. But in the *Laws*, he says that there should be common meals for women, and that 5,000 instead of 1,000 should be the number of those bearing arms.

6. Therefore, all the dialogues of Socrates use excessive language, lack profundity, try for novelty, and raise many questions. But it is perhaps hard to say everything well.

7. Take the aforementioned 5,000 warriors. We should not fail to recognize that they would need a territory the size of Babylon or a similarly large territory to support 5,000 men not engaged in productive work. In addition, there will be a far larger number of wives and slaves. Therefore, it is fitting to suppose whatever we wish but nothing impossible. And he says that the lawmaker needs to establish laws regarding two things: the territory and the population. Moreover, it is right to add regard for neighboring regions. First, this is necessary if the political community is to enjoy a political, not a solitary, life. For it is necessary that the political community use military force both within its own territory and against foreign lands. And if one should reject such a life, whether for the individual or the collectivity, it is still no less necessary to be formidable to enemies, both when they invade the territory and when they do not.

8. And we need to look at the amount of property, whether it is perhaps better to determine it more clearly in another way. For he says that there needs to be enough to live moderately. That is to say, one should live life well, since this formulation is more beneficial.

9. Moreover, it is possible to live moderately and be miserable. But a better determination is that one lives both moderately and generously, since if one takes each virtue separately, too much ease results from one, and too much toil from the other. Only these dispositions are virtues concerning the use of property (e.g., using property moderately and generously, not using it meekly or courageously). Therefore, these dispositions necessarily concern property.

10.   And it is also odd to equalize property regarding number of citizens but not to regulate the number of births, as if infertility will keep the birth rate constant, no matter how many births. This may also happen now with some political communities, but it is not necessary that there be such an exact balance in past or present political communities.

11.   For no one currently is uncertain about property, since it is divided among sons, however many. But in Socrates' scheme, the property is indivisible, and disinherited sons, whether few or many, necessarily get nothing.

12.   And one will surmise that we should regulate the birth rate more than property, so that no more than a certain number of offspring are born. And this number should take account of chance factors, namely, that some offspring may die, and that some couples may be childless. And allowing unrestricted births, as practiced in other political communities, necessarily causes citizens to become poor, and their poverty causes rebellion and wickedness.

13.   Therefore, Pheidon of Corinth, a lawmaker of antiquity, thought that estates should remain equal, and the population constant, even if the citizens originally were to have had unequal allotments of land. And it is the contrary in the *Laws*. But we think that we should speak later about how to arrange these things better.

14.   And Plato in the *Laws* left untouched things concerning rulers, and how they will differ from subjects. For he says only that, as a thread of wool is made of different material than a thread of linen, rulers should also be related to subjects in the same way.

15.   And since he allows all of one's personal property to increase up to fivefold, why will there not be a limit on real property? And we need to consider separate homesteads, lest the number perhaps be inexpedient for the management of one household. For Plato gave two separate homesteads to each citizen. But it is hard to live in two homes.

Comment

1.   After Aristotle argued against the position of Socrates regarding the common wives, children, and property that the latter proposed as the chief thing in his regime, as it were, he here inquires about other, later *Laws*. First, Aristotle describes them. Second, he argues against them [6]. Regarding the first, he does two things. First, he speaks about his aim. Second, he pursues his aim [2]. Therefore, he says first that, as there are many objections to the law about common wives and property, so also are there many objections to the other, later *Laws*. And so it is better that he say here a few things about Socrates' whole regime. For Socrates has determined about few things regarding the *Republic*, namely, how

common wives, sons, and property ought to be arranged, and he has determined the organization of political life over these things.

2. Then Aristotle, since he has said enough before about common wives and property, describes the things that Socrates said about the organization of the regime. First, Aristotle describes what Socrates said about the parts of the political community. Second, he describes what Socrates said about the education of citizens [3]. Regarding the first, Aristotle says four things. First, he says that Socrates divided the whole population of the political community into two parts, one of farmers and other artisans, and the other of men who are warriors. And Socrates also added a third part, namely, the council and rulers of the political community. Second, Aristotle says that Socrates failed to say anything about whether farmers and artisans should also have a share in ruling, and whether they should be warriors in some way. Third, he says that Socrates thought that women should be warriors and do other things the same as men. Fourth, he says that Socrates filled other parts of his constitution with many extraneous words irrelevant to the subject of regime, injecting many things about natural and other sciences.

3. Then Aristotle cites what Socrates said about education in the political community. Regarding this, Aristotle does three things. First, he says in general that Socrates said that the guardians (i.e., the city dwellers) should have a certain education.

4. Second, Aristotle lays out the things in which Socrates was in agreement with other regimes and says that most of the *Laws* that Socrates proposed are laws currently observed in political communities. For Socrates spoke about a regime (i.e., the life of a political community) and introduced a greater sharing in the political community than is customary, but he, by establishing the *Laws*, gradually arrived at a second regime,[15] one that is currently practiced. This is because, besides the common wives and property that belonged to the first regime, he treated of all the other things that could be common to both regimes, namely, the one that observes such sharing and the one that does not. For he said that the same education belongs to both. For example, he said that human beings in both communities were to live in moderation and restraint free of necessary tasks, and that they were to establish common meals in the city, meals that were also observed in other political communities, for the greater intimacy of citizens. But it would have been necessary to establish a very different education, as Aristotle said before [chap. 5, n. 6].

---

15. Aristotle says that Socrates returned to the other regime, meaning the one in the *Republic*. Aquinas reads the other regime as the one in the *Laws*.

5. Third, he cites some special things that Socrates proposed. One was that there were also common meals for women, and another was that the number of warriors in the political community was fixed, namely, at least 1,000 and at most 5,000 warriors.

6. Then Aristotle argues against the aforementioned other things that Socrates introduced. First, he argues against the education of the *Laws*. Second, he argues against their organization of the parts of the political community [chap. 7]. Regarding the first, he does two things. First, he lays out his aim. Second, he demonstrates what he proposes [7]. Therefore, he says first that Socrates' dialogues are extravagant, since Socrates inflates his constitution with extraneous discussions; carry little weight, since the arguments were inadequate or unsupported by experience;[16] try for novelty, since the dialogues were contrary to general custom; and raise many questions, since many problems result. But it is difficult to say that Socrates was speaking correctly in all things.

7. Then Aristotle demonstrates what he previously said. First, he argues against what Socrates said about the limits he laid out for the political community. Second, he argues against what Socrates said about differences [13]. Regarding the first, he does two things. First, he argues against what Socrates said about the number of warriors. Second, he argues against what Socrates said about the amount of property he allowed [8]. Therefore, he says first that if one should consider the aforementioned number of warriors that Socrates established in the political community, it is clearly evident that such a political community will need a very extensive territory, like the one around Babylon. This will be necessary in order to provide support from it for 5,000 warriors, who do no other work, and in addition for another, far larger number of wives and slaves. And so the founder of such a political community needs to have extensive territory at his disposal, and this is not impossible.

But one should consider that the would-be founder of a political community should not establish a law because he thinks it possible. Rather, he should do so with regard for the things that belong to it, and especially two things. These are the territory, so as not to establish a larger political community than the territory can support, and the population, so that the laws are suitable for human beings according to their circumstances. Third, the founder of a political community should also establish laws with regard for neighboring territories. First, this is necessary if the

---

16. Aristotle describes the Platonic dialogues as "light," possibly meaning light-hearted, but Aquinas reads it to mean of lightweight, which is also possible. I have translated Aristotle to accommodate Aquinas.

political community ought to have a political, not a solitary, life (i.e., a common life with many other political communities, with whom it is associated in both peace and war). The reason is because such a political community needs to use such arms for war, not only as much as is useful to defend its own territory, but also in foreign territories, in which both enemies and friends are active. Second, if one should not approve of the warlike life, whether the life of an individual human being or the common life of the whole political community, citizens in this regard still need to be armed and warlike in order to be formidable to enemies. Citizens need to be on guard both when enemies are actually invading the territory and when they are not.

8. Then Aristotle argues against the position of Socrates regarding the limit of property that Socrates established in the political community. Regarding this, Aristotle does two things. First, he argues against the limit of property proposed by Socrates in itself. Second, he argues against the position of Socrates insofar as Socrates failed to consider the birth rate [10]. Regarding the first, he gives two arguments. Therefore, he says first that we should consider whether we could perhaps in another way determine more clearly the amount of property that the political community ought generally to have than in the way that Socrates had determined. For Socrates says that there ought to be enough property of the political community to enable citizens to live moderately. But one would speak more intelligibly if one were to say that the political community ought to have enough property to live well with it. For the latter formulation is more beneficial, since enjoying the good life includes more things than living moderately.

9. Aristotle gives a second argument, saying that one may live moderately but miserably (i.e., in great poverty). And so it is clear that the aforementioned formulation of Socrates does not suffice. Rather, the better determination is that we say that one ought to have enough property to live moderately and generously, since if we should speak of one or the other separately, unfitting consequences will follow. For, on the one hand, if we should say only that one ought to live generously, he will consequently indulge in extraneous pleasures. And on the other hand, if we should say only that one ought to live moderately, he could then live in poverty and toil. Therefore, in order to exclude both unfitting consequences, we need to say that human beings ought to live moderately and generously. And this formulation is adequate, since only these two virtues make human beings well disposed regarding the use of their substance (i.e., their property).

And this is evident in contrast to other virtues. For we cannot say that one uses his property meekly or courageously, since the virtue of meekness concerns anger, and the virtue of courage concerns fear and boldness. And so the latter virtues in no way regard the use of property. But moderation, which concerns desires for food and sex, on which account many waste their substance, and generosity, which concerns giving and receiving, clearly regard the use of property. And so we can say that one uses one's property moderately and generously. And so, since there seems to be something improper about the use of property in each of these respects, we need to practice moderation and generosity regarding it.

10.   Then he argues against the position of Socrates because determining the amount of property did not determine the number of births. Regarding this, he does six things. First, he proposes that what Socrates said is unsuitable. And he says that it is odd that one wishes to equalize the property of the political community (i.e., limit it to a fixed amount) and at the same time does not establish something to fix the number of citizens and allows an unlimited birth rate. This is what Socrates did.

Second, Aristotle gave the argument that influenced Socrates. For many women in the political community may be childless and so, although other women beget many sons, the population of the political community will always remain constant, as we currently see happening in political communities. And so it did not seem necessary to Socrates that anything would be affected regarding the birth rate of sons.

11.   Third, Aristotle shows that this argument is inadequate. For in political communities today, because property is divided, and each citizen has his own, no problem can arise in regard to however many sons are born, since each citizen is anxious to provide in some way for his sons. But in Socrates' scheme, since property in his scheme was not divided among citizens, the disinherited sons, whether their number increases or decreases, would then receive none of the produce from property if the number of the powerful were to increase. For if the powerful in a political community were to take things necessary for themselves and their families first, the number of the powerful would then increase.

12.   Fourth, Aristotle proposes that the number of sons born should be limited, saying that one can think that one should limit the births of sons even more than the amount of property, namely, that no more citizens are born than a fixed number for whom the property of the political community is adequate.

Fifth, he shows what one ought to observe in making such a limit, saying that one should determine the number of sons in relation to fortuitous events (e.g., infant deaths and the infertility of women who do not conceive). That is to say, one only allows the number of births to increase so as to compensate for such chance deficiencies.

Sixth, he shows how necessary it is to limit the birth rate. And he says that it is necessary because, if one should allow an unlimited number of offspring, as is generally the case in political communities, this necessarily causes citizens to become poor. For many sons, having only what their wealthy father had, will be poor, and the poverty of citizens then causes them to be rebellious and wicked, since those without the necessities of life are eager to acquire them by fraud and robbery.

13.   Then he argues against the education of the *Laws* regarding differences that Socrates made in the political community. Regarding this, Aristotle does four things. First, he shows how Socrates disagreed with other lawmakers regarding the differences. And he says that a certain lawmaker, Pheidon of Corinth, said two things should be observed in the political community. The first is that the households of the ancient citizens would remain equal in wealth and honor, even if they were originally to have had unequal estates. (Aristotle will say later [chap. 8, n. 2] how they can be brought back to equality.) The second is that the number of citizens would always remain constant. But we find the contrary in the *Laws* of Socrates, since he neither directs how the number of citizens remains constant nor establishes what constitutes the equal wealth of citizens. Rather, Socrates allows some to have more wealth than others, as Aristotle will say later [15]. But Aristotle will determine later [chap. 8, nn. 4–8] about which is better, namely, whether or not all citizens have equal wealth.

14.   Second, Aristotle argues against Socrates' law regarding the difference between rulers and subjects. And he says that the *Laws* of Socrates did not determine how rulers ought to be distinguished from subjects, although Socrates said that there needed to be a difference between them. As a thread of wool is made of a different material than a thread of linen, Socrates said, so, by reason of their different condition, some citizens needed to be raised to be the ruling power, and others to remain subjects. For Socrates could not distinguish citizens by their ancestry, since he proposed common children and wives.

15.   Third, Aristotle argued against the position of Socrates regarding difference in property. And he says that Socrates allowed the wealth in personal property of one citizen to be five times greater than that of another. And he could by the same logic allow the same difference in real property, so as not to make all fields common.

Fourth, Aristotle argued against the position of Socrates regarding households, saying that we need to consider whether the different households that Socrates introduced are perhaps unbeneficial to household management. For Socrates said that each citizen ought to have two homesteads, perhaps because sons live separately. But it is difficult for one citizen to have a household large enough to be able to fill two homesteads, and it is also harmful to household management that one human being pay the expenses of two homes.

Chapter 7
The Second Regime of Socrates (2)

Text (1265b26–1266a30)

1.   And the whole arrangement aims to be neither a democracy nor an oligarchy but something in between, which people call a polity, since it consists of those who bear arms.

2.   Therefore, if he constitutes his regime to be most like the political communities of other regimes, he perhaps spoke well. But if he wishes his regime to be the second-best regime, he did not speak well. For one will perhaps prefer the Spartan one or another, more aristocratic regime.

3.   Therefore, some say that the best regime needs to be a blend of all kinds of citizens and so praise the Spartan one, which, they say, is composed of oligarchy, monarchy, and democracy. They say that kingship makes it a monarchy, the ruling power of the elders makes it an oligarchy, and it is democratically ruled by the ephors, since the people choose the ephors. But others say that the rule of the ephors is tyrannical, and that common meals and the rest of daily life are what make Sparta democratically ruled.

4.   But Socrates in the *Laws* said that it is fitting that the best constitution is composed of democracy and tyranny.

5.   But one will consider these regimes as completely unconstitutional or the worst of all regimes. Therefore, those who mix many regimes speak more correctly, since a regime composed of many kinds of regime is better.

6.   Moreover, the regime in the *Laws* seems to have nothing monarchic. Rather, it has only oligarchy and democracy, and Socrates wants to incline the regime more in the direction of oligarchy.

7.   And the way rulers are chosen shows this. For choosing rulers by lot from those elected is common to both oligarchy and democracy. But that only wealthier citizens are required to participate in the assembly, elect officials, and do everything else political is oligarchic. And so is the attempt to ensure that most rulers are from the wealthy, and to fill the highest offices from the highest ranks.

8.   And he also makes the election of councilors oligarchic. For all need to elect candidates, first from the highest rank, then an equal number from the second rank, then an equal number from the third rank. But it was not necessary that all elect candidates from the third and fourth ranks, and only the first and second ranks were required to elect candidates from

the fourth rank. Then Socrates says that there should be from these an equal number from each rank in the council. But the electors from the highest ranks will be more numerous and better off, since some of the lower classes, not being obliged to vote, do not do so.

9.   Therefore, it is clear from these things, and from what we are to say later when we shall come to consider such a regime, how we should constitute such a regime out of democracy and monarchy.

10.   And the way of electing rulers, namely, that those eligible come from the electors, is dangerous. For if some resolved citizens, even if few in number, should so wish, councilors will always be chosen as these citizens wish. Therefore, the things in the *Laws* regarding regime have this way.

Comment

1.   After Aristotle has argued against the position of Socrates regarding the education in the *Laws*, he here argues against the position of Socrates regarding the organization of the political community. First, Aristotle argues against this position regarding the people. Second, he argues against this position regarding the rulers [3].

And to evidence the things said here, we should consider that there are six kinds of organization of political communities, as he will say later [III, chap. 6, nn. 1–4], since either one or few or many rule every political community. If one person rules the political community, that one is either a king or a tyrant. He is a king if he should be virtuous, keeping as his goal the common benefit of his subjects. And he is a tyrant if he should be evil, turning everything to his own advantage and contemning the benefit of subjects. And if a few persons should rule the political community, those who look after the good of the people will be chosen because of their virtue, and we call such a regime aristocracy (i.e., rule of the virtuous or best citizens). Or a few persons, who will turn everything belonging to the community to their own benefit, will be chosen because of their power or wealth, not because of their virtue, and we call such a regime oligarchy (i.e., rule of the few). And likewise, if many persons should rule the political community, we call such a regime by the general name *polity* if many virtuous citizens rule. But there may not be many virtuous persons in the political community, except, perhaps, regarding military virtue. Therefore, this regime is one in which the men warriors in the political community rule. But if the whole people should wish to rule collectively, we call the regime democracy (i.e., rule of the people).

Therefore, he says first that, according to the *Laws*, the whole organization of the people, namely, the political community, is neither a democracy nor an oligarchy but a regime in between the two. And some call the regime by the general name *polity*, and it consists of those who bear arms. For Socrates divided the people of the political community into two parts, one of warriors and the other of artisans and farmers, and the farmers need to stay in the fields. And so Aristotle concludes that almost all the men living in the city would be warriors.

2.   Then Aristotle shows in what regard Socrates spoke well, and in what regard he spoke wrongly, saying that if Socrates established such an organization as one most common to other regimes, he was perhaps right. For oligarchy belongs only to the upper classes, and democracy only to the lower classes, but his regime consists of things in between both. And so his regime, as sharing in both regimes, is more common. But if Socrates established such an organization as the second-best, as it were, he was wrong. And Aristotle says that the first organization is the kingdom, whether because it is the first in time, since kings originally ruled all political communities, or because it is the best, provided that the king is good. And next to this first regime, we cannot say that the regime of warriors is the best, since aristocracy (i.e., rule of the virtuous) is much better. And Spartans were ruled in the latter way, even if other citizens are ruled still more aristocratically.

3.   Then he argues against the organization that Socrates established in the political community regarding the rulers. Regarding this, he does two things. First, he lays out the position of Socrates. Second, he argues against it [3]. Regarding the first, he does two things. First, he proposes that it is expeditious that the aforementioned regimes in political communities be mixed. Second, he shows how Socrates mixed them [4]. Therefore, he says first that some say that the best regime of a political community is one that is a mixture, as it were, of all the aforementioned regimes. And this is because the admixture of one regime moderates another, and there is less reason for rebellion if all the citizens share in the rule of the political community (i.e., if the people should rule in something, the powerful in another, and the king in another).

And so the organization of the Spartan political community will be most praiseworthy, although there were two opinions about it. For some said that it was composed of three political communities, namely, oligarchy (i.e., rule of the few), monarchy (i.e., rule of one person), and democracy (i.e., popular rule). For the Spartans in their political community had a king (this belongs to monarchy); elders drawn from the more important people in the political community (this belongs to oligarchy); and rulers chosen from the people, called ephors (i.e., providers), which belongs to democracy. And others were of the opinion that the rule of the ephors belonged to tyranny, since they ruled as they wished. But there were other rulers in the political community who arranged for the common meals and other things belonging to the daily life of the community (e.g., buying food and other commercial things). And those of the second opinion said that this belongs to democracy.

4.   Then Aristotle shows how Socrates composed the mixture of his regime, saying that Socrates in the *Laws* said that the best regime ought to be composed of tyranny and democracy. Socrates perhaps said this because the power of the tyrant would then restrain the power of the people, and the power of the people would restrain the tyrant.

5.   Then Aristotle argues against this statement of Socrates. First, Aristotle shows that this organization as such is improper. Second, he shows that the things Socrates established were not suitable for such a mixture [6]. Therefore, he shows first that we should not call the two aforementioned regimes, namely, tyranny and democracy, true regimes, since they follow the impulse of the will, not the order of reason. Or we should call them the worst regimes of all. And so it is unfitting that the best regime be composed of the worst regimes. Therefore, those who blend the organization of the political community out of many regimes do far better. For the more the regime is blended out of many regimes, the better it is, since many citizens share in ruling the political community.

6.   Then Aristotle argues against the statement of Socrates regarding the things he established, which were unsuitable for the aforementioned mixture. Regarding this, he does two things. First, he shows that the things Socrates established were unsuitable for the aforementioned mixture. Second, he shows that they were intrinsically dangerous [10]. Regarding the first, he does three things. First, he sets out his aim. Second, he proves what he proposes [7]. Third, he shows how the aforementioned mixture could be accomplished [9]. Therefore, he says first that Socrates wished to mix his regime from democracy and tyranny, which is a sort of monarchy. But nothing in the regime is monarchic (i.e., belonging to the rule of one person) if one should consider the things he established. Rather, all these things are oligarchic and democratic (i.e., belonging to the powerful or the people), but his organization inclines more toward oligarchy.

7.   Then Aristotle shows what he proposes. First, he shows it regarding the election of rulers. Second, he shows it regarding the election of the councilors [8]. Therefore, he says first that what he said is evident from the way Socrates established rulers. For Socrates says that some persons should be elected from whom the rulers would be chosen by lot. And this was common to both democracy and oligarchy, since those elected were from both the people and the upper class. But he established some other things belonging to oligarchy, namely, that it belonged to the wealthy of the political community to call an assembly, and that they report the rulers elected to the people. And he wanted only wealthier citizens to do all such

things belonging to the organization of the political community. Likewise, it was oligarchic that Socrates wanted most rulers to come from the wealthy and be established in the more important offices.

8.   Then Aristotle explains how Socrates inclined toward oligarchy in the election of councilors,[17] saying that Socrates distinguished citizens by four ranks, from all of which there were some who chose the councilors. All those of the first rank were absolutely obliged to vote. But only some of the second rank, who were equal in number to those of the first rank, voted, and they were also absolutely obliged to do so. Then an equal number were elected from the third and fourth ranks. But it was not required that all of those eligible out of those ranks vote, and only those of the first or second rank could vote for councilors from the fourth rank. And so Socrates said that an equal number of councilors came from each rank of the political community. But this is not necessarily so. Rather, there will always be more and wealthier councilors from the highest ranks, since not all of the lower classes will vote, inasmuch as they are not obliged to do so.

9.   Then Aristotle says that what he has just said, and what he will say later when he will come to consider a mixed regime,[18] can make clear how to establish such a regime out of democracy and monarchy.

10.   Then he shows that the election of the rulers that Socrates established is dangerous. And he says that the system of choosing rulers established by Socrates, namely, that those chosen were selected from previously elected electors, is dangerous for the political community. For those first elected, from whom the rulers are chosen, are few in relation to the whole population of the political community. And so it will be easier to corrupt them than to corrupt the whole population. And so, if there should be some who want to be always established in power, even if they should be slight in number, rulers will always be chosen according to the wishes of those citizens, since the latter will elect one another in turn and succeed one another in ruling.

In a final summary, he concludes that things in the *Laws* about the regime of Socrates have the aforementioned way.

---

17. Aquinas' description of the election process of the councilors differs in a few particulars from that of Aristotle. The Latin text of Aristotle is quite ambiguous, and this may explain the differences.

18. *Politics* IV, 9 (1294a30–b41).

Chapter 8
The Regime of Phaleas (1)

Text (1266a31–1267a21)

1. And there are also other regimes, some by uneducated people and some by philosophers and political leaders, but all describe constitutions closer to currently existing regimes than to either regime of Plato. For no one else suggested a regime with common wives and children, or common meals for women, but the others begin with essential things.

2. For it seems to some that it is most necessary that there be a good arrangement about property, since they say that all rebellions arise concerning property. And so Phaleas of Chalcedon was the first to reach this conclusion. For he said that the property of citizens needs to be equal. And he thought that it was not difficult for political communities to do this at the time of their foundation. And he thought that, although it is more difficult for established political communities to do this, it could be very quickly accomplished through dowries, with the rich giving but not receiving them, and the poor receiving but not giving them.

3. And Plato in the *Laws* thought that there ought to be the power to acquire property up to a point, but that no citizen should have more than five times the least property, as I have also said before.

4. And those who legislate in this way should not ignore, as they now do, that it is fitting that those establishing the amount of property also establish the number of offspring. For if the number of children should exceed the amount of property, the law necessarily fails. And if you do maintain the law, many of the rich become poor, and this is wrong, since it is necessary that there be no such rebellious persons.

5. Therefore, even some of the ancients seem to have recognized that equalization of property plays a role in the political community, as the law of Solon established. And with other ancients, there is a law that prohibits the acquisition of as much land as anyone desired. And laws likewise prohibit the sale of property. For example, in Locri, the law prohibits the sale of property unless the prospective seller should demonstrate that an obvious misfortune has happened. Moreover, other laws require that ancient lots of land be preserved. And the abrogation of such a law made the regime of Leucas too democratic, since it was no longer possible for citizens to advance by fixed property qualifications to ruling power.

6.   And the equal amount of property may be too high, so that citizens live luxuriously, or too low, so that citizens live tenuously. Therefore, it is clear that it will not be enough that the lawmaker makes property equal. Rather, he should estimate the mean.

7.   And if one should have arranged a moderate amount of property for all citizens, it may still bring no benefit. For it is more necessary to moderate desires than property, and this will not be so unless laws have sufficiently instructed the citizens.

8.   But perhaps Phaleas will say that this is what he himself says, since he thinks that two things should be equal in political communities, property and education. But one needs to say what the education will be. And saying that education should be one and the same for all citizens is not at all helpful. For there may be one and the same education but of such a kind that it will make citizens excessively desirous of wealth or honor or both.

9.   Moreover, people are factious both because of unequal property and because of unequal honors, but in contrary ways. For the many are unhappy because of unequal property, and the endowed unhappy because of honors if they are equal. And so also both the wicked and the good want honor.

10.   And human beings do not commit crimes against property only for the sake of the necessities of life. (Phaleas thinks that equality of property is the cure, so that people do not steal because of cold or hunger and enjoy what they have without desiring more.) For if they should desire more than necessary things, they will commit crime as the cure. Therefore, they will commit crimes both for this reason and also if they should desire to enjoy pleasure without pain. Therefore, what are the cures for these three things? For the first, there should be a modest amount of property and employment; for the second, self-control; and for the third, people, if they should be able to enjoy contemplating things in themselves, will seek the cure only in philosophy. For the other cures require human beings.

11.   And human beings most commit crimes for the sake of eminence, not necessary things. For example, human beings do not practice tyranny in order not to be cold. And so it is also more honorable to kill a tyrant than a thief. And so the method of the regime of Phaleas is helpful only for minor crimes.

12.   Moreover, many things whereby citizens live well with one another need to be established, but relations with neighboring and all foreign peoples also need to be arranged. Therefore, one needs to establish a militarily strong regime. And Phaleas said nothing about this.

Comment

1.   After Aristotle discussed the regime of Socrates or Plato, he here continues with a discussion about the regime of a certain man called Phaleas. Regarding this, Aristotle does three things. First, he describes the organization of Phaleas. Second, he approves it regarding what Phaleas said correctly [5]. Third, he argues against it regarding what it lacked [6]. Regarding the first, he does two things. First, he relates that regime and later regimes to the previous organization of Socrates or Plato. Second, he describes the organization of Phaleas' regime [2].

Therefore, Aristotle says first that there are other regimes (i.e., organizations of political communities) besides the aforementioned regimes of Socrates or Plato. Simple and uneducated people arrived at some of the regimes, and philosophers and those wise and expert in civic life arrived at others. Some of the regimes conceived by their authors never existed in any political community, but there were other regimes by which particular peoples organized their civic life. And all such regimes are more closely related to one another and to what is proper for a political community than to both aforementioned regimes of Socrates or Plato. The first regime of Socrates, previously considered, concerns common wives, sons, and property, and the second concerns the *Laws*, which Plato wrote later. For no other lawmaker arrived at the common sons and wives belonging to the first regime of Socrates or ordained anything regarding the common meals belonging to his second regime, as the foregoing makes clear [chap. 6, n. 4]. Rather, the lawmakers begin to organize a political community by more elementary things.

2.   Then Aristotle describes the regime that Phaleas ordained. Regarding this, Aristotle does four things. First, he shows what most lawmakers aimed at. And he says that it seemed to some lawmakers most necessary that there is a right order about property (i.e., the private property of citizens), since property most causes all the rebellions in political communities, which lawmakers strive chiefly to avoid.

Second, Aristotle shows what Phaleas ordained about this, saying that Phaleas was the first to determine something about it. For Phaleas wanted all property of citizens to be equal. And he said that this is not hard to do in political communities at the time of their foundation, since property could be equally divided among the citizens. But in already established political communities whose citizens have unequal property, it was more difficult. Nonetheless, one could quickly bring property back to this rule by dowries, namely, that the rich contracting marriage with the poor would give but not receive dowries, and the poor would receive but not give them, until the property of all was equal.

3. Third, he shows how Plato ordained about this in a different way. For Plato said that no citizen should be given the power to possess more wealth than five times above the citizen who had the least. But we need to understand this regarding the wealth of personal property, since he makes real property common.

4. Fourth, Aristotle shows in what all such lawmakers fell short. For they did not realize that, since they established a limit regarding the amount of wealth, it was also necessary to ordain a limit regarding the number of sons. For example, the limit could be that no one strove to generate more than a certain number, or that after a certain number of children, the extra men were sent to found other political communities, or some other way. This is because, if the number of sons born should surpass the amount of wealth allotted to each man, the law regarding equal property necessarily fails. For example, if one of two citizens having equal property begets four sons, and the other only one, then their sons do not inherit equal property.

And in addition to the law failing, another evil will result, namely, that many born of the wealthy become poor when the property of a wealthy citizen is divided among many sons. And this is an evil, since it is necessary for the peace of a political community that the sons of the wealthy, who can become rebellious, are not poor, since they might become robbers. But this will not result if the amount of property for each citizen should be unregulated, since each will be anxious to increase his wealth as the number of his sons increases. Therefore, we should either establish nothing about a limit on property or, along with this, establish some limit regarding the number of sons.

5. Then Aristotle approves the aforementioned arrangement insofar as Phaleas ordained some limit on property, lest Aristotle seem to have rejected the things because of their aforementioned defects. And he approves a limit for two reasons. First, he approves it on the authority of ancient lawmakers, saying that some of them seem to have recognized that equalizing the property of citizens has great power to preserve the well-being of the political community. And so Solon, who was one of the seven wise men and established the laws of Athens, established as law what other peoples also observe, that one could own land only up to a fixed limit, not as much as one wished. Similarly, there are laws in some political communities that prohibit citizens from selling their property. For example, there was from ancient times a law in the city of Locri in Calabria that no one was to sell property unless he were to show that he had suffered a serious misfortune (e.g., that he was captured by enemies or suffered some other such thing). Similarly, there are laws ordaining that the ancient lots of citizens are preserved intact. And all these things belong to equalizing the property of citizens.

Second, Aristotle shows the same thing by the unsuitable consequences, saying that, if there were no limit on property in a political community, the regime would then be too democratic (i.e., too favorable to the
common people). For, inasmuch as each citizen without distinction was
allowed to buy property, many of the lower classes were then elevated, and
members of the upper classes lowered. And so it followed that, because of
the added confusion regarding the status of citizens, human beings were
not chosen as rulers from certain fixed ranks of citizens.

6.   Then Aristotle argues against the aforementioned arrangement: first,
regarding its omissions; second, regarding its unsuitable equalization of
property [chap. 9, n. 1]; and third, regarding its unsuitable prescription
about artisans [chap. 9, n. 5]. Regarding the first, he does three things.
First, he shows that Phaleas omitted things belonging to the education of
citizens. Second, he shows that Phaleas omitted things belonging to the
peace of the political community [9]. Third, he shows that Phaleas omitted things belonging to civic life [12].

Regarding the first, he gives two arguments. The first is that there can
be equality of property among citizens, but it can be either too much, so
that citizens live too luxuriously with it, and so the morals of citizens are
corrupted, or too little, so that citizens live so stringently that they cannot
help one another. And both of these are harmful to the good education of
citizens. And so it is clear that Phaleas is an inadequate lawmaker, since he
only makes the property of citizens equal. But he needs to determine a
mean, namely, an amount of property such that citizens can neither strive
excessively for pleasures nor be forced to live too sparingly.

7.   Aristotle gives a second argument, regarding which he does two
things. First, he makes the argument, saying that even if one ordains moderate property for all citizens, this still does not suffice for the good life of
citizens. For it is more necessary to moderate internal desires of the soul,
namely, that citizens not desire immoderate things, than to regulate external property, namely, that citizens not possess excessive things. But
human desires can be moderated only if proper laws adequately instruct
human beings, and Phaleas did not propose such laws. And so he inadequately treated of things belonging to the instruction of citizens.

8.   Second, Aristotle excludes a possible rejoinder by Phaleas, who might
say in reply to this argument that the political community needs both,
namely, equal property and equal education (i.e., that the same education
should form all citizens). But against this rejoinder, Aristotle says that
Phaleas needed to say of what the education necessary to form all citizens
consists. For it is not enough to say that the education is one and the same
for all. Rather, the education forming citizens needs to be such and such,
so that some do not wish to surpass others, whether in riches or honors or

both. And so, since Phaleas omitted such an education, he was an inadequate lawmaker.

9. Then Aristotle shows that Phaleas omitted things belonging to the peace of the political community. Regarding this, Aristotle gives three arguments. The first is that citizens form factions both because of unequal property and because of unequal honors, although in different ways. For the lower classes care about wealth, not honors. And so they are factious because of unequal wealth. But endowed human beings, who surpass others in virtuous deeds, are factious about honors if even those of no distinction are rendered their equals. And so the lawmaker needs to ordain something regarding honors, namely, that there is one honor allotted only to the good, and a different honor that even an evil person (i.e., one lacking virtue) can enjoy. For peace will then be observed in the political community. Therefore, since Phaleas omitted this, he inadequately treated of things proper to the peace of the political community.

10. Aristotle gives a second argument, as follows. Human beings commit crimes against others to acquire the necessities of life, the foremost cause, and Phaleas thought that the cure for it was to make the property of citizens equal. And then all citizens would have the necessities of life, and so one human being would not rob another to avoid cold or hunger. But human beings do not commit crimes only for this reason; they also commit crimes against their neighbor in order to enjoy their pleasure and not to have any unfulfilled desire. This is because, if some should have greater desire of earthly necessities (i.e., *for* necessities, in Greek usage), that is, if they should desire more things than are necessary for them, they will commit crimes, taking the goods of others by force or fraud. They will do so as a cure (i.e., to satisfy their desires). Human beings commit crimes for the latter reason and also because some wish to enjoy pleasure without suffering any pain. And so they commit crimes against human beings who they fear can cause them pain, by oppressing them.

Therefore, it is necessary for the peace of the political community that the lawmaker devise cures against these three causes of crime. For a modest amount of property and the employment whereby one acquires one's livelihood suffice as a cure for those who commit crimes in order to acquire the necessities of life, since nature is satisfied with a few things. And self-restraint, which controls the desires in human beings for pleasure, is the cure for those who commit crimes because of desires for pleasure. And against the third group, namely, those who commit crimes in order not to suffer pain, the cure uses philosophy. This cure concerns those who can enjoy such painless pleasure, and causes human beings not to be anguished over misfortunes. But in the two former cases, human beings can help one another. And so, since Phaleas omitted the latter two cures and offered a cure only against the first cause of crime, he seems to have provided inadequately.

11. Aristotle gives a third argument, saying that human beings most commit crimes in order to acquire the distinctions of wealth and honors, not the necessities of life. For example, it is obvious that tyrants practice tyranny for the sake of the aforementioned distinctions, not in order to avoid cold or hunger. And so, because tyrants commit the greatest crimes in the political community, the reward of great honors is for this reason given to those who kill tyrants and not to those who kill other thieves. And yet Phaleas applied no cure against the crimes of tyrants. And so his way of organization clearly offers help only against minor, not major, crimes.

12. Then Aristotle shows that the organization of Phaleas was inadequate regarding civic life, since one needs to establish many things in the political community whereby citizens live well with one another. One also needs to establish things whereby they live well with their neighbors and any foreigners. And since some neighbors and foreigners are also enemies against whom one needs to wage war, one also needs to establish in the political community an organization regarding military strength. And Phaleas omitted all these things. And so it is clear that he inadequately organized the political community.

Chapter 9
The Regime of Phaleas (2)

Text (1267a21–b21)

1. And it is also the same about property. For property needs to be sufficient for external dangers as well as internal uses. Therefore, the total amount of property should not be so large that more powerful neighbors covet it, and the owners cannot repel the invaders. Nor should it be so small that the owners cannot support war against equal or like enemies. Thus Phaleas determined nothing about this, and it needs to be noted that abundant property is useful. Therefore, the best limit is perhaps that property not be so large as easily to induce the more powerful to wage war because of its abundance, but as if the citizens do not have so much property. For example, when Autophradates wanted to lay siege to Atarneus, Eubulus bade him consider how long it will take to capture it, and estimate the cost of a siege of that duration. For Autophradates ought to accept a lesser ransom and immediately abandon the siege. And Eubulus, having said this, got Autophradates to agree and call off the siege.

2.   Therefore, it is somewhat expedient to equalize the property of citizens in order to avoid civic strife, but this is not a great matter, so to speak. For the endowed, thinking themselves worthy of more, will be indignant, for which reason they also often seem to be troublesome and seditious.

3.   Moreover, the wickedness of human beings cannot be satisfied. They are at first satisfied with only a little money. And when this has become an ancestral right, they always demand more and more. For it is the nature of desire to be boundless, which most live trying to satisfy. Therefore, rather than equalize the property of rulers, it is better to ensure that those by nature just do not wish to act covetously, and that the wicked cannot do so. And this is so if the latter should be lesser but not treated unjustly.

4.   Nor was Phaleas right about equal property. For he makes only real property equal, but there is wealth in slaves, cattle, money, and much provision of things called personal property. Therefore, one should seek equality or a moderate limit of all these things. Or all property should be unlimited.

5.   And it seems from Phaleas' proposed laws that, if all the artisans will be public slaves and not augment the political community, he is constructing a small political community. But if there need to be public slaves performing public works, it should adopt the way it was done in Epidamnus and the way Diophantus once established in Athens. Therefore, one will judge mostly from the foregoing if there was anything right or wrong about the regime of Phaleas.

Comment

1.   After Aristotle argued against the regime of Phaleas regarding things the latter omitted about the education of citizens, the peace of the political community, and civic life, he here argues against what Phaleas inadequately ordained about property. Regarding this, Aristotle gives four arguments. In the first, he says that Phaleas has also not adequately determined about property. For, although Phaleas has established a limit on property among citizens in relation to one another, namely, that all have equal property, he did not determine how much property should belong to the whole political community. And this ought to be limited both in relation to sufficiency for civic uses, which pertain to food, clothing, and the like, and in relation to

the dangers that can threaten from external sources. And so we should consider two things regarding the amount of property of the political community. The first is that property should not be so large that more powerful neighbors are enticed to covet it, with the result that citizens cannot withstand the neighbors' incursions. The second is that property should not be so small as not to be enough to be prepared for war, by which citizens resist enemies equal and similar to themselves.

Therefore, one needs to recognize that abundant property is beneficial for the political community, since this will enable citizens to have sufficient property for both the expenses of civic life and the waging of war. But the best limit of the amount of property seems to be one not so large that citizens lightly presume to wage war against their more powerful enemies because of its abundance. And yet there should be enough property so that citizens can securely wage war against those who do not have so much property as to be able to resist them.[19]

Or we can understand the cited text in another way. The limit on the property of citizens should be such as not easily to cause the more powerful, enticed by the citizens' abundant property, to wage war against the political community. Rather, the limit should be such that the more powerful regard the citizens as not having so much wealth as to make it worthwhile for the more powerful to undergo the test of war for the sake of plundering it. And the example that he adds confirms this. For when a certain ruler called Autophradates wished to lay siege to a certain city called Atarneus, a certain wise man called Eubulus (i.e., wise counselor) led him to consider how long it could take to capture the city, and to estimate the expenses of a siege over so long a time. And if Autophradates were to find that he would gain less in capturing the city than he would spend in the siege, he should abandon it. The ruler agreed with this advice and called off the siege. But he would not done so if he were to have obtained greater wealth. And so the aforementioned limit on property seems to be useful for the political community. And since Phaleas omitted this, he seems to have inadequately ordained about the property of the political community.

2. And Aristotle gives a second argument, saying that it is in one respect expeditious for the political community that citizens have equal property, in order to avoid civic strife among them. But it is not important, so to speak, that this avoids civic disturbances by the lower classes when matter for strife by the upper classes remains. For the endowed in the political

---

19. This way of understanding the Latin text of Aristotle is possible but does not seem to fit the context of the example of Eubulus.

community (e.g., the noble and virtuous) will be indignant if they receive equal things but deserve greater things. For, as it seems to be contrary to justice that equal persons have unequal things, so it is unjust that unequal persons have equal things. And this is why the upper classes are often troublesome and factious. For justice preserves the peace of a political community, and violation of justice incites sedition. Therefore, Phaleas inadequately ordained about property.

3.   Aristotle gives a third argument, saying that the will of human beings, even if it could be satisfied regarding necessities, cannot be satisfied regarding vice. For it first seems to one who has nothing enough to have a little money. But when such a person has acquired or by paternal inheritance received a bit of money, it always seems that he needs more and more money. And this is so because the nature of desire is to be infinite. For desire seeks not only the necessities of life but also all the things that can be pleasurable for human beings, and such things are unlimited. And so, since most human beings strive to satisfy their desire, it follows that their desire cannot be infinitely satisfied. And since some desire things that belong to others, seditions arise in political communities. Therefore, the lawmaker needs to regulate the source of these things, namely, desire, rather than even property.

But this is done in one way regarding the good and in another way regarding the wicked. For the lawmaker needs to establish such a system that the just by nature (the virtuous by nature) do not want to act covetously (i.e., steal property belonging to others), and he can do this by accustoming them to the love of justice. But he ought so to deal with the wicked that they cannot steal property belonging to others even if they should want to. And two things are necessary for this. One is that the wicked in the political community should be lesser (i.e., left in the lowest class), so that they cannot harm others. And the second is that injustices, which provoke human beings to harm others, should not be inflicted on them. Therefore, since Phaleas omitted such education, he seems to have been an inadequate lawmaker.

4.   Aristotle gives a fourth argument, saying that Phaleas did not say enough about the equality of property, since he equalized the property of citizens only regarding real property, namely, ownership of land. But there is another kind of wealth (e.g., slaves, animals, money, and other things provided for enjoying life and called personal property). And Phaleas said nothing about the equality of these things. But one needs to establish the equality of both real and personal property, make dispositions about personal property in some other way, or omit limits on all of them. For the same argument applies to both real and personal property, since civic disturbances arise from both.

5.   Then Aristotle argues against the organization of Phaleas regarding artisans, saying that, because of the law of Phaleas regarding them, it followed that a small political community was established. For Phaleas wanted all artisans to work for the public, and their products distributed to citizens according to the latter's needs. And so the artisans would be slaves, as it were, of the community and would do nothing to augment the citizen-body of the political community. And so the political community would be small, since we currently perceive that a good part of the political community consists of artisans. But there need to be in a political community some public workers who perform the public works of a political community, as was observed in the city of Epidamnus, and as a certain lawmaker called Diophantus once established at Athens.

And in a final summary, Aristotle concludes that one can consider from the foregoing what is good or bad regarding the regime of Phaleas.

Chapter 10
The Regime of Hippodamus (1)

Text (1267b22–1268a15)

1.   And Hippodamus of Miletus, son of Euryphon, invented the division of cities and laid out suburbs. He was extravagant about a different kind of life because of love of honor, so that he seems to some rather odd because of his long beard and hair. Moreover, he wore cheap but warm clothes both in winter and summer. He also wished to be considered an expert on the whole of nature. He was the first nonpolitical practitioner to attempt to say something about the best regime.

2.   And he planned a city with a population of 10,000 men, divided into three parts: one of artisans, one of farmers, and one of warriors.

3.   And he divided the territory into three parts: one sacred, one public, and one private. And the sacred part was land out of which they produced things assigned to the gods. The public part was land out of which the warriors subsisted. And the private part was land belonging to the farmers.

4.   And he thought that there were only three kinds of laws, regarding which three kinds of lawsuits arose, namely, cases involving insult, damage, and homicide.

5. And he legally established a supreme court, to which all apparently erroneous lower-court decisions should be appealed. And elected elders were the judges on this court.

6. And he thought that the verdicts in the law courts should not be by simply collecting the juror-judges' votes. Rather, each juror-judge should have a tablet on which he wrote *guilty* if his verdict were such, or leave the tablet blank if his verdict were for acquittal. And if the juror-judge's verdict was qualified, he was to write this on the tablet. For Hippodamus thought the present law bad, since rendering a definitive verdict compelled juror-judges to violate their oath of office.

7. Moreover, he established a law concerning those who discover things useful for the political community, that they obtain honor. And he established that the children of those who died in battle should be supported at public expense, something he thought not hitherto legally established elsewhere. But this is the current law in Athens and other political communities. And the people, composed of the three parts of the political community, elect all the rulers. And those elected take care of public affairs, foreigners, and orphans. Therefore, these are most of the things of the organization of Hippodamus and the ones most worthy of comment.

Comment

1. After Aristotle attended to the regime of Phaleas, he begins here to treat of the regime of Hippodamus. Regarding this, he does three things. First, he explains the background of the lawmaker. Second, he describes the regime Hippodamus established [2]. Third, he argues against it regarding certain things [chap. 11, n. 1]. Regarding the first, he does three things. First, he says what Hippodamus devised in politics, saying that he devised dividing a city according to different classes of citizens. And he also laid out (i.e., carved out) suburbs. For he discovered how different kinds of suburbs ought to be carved out of the territory of a political community. And Hippodamus was the son of Euryphon and from Miletus.

Second, Aristotle explains Hippodamus' lifestyle, saying that Hippodamus, because he coveted honor, practiced extravagant things in his private life, which was different from his public life. For example, he seemed to be odd in his long beard and hair, and also in his cheap clothing, and he wanted to wear warm clothes in both winter and summer.

Third, Aristotle explains Hippodamus' interest. Hippodamus wished to study the whole nature of things, and he was the first politically inactive but theoretical philosopher to attempt to determine which is the best regime.

2.   Then Aristotle describes the organization of Hippodamus' regime. First, he describes the arrangement regarding the divisions Hippodamus devised. Second, he describes the arrangement regarding lawsuits [4]. Third, he describes the arrangement regarding the education of citizens [7]. Regarding the first, he does two things. First, he shows how Hippodamus divided the citizen population. Second, he shows how Hippodamus divided the property of the political community [3]. Therefore, he says first that Hippodamus determined that the optimum population of the political community is 10,000 men, and divided it into three parts: one of artisans, one of farmers, and one of warriors.

3.   Then he shows how Hippodamus divided the property of the political community, saying that Hippodamus divided the whole land (i.e., the territory) of the political community, into three parts. Hippodamus wanted one part to be sacred, namely, the part from which come the things that human beings assign for divine worship. Hippodamus wanted the second part to be public, or common, off which the warriors subsisted. Hippodamus wanted the third part to be private, and it was distributed among the farmers.

4.   Then Aristotle describes the arrangement of the regime regarding lawsuits. And regarding this, he does three things. First, he says that Hippodamus thought that there are only three kinds of laws, which correspond to the three things about which human beings dispute in lawsuits, namely, insults, damage, and homicide. Insult refers to things done in the verbal abuse of another, damage to things done to cause the loss to another's property, and homicide includes all the things done to the physical harm of another.

5.   Second, Aristotle says that Hippodamus established a supreme court to which all cases that did not seem to be correctly decided were brought on appeal, as it were. And Hippodamus wanted such a decision to be committed to elders of proven discernment and virtue elected for this purpose.

6.   Third, Hippodamus established the process that he wished to be observed in judging. For, although many juror-judges should bring in a verdict, he thought that juror-judges should not confer with one another about the verdict to be rendered. Rather, he thought each juror-judge would consider by himself about the verdict to be delivered and put down on a writing tablet what he thought. If it were to seem to the juror-judge that the accused should be condemned, the juror-judge would simply write *guilty*. And if it were to seem to the juror-judge that the accused should be acquitted, the juror-judge would leave the tablet blank. And if it were to seem to the juror-judge that the accused were partially guilty and partially not, the juror-judge would also specify this in writing. And so all the written statements would decide how it seemed to the majority. And he thought that what the law currently established, that juror-judges confer with one another before each votes, is wrong. For juror-judges are bound under oath to give their own opinion. But such collective discussions in such a place and regarding such things somehow compel the juror-judges to violate their oath if one of them does not dare to give his own opinion when the majority disagrees with him.

7. Then Aristotle describes Hippodamus' arrangement regarding the education of citizens. And Aristotle describes the four laws of Hippodamus. The first law is that those who discovered beneficial things to be established in the political community would obtain an honor.

The second law is that the sons of those who died for the political community in war were maintained out of the public treasury. Hippodamus thought that this was not yet established in political communities, but the law is currently observed in Athens and some other political communities.

The third law concerns the election of rulers, namely, that the whole people choose the rulers. For Hippodamus said that the people consist of the three aforementioned parts of the political community, namely, farmers, artisans, and warriors.

The fourth law concerns the duty of the rulers, namely, that those chosen to be rulers take care of the public property of the political community, foreigners, and orphans and other powerless persons.

Lastly, Aristotle concludes that he has spoken of most of the things about which Hippodamus ordained, and the ones most worthy of comment.

Chapter 11
The Regime of Hippodamus (2)

Text (1268a16–b22)

1. But someone will object first about the divisions of the citizen population. For artisans, farmers, and warriors all share in the regime. Farmers have no weapons, and artisans have neither land nor weapons. And so they are almost slaves of those who possess weapons. Therefore, they cannot share in every office, since generals, civilian governors, and the highest rulers, so to speak, need to be established from those who possess

weapons. And how can those not sharing in the regime be amicably disposed toward it?

2.   And those with weapons should be more powerful than both of the other parts, and this is not easy unless they are numerous. And if they are, why should others share in the regime and dominate the selection of rulers?

3.   Moreover, how are the farmers useful for the political community? For there need to be artisans, since every political community needs them. And as in other political communities, they can support themselves by their skills. And farmers, if they acquire food for the warriors, would reasonably be part of the political community. But in Hippodamus' regime, farmers own and cultivate their private land.

4.   Moreover, if the warriors themselves cultivate the public land to support themselves, there will be no difference between warriors and farmers, which Hippodamus wanted. And if others than the private farmers and the warriors cultivate the public land, there will then be a fourth part of the political community, one that shares in nothing of the political community and is estranged from the regime. And if one should suppose that those who cultivate their private land and those who cultivate the public land are the same, then there will not be enough produce for each one to maintain two households. And why will they not immediately support themselves and provide for the warriors from the land and the same lots? And so all these things are very confusing.

5.   Nor is his law about the verdicts in lawsuits good. He thinks that, even when the charge is absolutely clear, juror-judges should make qualifications, and he turns the juror-judge into an arbitrator. This happens in arbitration by many arbitrators. For they discuss their decision among themselves. But this is not the practice in courts, and many lawmakers establish the contrary, that juror-judges do not discuss cases with one another.

6.   Second, how will the decision be free of confusion if a juror-judge thought that damages ought to be awarded but a lesser amount than the plaintiff wanted? Suppose that the plaintiff demands 20 *minae*,[20] and a juror-judge awards 10. Or one juror-judge awards more, another less, one juror-judge 5, another juror-judge 4. And so it is clear that the juror-judges will undergo the same thing. Some juror-judges will award the full amount, and other juror-judges none. What will be the method of weighing the votes?

7.   Moreover, no one requires a juror-judge who unqualifiedly condemns or acquits a defendant to violate the juror-judge's oath if the indictment is

---

20. The *mina* was a Greek unit of currency roughly equivalent to a pound of silver.

framed in clear terms. For a juror–judge who rejects the plaintiff's demands does not say that nothing is owed to the plaintiff, but that 20 *minae*
is not the sum due him. Rather, a convicted defendant who thinks that he
does not owe 20 *minae* but pays the sum would be false to his oath.

Comment

1. After Aristotle laid out the regime of Hippodamus, he here argues
against it. First, he argues against it regarding the divisions of citizens
Hippodamus established. Second, he argues against it regarding things
Hippodamus said about lawsuits [5]. Third, he argues against it regarding
things Hippodamus established regarding the education of citizens [chap.
12, n. 1]. Regarding the first, he does two things. First, he argues against
the division Hippodamus established regarding the parts of the political
community. Second, he argues against the division Hippodamus established regarding property [4]. Regarding the first, he does three things.
He argues against the division of the parts of the political community:
first, regarding artisans; second, regarding warriors [2]; and third, regarding farmers [3].

Therefore, he says first that the first difficulty regarding the regime
of Hippodamus concerns the divisions of the citizen population. For
Hippodamus wanted artisans, farmers, and warriors all to share in the
regime of the political community, but in such a way that farmers would
have land but not weapons, and that artisans would have neither land nor
weapons. And this organization makes the artisans almost slaves of the
warriors. For artisans, who have no property of their own (which would
seem to belong to their usefulness) perform tasks in the service of the political community and especially of the warriors, who need to obtain a
greater share in the honors of the political community. Artisans cannot
share in every office, since it will be unbecoming that generals, civil governors, and other more important rulers are chosen from artisans. Rather,
only the warriors, who are more suitable for this, should be such. And because artisans have no share in the regime of the political community, they
cannot love such a regime. And so there remains matter for sedition.
Therefore, Hippodamus did not properly ordain regarding artisans.

2. Then Aristotle argues against the aforementioned organization regarding the warriors. For they need to be superior (i.e., more powerful)
than the other two parts, namely, the farmers and artisans. And this is because it belongs to warriors to defend the supremacy of the political community against both enemy attack and civil insurrection, which they could
do only if they were more powerful. And this is not easy unless they
should be numerous. And if the warriors should surpass the others in

number, virtue, and worthiness, there was no need that artisans and farmers share in the regime of the political community. And it was necessary that the establishment of rulers belong to the warriors, since this will always be done at their choice. Therefore, the choice is superfluously committed to others. Therefore, it is clear that Hippodamus improperly distinguished warriors from the others as parts of the political community.

3. Then Aristotle argues against the aforementioned difference regarding farmers, and the aforementioned organization does not make clear how they are beneficial to the political community. For it is obvious that artisans are necessary for the political community in order to provide various kinds of personal property, and artifacts will enable the life of citizens to progress well, as happens in other political communities. Or we can understand that the artisans can subsist (i.e., be maintained) by their skill and so do not need the farmers to support them. But the warriors' office cannot sustain them separately from the others, so to speak, and so warriors need others to sustain them. Therefore, farmers, if they were appointed to acquire food for warriors, would reasonably be considered part of the political community, since a part of the whole needs to provide for the good of the other parts. But according to the aforementioned arrangement, farmers will own and cultivate their private property and so be beneficial for themselves and no one else. Therefore, Hippodamus improperly considers farmers part of the political community.

4. Then Aristotle argues against the division of property. For Hippodamus considered one part of the property of the political community public, and it supported the warriors. Therefore, we should consider who will cultivate the public land, which needs to be cultivated in one of three ways. The first way is that the warriors themselves cultivate the public land, and so they will be warriors and farmers. But Hippodamus wanted to distinguish them. Therefore, the distinction was useless.

The second way is that others in between the warriors and farmers, who cultivate their own property, cultivate the public land. And so there will then be a fourth part of the political community that shares in no way in the regime of the political community and is completely estranged from it, since Hippodamus permitted only the three aforementioned parts into the choice of the rulers.

The third way can be that the farmers cultivate both their own property and public property. But then the supply of the produce of the land in the political community will be insufficient, since it will not be easy for an individual farmer adequately to cultivate so much land and manage the produce from it necessary for two households. Even supposing the third way, the division of property into three parts seems to have been superfluous, since it would have been possible at the beginning to give the whole land to the farmers. That is to say, each farmer, out of the land allotted to him, would get food for his own household and for some warriors. Therefore, the things that Hippodamus said about such divisions cause great confusion.

5.   Then Aristotle argues against the aforementioned regime regarding judicial verdicts, namely, that Hippodamus established that judicial verdicts are not determined by counting the juror-judges' votes. Regarding this, Aristotle does two things. First, he argues against the statute. Second, he argues against the reason for the statute [7]. Regarding the first, he gives two arguments. Regarding the first, he says that the law Hippodamus laid down about the verdicts is badly disposed. By that law, Hippodamus thought it worthy that individual juror-judges gave separate opinions, so that each individually wrote what seemed to him to be true about the case. And so Hippodamus wanted the juror-judge individually to investigate what the decision should be. But the several juror-judges might also collectively inquire into the particulars, since they could discuss with one another in their own homes about the decision to be rendered. As a result, they did not discuss in conference with one another in the courts (i.e., the public courthouse) regarding the verdict.

But this was most dangerous. For it could easily happen that one juror-judge, conferring with another juror-judge in private rather than in public court with everybody listening, perverted the other to render a verdict otherwise than it seemed to him. And so many lawmakers established the contrary, namely, that juror-judges confer with one another only in the courts and do not discuss the case with one another in private. Therefore, it seems that the aforementioned law was dangerous and contrary to the laws of other lawmakers.

6.   Aristotle gives a second argument, saying that there could not be verdicts in the aforementioned way without confusion. For it may not seem to a juror-judge separately that he should condemn the defendant to pay as much as the plaintiff seeks. Rather, perhaps the plaintiff seeks that the defendant be condemned to pay 20 *minae*, and the juror-judge will judge that the defendant be condemned to pay 10. Or perhaps one juror-judge will condemn the defendant to pay more (e.g., 5), and another juror-judge will condemn the defendant to pay less (e.g., 4). And the juror-judges in this way will need to undergo the same thing (i.e., confer with one another after they have written their opinions). This is as if they were not to have individually written their opinions, since some of the juror-judges will perhaps condemn the defendant regarding everything the plaintiff seeks, and others will not. Therefore, what will be the method of debating about the different opinions except by conferring? And so the aforementioned law could not avoid what it wanted to avoid,

namely, counting the juror-judges' votes. And so it is clear that it is superfluous.

7.   Then Aristotle argues against the reason for the statute, which was to avoid violation of the juror-judges' oath. And he says that if the juror-judges' votes about condemning someone were counted, no one thereby forces a participating juror-judge to commit perjury, although the plaintiff's charge is in proper form and the juror-judge disallows it. For the juror-judge will perhaps judge that the defendant owes only 20 *minae* when the plaintiff seeks more, not that the defendant owes nothing. Rather, a condemned defendant who does not think that he owes even 20 *minae* but agrees to pay seems to commit perjury. And so this law did not need to be established for such a reason.

Chapter 12
The Regime of Hippodamus (3)

Text (1268b22–1269a28)

1.   Moreover, making a law that an honor should be given to those who discover something beneficial to the political community is dangerous, although it looks and sounds good. For it involves calumnies and possible revolution against the regime. And it leads into another problem and another consideration. For some question whether it is harmful or expedient for political communities to abolish their ancestral laws if there should be another, better law. And so it is not easy to agree readily to the statement of Hippodamus if it is not expedient to change the laws. And it may induce abolition of laws or the regime as a public benefit.

2.   And since we have recalled this, it is best to expand on it further. For there is a question, as we have said, and it will seem better to change laws. For in other sciences (e.g., medicine, physical training, and generally all skills and abilities have moved away from ancestral ways), this was profitable. Therefore, since we should hold statecraft to be one of these, it is clear that this also holds about it.

3.   And one will say that there is evidence of this in history, since ancient laws were very simple and uncivilized. For example, Greeks used to carry weapons and buy wives from one another. And any remnants of ancient

laws in certain places are altogether foolish. For example, there is a law regarding homicide in Cyme that if a number of witnesses should be prosecuting the murderer of one who is a relative of theirs,[21] the defendant is guilty. And people generally seek what is good, not what is traditional.

4.   It is likely that our first ancestors, whether earth-born or the survivors of a catastrophe, were like ordinary and foolish people today, as people also say about the earth-born. Therefore, it is improper to adhere to their doctrines.

5.   Moreover, it is better not to adhere to written laws as if they were unchangeable. For, as in other skills, it is impossible that everything be prescribed in detail about a political organization, since one needs to write laws in general terms, but actions regard particulars. And so it seems from these things that some laws should sometimes be changed.

6.   And it will seem to those considering the matter in another way that there is need of great respect. For if there should be a small improvement by changing the law but harm in becoming easily accustomed to abolishing laws, it is clear that we should tolerate mistakes on the part of lawmakers and rulers. For the benefit from changing a law will not be as great as the loss from becoming accustomed to disobeying rulers.

7.   And the comparison with skills is false, since changing a skill and changing a law are different things. For law has no power besides custom to ensure obedience, and it takes a long time to establish custom. And so easily changing from current laws to new ones weakens the power of law.

8.   Moreover, if laws are to be changed, should all of them and those in every regime be changed? And should anyone or only certain persons change them? For this makes a big difference. And so we now leave off this consideration, since it belongs to other occasions.

Comment

1.   After Aristotle argued against the regime of Hippodamus regarding its divisions and judicial verdicts, Aristotle argues here against it regarding the education Hippodamus ordained, namely, regarding the statute

---

21. I have supplied the phrase *of one* to the text. This seems necessary if the text is to be consistent with Aquinas' commentary on it. If the phrase is not supplied, the text would say that the *defendant's* relatives support the prosecution, and that a law requiring the defendant's conviction under those circumstances is irrational. But the conviction of a defendant whose own relatives testify against him hardly seems to be irrational. Moreover, the statement that the defendant's relatives support the prosecution is contrary to the statement of the extant Greek text that the *prosecutor's* relatives support the prosecution.

that those who discovered something beneficial to the political community were honored. Regarding this, Aristotle does two things. First, he argues against the law. Second, he raises questions [2]. Therefore, he says first that it is not safe for a political community to establish the aforementioned law, which seems good only at first glance and first hearing. For if such a law should happen to be established, it will involve many calumnies when some will think the discovery useful, and others the contrary. It will also involve regime changes, since changing one law sometimes changes the whole condition of the political community.

And this law causes us to incur another problem (i.e., another question and another consideration), since some will ask whether it is expedient or harmful for the political community to abolish ancestral laws if a better law should be discovered. And so it is not easy for human beings to agree readily with the dictum that inventors of new things should be honored, and with whether it is expedient for political communities that ancestral laws be abolished. And under the appearance of public benefit, some may bring about the abolition of laws and the whole regime when they are incited to discover new things in order to gain honor. And this is very dangerous. Therefore, the statute is improper.

2.   Then Aristotle raises some questions. First, he asks whether it is necessary to change laws. Second, if they should be changed, he asks by whom, and how [8]. Regarding the first, he does two things. First, he gives arguments to show that it is necessary to change them. Second, he gives arguments to the contrary [6]. Regarding the first, he proposes four arguments. In the first, he says that, since we have commented little on changing laws, it is advisable to elaborate a little more fully about it. As he has said before [1], the matter raises a problem, and it seems to some that it is better to abolish ancient laws if a better law should be discovered. For we see that this is of great profit in other sciences, namely, that some things about what our ancestors observed have been changed. In medicine, for example, later doctors discovered many things, changing things that the first doctors practiced. And the same is true in gymnastics (i.e., physical training, since certain places in which nude men exercised were called gymnasia, from *gymnos*, the Greek word for nude). And so also we perceive the same in all the other skills and practical abilities, among which is statecraft, which directs the political community. Therefore, we also need to change things in the regime of a political community that our ancestors observed, if better things should result.

3.   Aristotle gives a second argument, saying that one can understand why laws should be changed from their works (i.e., their results). For we perceive that ancient laws were very simple and uncivilized (i.e., irrational and strange). For example, ancient Greeks had a law allowing them to buy

wives from one another, carrying iron as the medium of exchange, perhaps because other metals were not in use.[22] And we likewise perceive that if some laws still remain from antiquity, they are all foolish things. For example, there was in a certain locale a law on homicide that if a relative of the victim were to prosecute someone as the murderer, and the defendant were to face many prosecution witnesses, the defendant would be considered guilty of homicide, which is altogether irrational. (This may have led to the custom of dueling.) And human beings in establishing laws ought to seek what is good to be observed, not what their ancestors observed. And so it is proper to alter ancient laws if better ones should be available.

4.   Aristotle gives a third argument. To understand this, we need to consider that Aristotle thought that the world existed eternally, as the *Physics*[23] and the *De coelo*[24] make clear. And yet it is clear from ancient history that lands began to be inhabited at a certain time, and this seems to be contrary to the eternity of the world. But to resolve this problem, Aristotle introduced the idea that some floods or whatever destructions very often caused general devastations of the lands, which afterwards began to be re-inhabited. And this could happen in two ways.

It could happen in one way such that human beings were generated out of the earth. For some held that human beings were by nature generated from the earth in an analogous way, just as it is certain that field mice are generated out of the fields. But this does not seem fitting, since nature produces its effects by fixed causes and with fixed means. And so only semen can generate perfect animals. And so we believe that only divine power can make human beings, and that nature cannot produce them out of the earth.

In a second way, it could happen that some human beings were preserved in a general destruction, whether in the mountains or in some other way. For example, we hold that Noah was preserved in the ark at the time of the general flood,[25] and Deucalion was preserved in the mountains during the flood that happened at the time of King Ogygus in Greece.[26] But in whichever of these ways this happened, it seems that the first human beings were ordinary (i.e., of any sort, not outstanding), and that

---

22. The iron mentioned by Aristotle refers to weapons, not a medium of exchange.

23. *Physics* VIII, 1–4 (250b11–255a21).

24. *De coelo* I, 22–27 (279b4–283b22).

25. Gen. 6:14–8:14.

26. Cf. Augustine, *The City of God* XVIII, 8 (PL 41:566).

they were foolish, as the famous story says about those produced from the earth at the time of Deucalion. And so it seems improper that one continues to live under the laws and statutes of the first human beings.

5. Aristotle gives a fourth argument. For one could say that changing the customs of foolish ancients was timely, but the laws written by wise men ought not to be changed. But to exclude this, he counters that it is not better if even written laws remain changeless. For we perceive that no one, not even however many wise men, can carefully and completely write everything about the organization of a political community, just as this is impossible regarding other skills. This is because the wise write laws in general terms and cannot consider all particulars, but actions concern particulars. And so the wise could not completely write down everything that belongs to directing actions. And so it is better to change laws when something better is discovered. Therefore, such arguments show that we should sometimes change some laws.

6. Then he proceeds to the contrary, showing first the truth about the question. Second, he analyzes one of the arguments advanced [7]. Therefore, he says first that if one should consider in another way, it will seem that there is much to be feared about changing ancient laws, even for better ones. For it can happen that what will be innovative is a little better, but growing accustomed to abolishing laws is very bad. And so it is clear that we should tolerate slight deficiencies and mistakes that happen to rulers and the wise when they make laws. For one who wishes to change a law for the sake of something better will not gain as much by the change as he will lose when citizens grow accustomed to not observing the laws and commands of rulers.

7. Then he analyzes one of the arguments introduced to the contrary, saying that the example taken from skills, in which it was profitable to have changed many things, leads us into error, since there is a difference between changing a skill and changing a law. For things belonging to skills get their efficacy from the power of reason, but laws have no power to persuade subjects that obeying the law is good other than custom, which evolves only over much time. And so one who easily changes laws as such weakens the power of law.

And this is the response to the other arguments, since they infer that some laws, namely, bad ones, should sometimes be changed, which is true, not that laws should be easily changed.

8. Then he raises another question, saying that if laws should sometimes be changed, we should ask whether all kinds of laws and those in any regime should be changed, and whether anybody or certain determined persons should change them. For what is better in this regard varies

greatly. And so this consideration is put aside for the moment and re-
served for later.[27]

Chapter 13
The Regime of Sparta (1)

Text (1269a29–b6)

1.   There are two considerations about the Spartan and many other
regimes. One is whether there is anything good or bad in them in relation
to the order of virtue established by law. And the second is whether there
is anything in them contrary to the presupposition and method of the proposed regime.
2.   Therefore, it is agreed that the well-being of a proposed regime requires that there be instruction of persons performing necessary tasks. But
it is not easy to understand how this is to be. For example, the underclass in
Thessaly very often rebelled against the Thessalians. Slaves did the same
to their Spartan masters, as if the former were always waiting to attack the
latter in their misfortunes. But nothing like that ever happened with the
Cretans. The reason for this is perhaps that, although neighboring political communities war against one another, none of them allies itself with
disaffected Cretans. For it was not expedient for the neighboring political
communities to do so, since they also had estates near their households.
But Sparta's neighbors, the Argives, Messenians, and Arcadians, were all
her enemies. And the underclass from the beginning rebelled against the
Thessalians because the latter were constantly at war with their neighbors: the Achaeans, Perrhaebians, and Magnesians. And it seems that
even if there is nothing else to cause trouble, there is need for care about
how one ought to deal with a subject class. If members of that class are allowed too much freedom, they commit crimes and deem themselves the
equals of their masters. And if they are badly treated, they are rebellious
and hate their masters. Therefore, it is clear that those to whom this happens have not found the best way to deal with the problem of slavery.

---

27. Aristotle does not return to this consideration.

3. Moreover, laxness toward women is harmful both for regime choice and the happiness of a political community. For, as men and women are parts of a household, it is clear that we should regard the political community as almost equally divided into two parts, one of men and the other of women. And so, in whatever regimes there is a bad arrangement regarding women, we need to think that half of the political community is ill-regulated by law.

4. And this happened in Sparta. For the Spartan lawmaker, who wished to preserve the whole political community, did so regarding men but neglected to do so regarding women, since they live altogether voluptuously, and luxuriously.

5. And so wealth needed to be honored in such a regime, particularly if the men should live in abstinence from women, as is common in military and warlike peoples, or if some other peoples honored male homosexuality. For it seems that the one who originated the story about the union of Mars and Venus spoke reasonably, since all warlike men have sex drives, whether for intercourse with men or intercourse with women. And so this was the condition in Sparta, and the women in the Spartan regime managed many things. But what is the difference between women ruling and rulers ruled by women? For the result is the same.

6. Boldness is not useful for daily life but only for war, and the Spartan women were most harmful even in that regard. They demonstrated this when Thebes invaded Sparta. For they were completely useless, unlike women in other political communities. And they caused more confusion than the enemy did.

7. Therefore, the freedom of Spartan women seems to have originated reasonably. For Spartan men were away from home for long periods of time warring against the Argives, Arcadians, or Messenians. And returning home and conditioned by military life, which has many virtues, the men showed themselves ready to follow the lawmaker Lycurgus. But people say that Lycurgus tried to bring the women under the laws, and that he yielded when they resisted. Therefore, these are the causes of the things that happened, and so it is clear that they are also the causes of this error. But we are considering about what is right or wrong, not whom to pardon or censure. And as we have said before, the wrong dispositions regarding both caused the regime itself to be unfitting and contributed to love of money.

8. Next, one will criticize the inequality of property. For some of them may own very much property, and others very little. And so the land comes to a few.

9. And the laws also badly ordained this. For the lawmaker rightly disallowed buying and selling current estates but empowered those who so

wished to give away or bequeath their estates. But the result either way is necessarily the same. Almost two fifths of all the land belongs to women, since there are many heiresses, and dowries are large, but it would have been better to have prohibited dowries or made them small or moderate. And it is currently allowed to give an heiress in marriage to whomever the citizen wishes. And if a man dies without indicating his wishes in the matter, he bequeaths her in marriage to whomever he wishes.

10.   Therefore, although the land could support 1,500 cavalry and 30,000 equipped infantry, there was a population of less than 1,000 citizens. And their history has made clear that the things they instituted in this regard were bad for them. For the political community did not survive a single defeat and perished for want of manpower. And they say that they under previous kings opened their regime to others so that there was then no shortage of manpower despite waging lengthy wars. And they say that there were at one time 10,000 Spartiates. But, whether these things are true or false, it is better to supply the political community with manpower by equalizing property.

11.   But there is also a contrary law to encourage population growth. For the lawmaker, wishing to increase the number of males, encourages citizens to have many children. And they have a law that the father of three sons is exempt from military service, and the father of four from taxes. But it is clear that if many sons have been born, and the land divided accordingly, there will necessarily be many poor citizens.

Comment

1.   After Aristotle laid out the regimes established by wise men, he now deals with the regimes observed in political communities. And he deals first with the Spartan, or Lacedaemonian, regime. Second, he deals with the Cretan regime [chap. 15, n. 1]. Third, he deals with the Carthaginian regime [chap. 16, n.1]. For people praised the regimes of these political communities. Regarding the first, he does two things. First, he lays out the way of consideration required regarding these regimes. Second, he deals with the Spartan regime [2].

Therefore, he says first that two considerations occur regarding the Spartan and other regimes. One is to consider whether what is legally established in them is fitting for the order of virtue. For this is the end of every law. And so a law will not be a true law if it should not be related to virtue. The other consideration is whether there is anything in the regime ordered according to the presupposition and method of a regime contrary to the one proposed. For example, such would be the case if a lawmaker should aim to establish a democracy but lay down laws suitable for an oligarchy, which is a contrary regime. For so also does one refute something in the sciences, whether because it is incompatible with truth, or because it is incompatible with a proposition.

2. Then he deals with the Spartan regime. And he deals first with the things citizens possess. Second, he deals with the organization of the citizens [chap. 14, n. 1]. Regarding the first, he does three things. First, he pursues things that belong to slaves. Second, he pursues things that belong to women [3]. Third, he pursues things that belong to property [8]. Therefore, he says first that all profess it to be expedient that a political community, which ought to enjoy the right kind of political life, provide instruction for necessary persons (i.e., slaves or any necessary servants),[28] namely, that they get correct instruction. But we cannot easily understand how this is done.

And he then shows that this is necessary by the unsuitable things that result if they are poorly instructed. For the poor in Thessaly very often attacked the wealthy. And likewise, Lacedaemonian (i.e., Spartan) slaves were often hostile to their masters, since the slaves were lying in wait to attack their masters when any misfortune befell the masters, who would then be unable to crush them, and the slaves attacked their masters in such misfortunes.

But nothing like this happened to the Cretans. And the reason for this is perhaps that, although the neighboring political communities war against one another, none wars against distant peoples,[29] since this is not expedient for them. For they have estates near their cities and households. And so, if they were to undertake a long war, they could not take care of their own estates. And since the Cretans did not have neighbors (e.g., peoples living on nearby islands) who warred against them, misfortunes rarely threatened them, during which slaves and the underclass could lie in wait to attack them.

But all the neighbors of the Lacedaemonians (i.e., Spartans) were hostile to them, since the Spartans were completely devoted to military affairs, as Vegetius says in his work *On Institutes of Military Affairs*,[30] and as Athenian philosophers also relate. For the Argives, Messenians, and Arcadians were their enemies. (There were also from the beginning slave

---

28. I think that Aquinas' reading of the Latin text of Aristotle is correct, but if so, it differs from the usual reading of the Greek text.

29. Aquinas' reading of the text of Aristotle is possible but unlikely. The context is one of intervention in civil wars and the vulnerability of Crete's neighbors to retaliation if they do.

30. *On Institutes of Military Affairs* III, Prologue.

uprisings against the Thessalians, who were waging wars with their neighbors: the Acheans, Perrhaebians, and Magnesians.) And so misfortunes often threatened the Spartans, at which times their slaves laid in wait to attack them.

Therefore, it is clear that slaves and other necessary persons need to be instructed, but he then shows that this is not easy, saying that, if nothing else, it seems difficult, regarding the care that one needs to have about slaves, how we ought to deal or live with them. For on the one hand, if one should be benignly disposed toward them, they become insolent and criminal and consider themselves the equals of their masters. And on the other hand, if masters should always mistreat their slaves, the slaves hate their masters and lie in wait to attack them. And so it is difficult to see how they are to be treated. For one needs to be disposed toward them in a middle way, that they are neither unjustly treated nor shown too much intimacy. Therefore, he concludes from these things that the Spartans, whose slaves attacked them, are not a people who discovered the best way regarding the governance of slaves.

3.   Then he deals with the Spartan regime regarding women. Regarding this, he does four things. First, he shows that women in a political community need to be well instructed. Second, he shows what the Spartans observed in that regard [4]. Third, he shows what improper things resulted from this practice [5]. Fourth, he shows what caused this practice [7]. Therefore, he says first that lax laws regarding women, namely, that they live in a political community without suitable instruction, is harmful in two regards. First, laxness regarding women is harmful regarding regime choice, since their disorder results in a change in the whole regime, as he will say later [5]. Second, the laxness is harmful in regard to the happiness of the political community, since their disorder can cause many improper things in the political community. And he shows this by the fact that, as the parts of the household consist of a man and a woman, as he has said in Book I [I, chap. 1, nn. 6 and 11; chap. 2, n. 2], so the whole political community, as it were, which is composed of households, needs to be divided into two parts, one of men and the other of women. And so, in whatever political communities the arrangement of women is badly disposed, we should judge that the laws have poorly ordained the middle course for a political community.

4.   Then he shows what was observed in this regard in Sparta, since the aforementioned disorder of women happened there. For although the lawmaker intended that the whole political community endure (i.e., be able to resist and abstain from pleasure), he rightly attended to this regarding men but failed to establish it for women. For Spartan women live voluptuously regarding every kind of intemperance, and luxuriously.

5.   Then he shows what improper things resulted and indicates four. The first is that in such a regime, in which women live so luxuriously, men necessarily value highly and desire wealth, so that they can thereby satisfy the pleasure of women, which requires large expenses. And the fact that they care greatly about wealth does a great deal to destroy morals in the political community. For then all things in the political community are up for sale, and this corrupts the condition of the political community.

Aristotle gives a second impropriety, saying that if most citizens should be forced to abstain too much from women, they then fall into a shameful vice, namely, homosexuality, as happens to many soldiers, warriors, and any such like.[31] For the one who originated the story that Mars was the husband of Venus spoke reasonably, since warrior (i.e., martial) men are lusty and desire sexual intercourse, whether with men or women. For the work *Problems* says that cavalry continually on the march become lustier, since they experience the effect of sexual intercourse because of the heat and motion of riding.[32] Idleness also frequently makes them lusty. And this also happened to the Spartans, since the lawmaker induced them to too much abstinence from women.

He gives a third impropriety, saying that Spartan women, because they lived pleasurably, became presumptuous and wanted to intrude themselves into all things, so that women managed many things even regarding governance of the political community. And yet it makes no difference whether the women themselves rule, or the rulers rule under the women, the rulers being subject to the women, as it were, because of the latter's arrogance. For the same thing results either way, namely, that the political community is badly governed, since women lack reason.

6.   He gives a fourth impropriety. For the Spartan women became arrogant and bold for the sake of pleasure. And boldness can be of no use in the political community for daily affairs (i.e., local occupations) but only for war, and yet the boldness of these women was harmful even in this regard. And this was clear in the war the Spartans waged against the Thebans, in which the women, unwilling to perform the services that women perform in other political communities, were completely useless. Rather, with the men waging the war, the women, perhaps wishing to intrude themselves into everything, caused more disturbance than even the

---

31. Aquinas' reading of the Latin text of Aristotle to mean that the men abstained from women seems correct but differs from the extant Greek text. But the Latin text does not say, as Aquinas does, that the abstinence led to the practice of homosexuality, nor, as the extant Greek text does, that the Celts honored the practice.

32. Pseudo Aristotle, *Problems* IV, 11 (877b14–16).

enemy. And so these things show that laxness regarding women was harmful.

7.   Then he shows the cause of the aforementioned practices, saying that the laxness of instruction regarding women reasonably happened to the Spartans at the beginning. For the Spartans, because of the military spirit to which the political community was completely devoted, waged lengthy wars abroad against the Argives, Arcadians, and Messenians. And so the women stayed at home without the men and lived as they wished, having no instruction from the men. And this is also the reason why the men became virtuous in many regards. For they, when free of military duties, showed themselves ready to obey the lawmaker because they were accustomed to military life, which includes many kinds of virtue. For such a life requires the greatest obedience and abstinence from pleasure, and perseverance in works and painful things. Later, the Spartan lawmaker Lycurgus tried to bring the women back to the right instruction of the laws. But the women completely resisted because of their wicked habits. And so the lawmaker had to stop what he started.

Therefore, these are the reasons for the things done in Sparta and the power of the women there. And although this happened reasonably without any fault on the part of the Spartans, and so they are to be excused, we do not consider now those whom we should pardon or not pardon, since we aim not to praise or blame them. Rather, we aim to show what is rightly or wrongly disposed. For it is clear that the things the Spartans badly disposed regarding women were intrinsically unbecoming to the Spartan regime and also increased lust for money in the souls of citizens, as Aristotle said [5].

8.   Then he deals with the Spartan regime regarding property. First, he argues against the Spartan regime regarding property, showing that it is harmful for the political community. Second, he shows that it is contrary to the aim of the lawmaker [11]. Regarding the first, he does three things. First, he says that there was inequality of property with them. Second, he shows why there was [9]. Third, he shows the harm that resulted from it [10]. Therefore, after the aforementioned things in this regime of which we should disapprove regarding slaves and women, he says first that one can also reproach them because they forsook concern about inequality of property. For it happened among them that some had very great property, and others very little, so that almost all of the land came into the control of a few people.

9.   Then he shows what caused this inequality, saying that it comes from a bad legal arrangement. For the Spartan lawmaker established that a citizen had no right to sell or buy property, namely, that he could not sell his own or buy another's for any reason. And the lawmaker did this good

thing in order to equalize property, but he did not do it correctly, since he did it inadequately. For he gave citizens the power to give their property away during their life, or bequeath it at their death, to whomever they wished. And inequality of property resulted from this, as it does from buying and selling property, so that if all of the Spartan land were divided into five parts, two fifths now came to women. This is both because many women became heiresses at the death of their husbands, and because women received large dowries when they married, although it is far better if no dowry, or a small or moderate one, is given. But any Spartan was allowed in his will to designate anyone he wished as his heir, and if he should not wish at his death to designate an heir, he can distribute his property to whomever he should wish.[33]

10.   Then Aristotle shows what harm resulted from the inequality, saying that, although the Spartan land (i.e., the territory) is large enough to be able to support 1,500 cavalry and 30,000 infantry, the Spartans became so few, with property belonging to the few, that there were only 1,000 warriors in the political community. And so their history demonstrated that the aforementioned arrangement was bad. For it caused the demise of the political community when it did not survive a severe enemy attack.

And he says that, in order to have many warriors, they expanded their regime in ancient times as far as they could, so that the Spartiates (i.e., Spartans) sometimes had 10,000 equipped warriors in their army, so people say. But whether or not these things are true, it is expedient that equalized property provide the political community with men. And it cannot be done in any other way, since, if property should devolve to a few people, the rest of them, because of their poverty, would abandon the political community.

11.   Then he shows that the aforementioned inequality of property was contrary to the aim of the lawmaker, who had proposed a law about fathering sons contrary to the aforementioned arrangement from which the inequality of property resulted. For the lawmaker intended that there would be many citizens in the political community and encouraged the Spartans to father many sons by exempting some from public duties. For the law established that a man who fathered three sons was exempt (i.e., free from military duty), namely, not bound to go to the defense of the political community. And a man who fathered four sons was exempt from all taxes and levies. And yet it is clear that if the aforementioned rule regarding the division of property should be observed, there will necessarily be many

---

33. Aquinas is clearly erroneous about what is at issue here, namely, the disposition of an *heiress*. The Latin text of Aristotle is explicit about this, whatever other ambiguity there may be.

poor in the political community if many sons were born. And this is harmful to the political community, as he said before [chap. 6, n. 12].

Chapter 14
The Regime of Sparta (2)

Text (1270b6–1271b19)

1.　And things regarding the Spartan office of ephor are badly disposed. For it belongs to this ruling power to control the most important things. And all of the ephors come from the people, so that very poor men may very often hold this office, and such men were open to bribery because of their poverty. And they showed this very often in the past, and now regarding the Andrians. For certain ephors, corrupted by taking bribes, ruined the whole political community insofar as it was in their power.

2.　And because their ruling power is very great and equivalent to tyranny, they forced the kings of Sparta to let them rule over the people. And so the regime is then injured, since aristocracy became democracy. Therefore, this ruling power holds the regime together. For the people are content, since they share in the most important ruling power. And so, whether this is due to the lawmaker or good fortune, it has utility for human affairs. For all parts of a political community should want a regime to be preserved and the parts to remain intact. Therefore, the kings have this opinion because it confers honor on them. The best men have it because of their membership in the council of elders, since that ruling power is the reward of virtue. And the people have it because of the office of ephors, since the latter are chosen from all the people.

3.　The ephors should have been chosen from all the people but not by the present method, since this method is very childish.

4.　Moreover, the ephors, ordinary people, have power to decide matters of importance. Therefore, it would be better that they have power to decide cases on the basis of documents and laws, not their own opinion.

5.　And the lifestyle of the ephors does not conform to the aim of the political community. For their manner of living is very lax in some things but so harsh in other things that they cannot endure it, and they secretly disobey the law and indulge in forbidden physical pleasure.

6.   And the Spartans have things regarding the ruling power of the elders that are ill-disposed. For if men are equitable and sufficiently well-educated in manliness, one will perhaps say that this is beneficial for the political community, but it is worrisome that the ephors with life tenure make important decisions. For as the body grows old, so too does the mind. But when men have been educated in such a way that even the law-maker himself doubted whether they are good enough, it is risky. And participants in this office seem to wish to be perceived as benefactors, and they give away many public things without benefit to the community. And so it is better that the elders are subject to supervision, which they now are not. Although it will seem that the body of ephors supervises all the rulers, this gives too much power to the ephors, and we are not saying that one should supervise in this way.

7.   Moreover, the method of choosing the elders is childish. And it is wrong for one who will be honored with office to seek it. For one who is worthy of ruling ought to rule, whether wanting to or not. But the law-maker seems also to produce something like the other part of the regime, since he makes citizens desirous of honor and uses this for the election of the elders. For only one who desires honors will seek to rule, but most deliberate injustices happen to human beings almost always because of love of honor and money.

8.   And about kingship, it is another question whether it is better for political communities to have kings or not. Rather, we are here speaking about whether it is better to choose each king on the basis of his life, not in the Spartan way. And the Spartan lawmaker himself clearly thinks it impossible to produce the best men, since he has no confidence that there are sufficiently good men. And this is why they sent joint ambassadors who were hostile to one another, and why they thought disagreement between the kings to be salutary for the political community.

9.   Nor did the originator legislate well things regarding the common meals (called friendship meals), since the latter should rather have been at public expense, as in Crete. But with the Spartans, every individual must contribute, although some are very poor and unable to bear this expense. And so the result is contrary to the aim of the lawmaker. For he wishes provision of the common meals to be something democratic, but what the law established is not at all democratic, since participation by the very poor is difficult. But the regime determines that those unable to pay this levy do not share in the regime.

10.   And others have rightly objected to the law regarding naval commanders, since it causes civic unrest. For the kings are the permanent commanders of the army, but the naval command is almost another kingship.

11. And one will object to the presupposition of the lawmaker, something that Plato also does in the *Laws*. For all of the Spartan laws are directed to only partial virtue, namely, military virtue, since this virtue is useful for domination. Therefore, the Spartans prospered when at war but perished when ruling, since they did not know how to use leisure or train for virtue in any other, more important way than the military way. And this is no small error. For they think, and rightly so, that virtue more than military tactics causes good results in warfare, but they wrongly think that the good results are better than virtue.

12. And the Spartans also arrange their public finances badly, since there is no money in the public purse of the political community, although they are forced to fight large-scale wars. And they are delinquent in paying taxes. For, inasmuch as most of the land belongs to Spartiates, they do not require levies from one another. And the result is contrary to what the lawmaker envisioned. For he produced an impoverished political community and made simple people lovers of money. Therefore, this is enough said about the regime of the Spartans, since these are the things that one will most object to.

Comment

1. After Aristotle treated of the Spartan regime regarding things possessed by the citizens, namely, slaves, women, and property, he here treats of the same regime regarding the citizens themselves. First, he treats of the rulers; second, of the people [9]; and third, of the warriors [10]. And there were three ruling powers with the Spartans, as he also touched on before [chap. 7, n. 3]. There were ephors (i.e., providers), and he treats of these first. And there were also certain elders, and he treats of these second [6]. And there was also a king in the political community, and he treats of this third [8].

Regarding the first, he argues against the rule of the ephors in five regards. First, he argues against it regarding the condition of the persons constituted in it. And he says that the Spartans badly arranged things regarding it, since these rulers had control and power over the most important things in the political community (e.g., declaring war or making peace, selecting soldiers, and the like). But all the ephors were chosen from the people for this office. And so it sometimes happened that very poor men were assumed into it, and such men were open to bribes because of their poverty and were easily corrupted with gifts. And the ephors had very often showed this in the past, and they showed it recently in some business they had with the Andrians. For the ephors were corrupted by money from them, so that the ephors exposed the whole political community to danger as far as it was in their power to do so.

2.   Second, he argues against the aforementioned ruling power of the ephors regarding the great power they had. And he says that, since this ruling power was very great and the equivalent, as it were, to tyranny, the ephors so weakened the power of the kings that they forced the kings to permit the people to rule over themselves in disobedience of the law.[34] And so the whole Spartan regime was corrupted, since it degenerated from aristocracy to democracy. And yet this ruling power was beneficial in one respect, since it kept the political community peaceful. For the people were free of civic unrest because they had a share in great ruling power. And this benefit resulted through experience in these matters, whether this was as the lawmaker intended or happened by chance. For, in order to preserve the regime, all classes of the political community should want it to exist, and any section of the political community should be satisfied to remain as it is. And this happened in Sparta. For kings accepted the regime because of the honor they held in it. The best men (i.e., men of virtue) accepted the regime because of their membership in the council of elders (i.e., because of their noble rank). For this ruling power was the reward for virtue, so that none but the virtuous were assumed into it. And the people accepted the regime because of the ruling power of ephors, in which office all the people shared.

3.   Third, he argues against the aforementioned ruling power of the ephors regarding the election process. For although it was commendable that the ephors were assumed into this office by election from the people, the election process was very childish, since they were perhaps chosen by lot or in some other unsuitable way. And so the ruling power sometimes came to the poor, as he said [1].

4.   Fourth, he argues against the aforementioned ruling power of the ephors regarding the discretion that they had, saying that it was objectionable that any ephors had in their power the discretion to decide about important matters. For it was better that they judge according to particular documents and laws, not according to their whim.

5.   Fifth, he argues against the aforementioned ruling power of the ephors regarding their lifestyle, saying that their manner of living (i.e., their customs in food, drink, clothing, and the like) was incompatible with

---

34. Aquinas has the people ruling over themselves, but the Latin text of Aristotle seems to have the ephors ruling over the people. The extant Greek text has the kings forced to curry favor with the ephors.

the aim of the political community. For their customs were very lax in some things (e.g., perhaps clothes or leisure), but a harsh law was imposed on them in other things (e.g., perhaps food and sex), perhaps in order that they did not become soft. And so they were unable to keep the law imposed on them and secretly disobeyed it by indulging in forbidden physical pleasures. And so their lifestyle was contrary to the aim of the political community.

6.   Then he argues against the aforementioned regime regarding the ruling power of the elders. First, he disapproves of their power. Second, he disapproves of the way in which they are chosen [7]. Therefore, he says that the Spartans wrongly disposed things belonging to the ruling power of the elders, since the elders remained in power for life. For one could perhaps say that it would be beneficial for the political community that elders remain in power for life if one could find such elders who were equitable (i.e., virtuous) and sufficiently educated in manliness (i.e., manly virtue, or activity). But even if they were completely virtuous, it would be a fearsome prospect for the political community that some persons had control and power over its important decisions, and this for the whole of their lives. For, as old age weakens the power of the body, so also it generally weakens the power of the mind. For human beings in their old age do not have the strong spirit and lively mental power that they had in their youth, since the sense powers serving their intellectual part are weak.

Therefore, much more should we fear that some persons rule for life if they are educated for virtue in the way that the Spartans were. And so even the lawmaker does not consider them as altogether good men, since he does not commit all things to them. Moreover, such persons often wish to seem generous regarding the common people in order to get their favor, and so they dispense public goods without benefit to the political community. And so it is better that they be subject to some supervision, namely, that they could be removed if they should be found lacking. But there is currently no such supervision. They were subject to supervision, since the ruling power of the ephors could overrule the other rulers, namely, prevent the execution of the other rulers' decisions if the decisions seemed injurious. And this was the special merit of the ephors. But we are considering another kind of supervision, namely, the power to remove the other rulers, which the ephors could not do.

7.   Then he argues against the aforementioned ruling power of the elders regarding their election, and this by two arguments. Regarding the first, he says that the Spartan election of elders was very childish, since the Spartans ordained that those who seemed worthy of such ruling power were to seek it. And this is wrongly disposed, since no one would then be elevated to the ruling power unless he wanted it. But one worthy of the

ruling power should be elevated to it whether he should want it or not, since one should prefer the common benefit to one's own preference.

He proposes a second argument, saying that, by this arrangement about the election of elders, the lawmaker seems to make citizens lovers of honor, like the arrangement about the other part of the regime (i.e., the election of ephors), or any other things by which the lawmaker made citizens such. And it is clear that the lawmaker did this in the election of elders, since one would seek the office only if he were willing to rule, and this is to love honor. Therefore, if no one were to hold ruling power unless he were to seek it, then only lovers of honor would rule, and so all would be motivated to love honor. And this is very dangerous for the political community, since most deliberate injustices in the political community (e.g., acts of violence, robberies, and the like) happen because of love of honor and money. And so it is clear that such an arrangement is dangerous for the political community.

8.   Then he argues against the aforementioned regime regarding the ruling power of the kings, saying that he will consider later whether having or not having a king is beneficial for the political community.[35] But assuming that having a king is better, it was worse to have one who did not rule for life, as was the case in Sparta.[36] Rather, it is better that each one has regal power for life, since a king is beneficial for the political community in order to effectively preserve its condition by his power. And unless he should rule for life, this cannot be done, since he will be afraid to offend others, and others will also be less afraid of him. But it is otherwise regarding the elders, who were chosen for deliberations or particular decisions.

And the reason why the Spartan lawmaker established that the kings were not tenured for life is because he thought that he could not make any citizens perfectly good (i.e., completely virtuous). And so he did not trust citizens, as if they were not completely virtuous. And so, when the Spartans sent ambassadors or messengers to foreign cities, they chose individuals who were enemies or adversaries of one another, so that one would frustrate the other if one or the other were to wish to act contrary to the good of the political community. And likewise, they thought that the political community was safe if kings, who succeeded one another, disagreed, since one corrected what the other had done wrongly.

---

35. *Politics* III, 8–17 (1281a11–1288b6).

36. Aquinas misinterprets the phrase about life in the text of Aristotle and so erroneously says that the kings of Sparta did not rule for life.

9. Then Aristotle argues against the aforementioned regime regarding things that belong to the people, namely, the public common meals in the city, saying that the law had not rightly disposed about such common meals. For it would be better that the assembly of such a common meal were financed out of the common funds of the political community, as the Cretans did, than out of the pockets of individuals, as the Spartans did. With the Spartans, even the very poor had to bear part of such expense, and this destroyed the poor, who could not afford it. And so, in this regard, the result was contrary to the aim of the lawmaker, who established such common meals as something democratic, as it were (i.e., favorable to the people), namely, that the people had a period of recreation during the meals. But this law of common meals resulted in great detriment to the people, since the common people could not then easily rule. For there was a Spartan law that those who did not contribute to such costs had no share in the regime, since they could not become rulers or have a voice in the choice of rulers.

10. Then he argues against the aforementioned regime regarding the warriors. First, he deals with naval warriors. Second, he deals generally with all the warriors [11]. Third, he deals with their pay [12]. Therefore, he says first that some others rightly criticized the Spartan law regarding naval commanders, since it caused civic unrest. For, while the Spartans had quasi-permanent kings in charge of the army, the naval command (i.e., the ruling power over the fleet) became another kingdom, as it were. And so they had two kings, as it were, and this could be a source of disunion.

11. Then he argues against the aforementioned regime regarding all the warriors in general, saying that one can rightly criticize the assumption of the lawmaker (i.e., what he assumed as the end in relation to which he directed the whole regime). And Plato in the *Laws* also criticized the fact that the Spartans directed all their laws to one part of virtue, namely, military virtue, since it was useful for dominating others. And they were well disposed regarding things belonging to war but badly disposed regarding things that belong to governing the political condition. Consequently, they survived in wars, but many dangers threatened them after they had acquired ruling power, since they did not know how to enjoy leisure (i.e., live in peace) and were not practiced in anything more important than waging war. And this was no small error.

The Spartans rightly thought that the virtue of human beings handles warfare better than military tactics. For, as the *Ethics* says,[37] virtuous

---

37. Aristotle, *Ethics* III, 16 (1116b15–23).

human beings do not spare their lives when it is virtuous to continue fighting, although soldiers, after they have overcome dangers, fall short of virtue, since they do not, in addition, have confidence that the trials and efforts of war can free them for other things. But the Spartans wrongly thought that the virtue whereby human beings are rightly disposed in wars is the best virtue, since other virtues, namely, practical wisdom and justice, are more worthy than courage. And even war itself is for the sake of peace, and not the converse.

12. Then he argues against the aforementioned regime regarding the soldiers' pay and the public treasury, saying that the Spartiates (i.e., Spartans) did not make good arrangements about their public funds. For the political community had none, although it was often forced to wage large-scale wars. Moreover, individual citizens badly administered things necessary for such expenses, since no public authority required contributions from individuals. Rather, it was left to the discretion of any citizen to give whatever he wished. And the lawmaker established this because citizens had much property and could give much without any burden. But the result was contrary to the benefit that the lawmaker intended, since he left the political community without public funds and made simple people (i.e., private and common persons) lovers of money when they attempted to gain as much as they could to provide for themselves and the community.

And in a final epilogue, Aristotle concludes that the things mentioned seem objectionable in the Spartan regime.

Chapter 15
The Regime of Crete

Text (1271b20–1272b23)

1. And the Cretan regime is very like the Spartan. The former has a few things no worse than those of the latter but is for the most part less detailed.

2. For it seems, and people say, that the Spartan regime is modeled on the Cretan in most respects. (Most things of antiquity are less detailed than those of more recent times.) For they say that Lycurgus, after he

relinquished the regency for King Charillus and traveled abroad, spent most of his time in Crete because of the kinship of the Spartans and the Cretans. For the Cretans were related to the Spartans. And the Spartans who had settled with the Cretans adopted the laws established at that time among the inhabitants. And so the inhabitants even today use the laws in the same way that Minos first established them.

3.   And the island seems to be suitable and well positioned to rule over the Greeks, since it dominated the entire Aegean, with almost all the Greeks located around the sea. For the island is not far from the Peloponnese and across from Asia around Triopium, and Rhodes. And so Minos obtained maritime dominance and conquered some islands and colonized others. And finally, he attacked Sicily and died there near Camicos.

4.   And the Cretan organization is analogous to the Spartan. For serfs took care of farming for the Spartans, and resident noncitizens took care of it for the Cretans. Both have common meals, and the Spartans in ancient times called them manly meals, as the Cretans do, not friendship meals. This indicates that the custom came from Crete. And there is the organization of the regime. For the ephors in Sparta have the same power as those called cosmoi in Crete, but there are five ephors and ten cosmoi. And the elders in Sparta and the elders that the Cretans called the *boulē* (i.e., the council) are the same. And there was originally a kingship in Crete, but the Cretans later did away with it, and the cosmoi exercise that leadership in war. And all the people participate in an assembly, but the assembly has only the power to ratify the wishes of the elders and the cosmoi.

5.   And the Cretans had a better arrangement for the common meals than the Spartans did. In Sparta, individuals contribute a specified amount per capita, and the law prohibits participation in the regime if the individual does not pay, as we said before. But in Crete, it is more communal. Out of the farm and animal produce from public lands, and the taxes paid by resident noncitizens, one part is allotted to the gods and public religious rites, and another part for the common meals. And so all men and women, adults and children, were fed at public expense. And the Cretan lawmaker wisely considered many things regarding the utility of frugal meals and promoted sexual intercourse between men in order to keep men apart from women and so control the population. (There will be time later to consider whether or not sexual relations between men are wicked.) And it is clear that the Cretans made better arrangements for the common meals than the Spartans did.

6.   But things concerning the cosmoi are still worse than those that belong to the ephors. It is true that both ruling powers have the defect of being chosen indiscriminately. But it is beneficial to the regime in Sparta and not to the regime in Crete. For the people in Sparta, because the

ephors are chosen from all of them, participate in the most important ruling power and desire to preserve the regime, but citizens in Crete choose
the cosmoi from certain elders, not from all the people, and choose elders
from those who have been cosmoi.

7.   And one will say the same things about the Cretan elders as about the
elders in Sparta. For being free of any supervision and having life-tenure
exceed the merit of age, and ruling according to their whims, not according to documents, is dangerous.

8.   But that the people are content not to share in the power of the cosmoi is not a sign that the system is well-ordered. For there is no opportunity for the cosmoi to profit, as there is for the ephors, since the Cretans
live on an island far away from foreigners.

9.   And they institute an unsuitable, coercive, and irregular cure for such
a defect. For conspirators, whether colleagues or ordinary people, very
often turn cosmoi out of office. And cosmoi are permitted to resign their
office. But law regulates all these things better than the human will, since
the latter is not a safe rule.

10.   And being without cosmoi is the worst possibility of all, which sus-
pension the Cretans often ordain because they do not wish to render judgments against powerful persons.

11.   Or it is at least clear that the Cretan arrangement has an aspect of
regime, but one based on power and not a true regime. And powerful persons are accustomed to use the people and friends to institute a monarchy,
cause disturbances, and war against one another. For what is the difference between this, namely, the disintegration of a political community
over time, and the dissolution of the political association? And a political
community in this condition, when those who wish to attack it are also
powerful, is very dangerous. But as we have said, Crete's location is its sal-
vation, since it kept the Cretans remote from expulsion. And so also resident noncitizens remain peaceful with the Cretans, while serfs often
abandon the Spartans. For the Cretans do not participate in any overseas
dominion. But a foreign war recently came to the island and made clear
the weakness of their laws. Therefore, we have said enough about the Cretan regime.

Comment

1.   After the author dealt with the Spartan regime, he deals here with
the Cretan regime. First, he relates the latter regime to the former. Second, he argues against the Cretan regime [7]. Regarding the first, he
does three things. First, he establishes the relation of these regimes in
general. Second, he assigns the reason for that relation [2]. Third, he

explains the aforementioned relation in particular [4]. Therefore, he says first that the Cretan regime is like the Spartan regime in some things but differs in others. In a few of the latter, the Cretan regime is better disposed than the Spartan, but in many of them, it is less fully developed (i.e., less beneficially and suitably for the good condition of the political community).

2.   Then he assigns the reason for the foregoing relation, showing first that the reason is that the Spartan regime is derived from the Cretan. Second, he assigns the reason why the Cretan regime was first [3]. Therefore, he says first that the reason for the aforementioned things is that the Spartan regime is modeled on the Cretan regime in many respects, as a more ancient one. And so the Cretan regime is worse disposed in many things, since we perceive that most of the things that thinkers of antiquity discovered are less detailed (i.e., less carefully distinguished), than things later thinkers discover. For people say that Lycurgus, who established the Spartan regime, left the kingdom of King Charillus of Sparta and was engaged for a long time at Crete because of the friendship and kinship between the Spartans and Cretans. And so the Spartans, who had come to Crete because of friendship, received the established laws of those then dwelling there. And so we perceive that the inhabitants of Crete use laws in the same way as the Spartans do, and the institution of Minos, the King of Crete, established them.

3.   Then Aristotle assigns the reason why the laws among the Greeks were discovered first at Crete. For he says that the island of Crete seems best disposed by its location to rule over the Greeks, almost all of whom dwell around the Aegean. The island is adjacent, as it were, to the whole coast of Greece and only a short distance from the peninsula called the Peloponnese, now called Achaia. And Crete is likewise opposite Asia, close to the place in Asia called Triopium and to the island called Rhodes. And so Minos, who was King of Crete, obtained the ruling power in the whole sea around Greece, forcibly conquered already inhabited islands, settled colonists on uninhabited islands, and imposed his laws on both. And finally, he crossed to the island of Sicily and died there near Camicos (i.e., near Mount Vulcano or Mount Etna, out of both of which fire erupts).

4.   Then Aristotle explains that relation in particular, showing first in what things the two regimes agree. Second, he shows in what things the Cretan regime is superior [5]. Third, he shows in what things it is worse [6]. And he shows first that the two regimes are related and agree in three things. First, they agree in farming, which the Spartan serfs and the Cretan resident noncitizens (i.e., peasant residents on the island) do.

    Second, they agree regarding the public common meals that they both have. The Spartans now call them friendship meals, from *philos* (i.e., love), since they were established to preserve mutual love among citizens. But they originally called them manly meals, from *aner* (i.e., man), since only men and no women attended the meals, and the Cretans still use that name. And so it is clear that that the Spartans took the custom from the Cretans.

Third, they agreed regarding the organization of the regime, since the Spartan ephors had the same power as those the Cretans called cosmoi (i.e., nobles). The ephors and cosmoi differ only in number, the Spartans having five ephors, and the Cretans ten cosmoi. Likewise, the number and power of the elders in Sparta and Crete were the same, and the Cretans called their elders the *boule* (i.e., the council). There was originally a kingship in Crete, but the Cretans later abolished it and committed the leadership in wars to the cosmoi. The Cretans also have an assembly (i.e., a popular assembly) for both, but it has only the power to ratify decisions of the elders and cosmoi.

5.   Then he shows in what things the Cretan regime was superior, saying that the arrangement of the common meals by the Cretans was better than that by the Spartans. For individual citizens in Sparta who attended the common meals were required to make per capita contributions and otherwise could not participate in the regime, as he said before [chap. 14, n. 9], but the practice in Crete belonged more to the public. For one part of public property, both agricultural produce and cattle, and the taxes that resident noncitizens who cultivated the land paid, was set aside to be spent on religious sacrifices, and another part was set aside to be spent on the common meals. As a result, men and women, adults and children, were all fed at the common meals from the public purse.

And something else was also proper to the Cretan regime. The lawmaker wisely provided that citizens eat frugally at the meals, as this would be very beneficial, as it were, to both individuals and the community. Wishing also to avoid overpopulation, lest the population were to exceed the resources to support it, he wanted men not to mingle much with women, and he for this reason allowed base sexual intercourse between men. But Aristotle will consider later whether the lawmaker provided well or ill in this.[38] Still, it is clear that the Cretan arrangement of common meals was superior to that of the Spartans.

6.   Then Aristotle shows in what the Cretan regime was worse than the Spartan, saying that the Cretan arrangement of the cosmoi was worse than the Spartan arrangement of the ephors. There is indeed one bad feature common to both, namely, that both indiscriminately recruit individuals to

---

38. Aristotle does not return to this consideration.

such ruling power (i.e., men who are neither excellent nor virtuous). But the Spartans had something good, since the ephors could be chosen from any class of citizens, and so the people, participating in the most important ruling power, as it were, rightly desired the preservation of such a regime. On the other hand, the Cretans chose the cosmoi only from those who were or had been elders, not from any class of citizens, and the Cretans likewise chose elders from those who had been cosmoi, who were allowed to relinquish their office, as he will say later [9]. And so the people had no share in the ruling power of the cosmoi.

7.   Then he argues against the Cretan regime, first regarding the laws the Cretans established. Second, he argues against the regime regarding the cures they employed [9]. Regarding the first, he does two things. First, he argues against their laws. Second, he answers a rebuttal [8]. He disapproves of the Cretan regime regarding two things that he disapproved of in the Spartan regime [chap. 14, nn. 2, 3, 4, and 6]. One of these is that the cosmoi and elders rule for life without supervision (i.e., without the possibility of removal for wrongdoing), and so they had greater ruling powers than would be merited. The second is that they did not rule according to documents (i.e., written laws) but according to their whims (i.e., as they by themselves decide or choose). But this was not safe for the political community, since love or hate could pervert their judgment.

8.   Then he answers a potential rebuttal, which could argue that the survival of the Cretans without civic unrest is a sign that their regime is well ordered. In response, he says that the fact that the Cretan people, who do not share in the ruling power, refrained from disturbances is no sign that their regime is well ordered. For this resulted because the Cretans dwelt on a remote island very far from other peoples and so did not have wars with their neighbors, as he said before [chap. 13, n. 2]. And so the Cretan cosmoi did not have to levy taxes or spend money on wars, as the ephors of Sparta did. And so the people did not care much about sharing in such ruling power.

9.   Then he argues against the cures that the Cretans used against the dangers, first laying out the cures. Second, he argues against them [11]. Regarding the first, he does two things. First, he lays out the Cretan cures against persons who rule badly. Second, he explains the cure against the ruling power itself [10]. Therefore, he says first that the cure the Cretans use against the aforementioned error regarding the lack of supervision of the rulers is unsuitable. The cure is oppressive and tyrannical, not political, not cognizant, as it were, of the public order of the political community. And this is contrary to reason and coercive. For some Cretans, whether rulers or private persons, very often conspire and forcibly remove the cosmoi. And there was another cure, namely, that the cosmoi could

resign their office. But it was better that these two things were regulated by law, namely, that cosmoi should be dismissed from office or resign according to settled law than that this be done at the whim of human beings. Doing things at the whim of human beings is not a safe standard (i.e., a safe rule), since the human will is often unreasonable and unjust.

10.   Then he lays out the cure that they had against the office of cosmos itself. And he says that the worst of all the cures was that the Cretans often eliminated the office of cosmos (i.e., suspended the ruling power of the cosmoi) when the latter wanted to render decisions against powerful persons. For the Cretans altogether forbade such ruling power for a time. And he says that this is the worst thing, since it was not only against persons but also against the entire office, or ruling power, from which the political community derived much benefit.

11.   Then he argues against the aforementioned cures. And he says that the last institution about suspending the cosmoi has something of regime insofar as it derives from the common consent of the people, but that it is coercive action by the power of the people and a road to tyranny rather than a true regime. For some, who hate the cosmoi, often mobilize the people and other friends to their side and set up a monarchy, namely, that one of them rules over the political community instead of all ruling. And when they cannot do this at once, they cause rebellions, and citizens war against one another. And this does not differ at all from the demise of the political community after some time and the dissolution of the whole political association, since there cannot be a political community if citizens do not live in peace. And so the political community as such is dissolved. But even before the political community as such is dissolved, enemies who wish to invade it and are powerful enough threaten danger to it, since citizens cannot be united in resisting enemies if they war against one another. And one faction sometimes invites enemies to help it.

But as he said [chap. 13, n. 2], the Cretan regime was free of such dangers from enemies because of its location, since the Cretans dwelt on an island far from other political communities, and so the distance made them secure from expulsion (i.e., from enemies expelling them from their territory).[39] And he gives two evidences of this. One is that the condition of the resident noncitizens persisted with the Cretans because of the custom of friendly intercourse between them. But foreigners who come to serve the Cretans cannot stay with them for long, since the foreigners cannot have any ruling power with them. For the Cretans did not want to

---

39. Aquinas' reading of the Latin text of Aristotle seems reasonable, although the usual reading of the extant Greek text differs.

have foreign rulers.[40] The second evidence is that foreign invaders had recently brought war to the island, and it is clear from this that the Cretan
laws were not good enough to preserve their regime. Rather, the Cretans
were preserved because they did not have enemies warring against them.

And in a final epilogue, he concludes that he has said enough about the
Cretan regime.

Chapter 16
The Regime of Carthage

Text (1272b24–1273b26)

1.   The Carthaginians also seemed to manage their political affairs well
and better than others in many things, and some particulars were very
similar to those of the Spartans. For the three regimes, the Cretan, the
Spartan, and the Carthaginian, resemble one other in some respects and
differ greatly from other regimes. And many of the Carthaginian institutions are well disposed. And an indication of their well-ordered regime is
that the people rest content with its institutions, and there is no serious
internal strife or tyranny.
2.   The Carthaginian regime has common meals of associations like the
friendship meals of the Spartan regime, and the Carthaginian board of
104 directors corresponds to the Spartan ephors. But the directorate is
better, since the Carthaginians choose virtuous directors, but the Spartans
choose ephors indiscriminately. And the Carthaginian kings and elders
correspond to those of Sparta.
3.   But it is better that the kings are chosen neither from only one family
nor indiscriminately. And if a family is distinguished in virtue, kings
should be elected from it rather than on the basis of seniority. For those
constituted masters of important things, if they should belong to the
lower classes, cause much harm and have already done so to the
Carthaginian political community. Therefore, most of the objectionable

---

40. Aquinas misinterpreted the Latin text of Aristotle on this point, although his
reading of the text is theoretically possible.

things in the Carthaginian regime because of errors are things common to all the aforementioned regimes.

4.   And of things related to the presuppositions of aristocracy and polity, some at Carthage favor the people, and others oligarchy. For kings with the elders, if they all agree, decide whether to refer particular matters to the people, but if they do not agree, the people also decide. And when they have brought matters to the people, they allow the people not only to hear the decisions of the leaders but also to decide the matters, and anyone who wishes may oppose the proposals. This is not the case in the other two regimes. And as for oligarchy, committees of five, which control many, important matters, elect their own replacements, and choose members of the directorate, the supreme ruling body. Moreover, members of the committees of five rule for a longer time than other officials, since members rule before and after their term of office, and this is oligarchic. But we should hold it to be aristocratic that they do not buy their office, that they are not chosen by lot or some such other way, and that they decide all lawsuits, not some rulers some suits, and other rulers other suits, as in Sparta.

5.   But the Carthaginian institution of aristocracy especially transgressed into oligarchy by reason of a rather common understanding. For they think that they ought to choose a ruler who is both virtuous and wealthy. For one without means cannot rule well or have the leisure to do so. Therefore, if choosing a wealthy ruler is oligarchic, and choosing according to virtue aristocratic, the organization that the Carthaginians had regarding their regime will be a third kind. For they consider both virtue and wealth when they choose officials and especially their highest officials, kings and generals.

6.   And we should think that this deviation from aristocracy is an error by the lawmaker. For it is most necessary from the beginning to see how the best people can have leisure and not be debased, whether as rulers or private citizens.

7.   But although we need to look to wealth for the sake of leisure, it is wrong that the highest offices, namely, kingship and military command, are for sale. For the Carthaginian law makes wealth more valuable than virtue, and the whole political community loves money. Whatever the chief part of the regime esteems valuable necessarily also becomes the opinion of the rest of the regime, and wherever virtue is not the highest honor, the regime cannot be firmly ruled according to virtue. And it is reasonable that those buying offices, when they obtain ruling power by spending money, grow accustomed to profiting from their investment. For if a poor but honest man will want to make profit, it would be odd if a less honest man will not want to do so when he has spent money to obtain office. Therefore, those who can rule best should rule.

8.   And it would be better if the lawmaker were to prefer the virtuous poor to rule but also provide for the leisure of rulers.

9.   And it seems to be wrong that the same man holds many offices, which the Carthaginians accepted, since one person best performs one task. And the lawmaker should provide how this is done and not command the same person to be a musician and a cobbler. Therefore, where the political community is not small, it is politically wiser and more democratic that many people share in the offices. For, as we have said, it is more communal, excellent, and expeditious that the same people perform individual tasks. And this is clear in the case of the army and the navy, since ruling and being ruled reach throughout the ranks of both, so to speak.

10.   And although the regime is an oligarchy, the Carthaginians, in acquiring wealth, escape civic unrest in the best way by regularly sending part of the people to outlying cities. For they thus cure the problem and ensure an enduring regime. But this needs luck, and there should be no rebels because of what the lawmaker provides. And if something unfortunate should now happen, and the subject population should rebel, the laws provide no remedy to restore peace. Therefore, this is the mode of the Spartan, Cretan, and Carthaginian regimes that we rightly respect.

Comment

1.   After Aristotle dealt with the Spartan and Cretan regimes, he deals with the Carthaginian regime, doing three things in this regard. First, he commends the latter regime along with the others. Second, he shows the agreement of the Carthaginian regime with the others [2]. Third, he disapproves of some things about the Carthaginian regime [3]. Therefore, he says first that the Carthaginians seemed to live well politically, better than other regimes in many regards and especially in things in which they resembled the Spartan regime. For these three regimes, namely, the Cretan, the Spartan, and the Carthaginian, resembled one another and differed much from other regimes, and the Carthaginians established many things well. And an indication that their regime was well organized is that the people remained content in such a regime, and there was no popular revolt of any significance there, nor did their regime decline into tyranny.

2.   Then he shows the agreement of this regime with the Spartan regime, first regarding the fact that the Carthaginians had the common meals of associations that the Spartans called friendship meals. Second, he shows the agreement of the regime with the Spartan regime regarding governance of the political community, since the Carthaginian ruling power of the 104 was like the ruling power of the Spartan ephors. But in this

regard, the Carthaginians arranged the power better, since the Spartans chose the ephors indiscriminately (i.e., from any persons and even persons unproven in virtue), while the Carthaginians chose only virtuous citizens for such ruling power. Similarly, the Carthaginians, like the Spartans, had kings, and they had elders (i.e., worthies or nobles) corresponding to those of Sparta.

3. Then he disapproves of the aforementioned regime in the two ways mentioned before [chap. 13, n. 1]. First, he disapproves of the regime in that it was not well established. Second, he disapproves of the regime in that it was not in accord with the aim of the lawmaker [4]. Therefore, he says first that it would be better that the kings were chosen from any virtuous citizens and not from only one family. And if they ought to be chosen from one family, the family should be one that generally produces good men, not any kind of family. Moreover, if a family distinguished in virtue from others, one from which the kings are taken, should be chosen, it would be better to choose kings from that family by election rather than seniority (e.g., primogeniture). And when this is done in other ways, it often happens that men of the lower classes come into the kingship. And it is very dangerous if men of the lower classes are constituted to have authority over important things. For this does much harm to political communities, and such kings from the lower classes harmed the Carthaginian political community in many things. He also concludes from the aforementioned things that, since these three regimes are similar, there are things common to all of them worthy of reproach. And so we also need to understand here things mentioned regarding the others.

4. Then he disapproves of the regime regarding the fact that it departs from its proposed aim. And regarding this, he does three things. First, he shows that it diverged toward democracy in some things and toward oligarchy in other things. Second, he shows that it diverged more toward oligarchy [5]. Third, he disapproves of the cure the Carthaginians applied to counter this [10]. Therefore, he says first that, although the presumed aim of the Carthaginian lawmaker was to establish a polity[41] or aristocracy, some of its laws favored the people (i.e., the common people), others oligarchy. For the Carthaginians had a law that the kings with the elders, when all of them agreed, had it in their power to bring or not bring some matters to the people. And if not all of them were to agree, the people had it in their power to decide what ought to be done in these matters. Likewise, when the kings with the elders by common consent referred things

---

41. Polity as a particular regime is a moderate (i.e., constitutional or limited) democracy. It is a republic as distinguished from a pure democracy.

to the people, the people had not only the right to listen to what was proposed and approve it but also the power to decide whether it was good or
bad. And if the people wanted to, they could reject the proposal, and this
was not done in the other two regimes. And so the people prescribed to
the rulers what was to be done, and this was democratic.

On the other hand, they had pentarchies (i.e., committees of five men
who had the power to interpose themselves in many important matters of
state), and only these rulers chose their replacements. Likewise, they
alone chose the 104 directors whom he mentioned before [2]. Likewise,
these more important officials ruled longer than other officials, since
predecessors were associates in the ruling power of their successors, and
so their time in office was increased, something not done in the case of less
important officials. And this was oligarchic.

They also had something aristocratic, namely, that their rulers were
chosen without having to buy their offices. Moreover, they were chosen
because of their virtue, not by lot or other like things. And so they did not
depart from aristocracy in all things. And they had something else oligarchic, namely, that the most important rulers decided all lawsuits, not
different rulers different lawsuits, as was done in Sparta.

5.   Then he shows that this regime inclines more toward oligarchy, and
this in two respects. (He posits the second later [9].) Regarding the first,
he does two things. First, he shows in what the regime favors oligarchy.
Second, he argues against this [6]. Therefore, he says first that the institution of the Carthaginian regime, which the Carthaginians wanted to be
aristocratic, inclined more toward oligarchy, as it seems to many. For they
thought that not only virtuous but also wealthy rulers should be chosen,
and they reasoned that a poor person could not rule well and have the
leisure for affairs of state. For their rulers did not receive a salary from the
public purse. And so virtuous poor persons, if they were chosen as rulers,
would have neglected the affairs of state and necessarily aimed to obtain
means to support themselves. But since choosing wealthy men as rulers is
oligarchic, while choosing virtuous men is aristocratic, it is clear that
choosing rich virtuous men as rulers will be a third kind of regime, and
the Carthaginians had this kind. For in choosing the most important
rulers, kings and generals, the Carthaginians regard both wealth and
virtue.

6.   Then he argues against the aforementioned arrangement. First, he
rejects the reason that motivated the Carthaginians. Second, he rejects the
arrangement itself [7]. Therefore, he says first that this departure from
aristocracy should be imputed to the lawmaker. For it was most necessary
to see to it from the beginning how the virtuously best men could have the
leisure for virtuous deeds without being debased by engaging in coarse

work, and this was necessary both when they were ruling and when they were in private life. That is to say, the lawmaker needed to institute rewards for virtue to support the virtuous.

7. Then Aristotle disapproves of the arrangement for two reasons. First, he shows that it is dangerous. For if, in choosing rulers, it is necessary to regard wealth in order that they have leisure without working to earn their livelihood, the very bad result will be that the most important offices, namely, kingship and command of the army, are for sale. That is to say, the offices are awarded for having abundant money. So also he says that this is wicked, since the law results in the whole political community loving money even more than virtue. This is because citizens then think that whatever they perceive to be valuable in the eyes of the ruling powers is valuable. And in whatever political community virtue is not the highest honor, namely, that the honor of ruling is not related to virtue alone, human beings cannot unerringly rule according to virtue. And because ruling power is in a way bought by wealth and awarded on account of wealth, it is likely that citizens become accustomed to want to make money if they could acquire office by spending money. For it is very odd to say that one who is poor and virtuous will want to profit when in office,[42] but that one who is less virtuous, after having spent much money to acquire office, will not want to, since this is altogether improbable. And so we should not ask whether those to be installed as officials are wealthy. Rather, those who can be the best officials (i.e., rule according to virtue), whether rich or poor, ought to be installed.

8. Second, he disapproves of the aforementioned law because it omits a more suitable cure that it could use. For it would be better if the lawmaker, disregarding wealth, were to prefer the virtuous poor to rule and add a cure so that they could have leisure at least when in office.

9. Then Aristotle lays out the second respect in which this arrangement favors oligarchy, saying that what the Carthaginians practiced, that the same individual held several ruling powers, or offices, is wrong, since one individual best performs one task. But if the same individual should be obliged to perform several tasks, there is necessarily an impediment to performing the second task or both tasks. And so the lawmaker needs to see to it that he does not impose several tasks on one individual (e.g., that he does not command that the same person be a musician and a cobbler). And so, unless the small size of a political community should prevent it, it seems to be politically wiser and more democratic (i.e., in accord with a popular regime) that many share in different offices, not that the same

---

42. "When in office" is implicit in the cited text of Aristotle.

person holds many offices, since the latter is oligarchic. And so this is better, since the same individual performs each task better and more quickly,
as he has just said, so that one person is not forced to do many things. And
we see this in the army and navy. For, because of different duties, ruling
and being ruled, namely, when some subjects are in charge of others, extends in some respect to all in the military, even the lowest ranks.

10.   Then he argues against the cure they had regarding the aforementioned inclination toward oligarchy. And he says that, although the
Carthaginian regime was oligarchic, the Carthaginians found the best way
to avoid popular revolutions, since they regularly sent some of the people
to rule cities subject to them, so that the Carthaginians became wealthy.
And they thereby somehow preserved their regime and caused it to endure. But this, namely, that the cities subject to them had not rebelled,
was the result of luck. But citizens need to be loyal because of the providence of the lawmaker, not because of luck. And if some misfortune
should befall the Carthaginians, so that the large subject class casts off
domination by them, the laws they established will be no cure for the in-
surrections.

And in a final epilogue, Aristotle concludes that we can rightly respect
the aforementioned things regarding the Spartan, Cretan, and Carthaginian regimes.

Chapter 17
Other Regimes

Text (1272b24–1273b26)

1.   Some of the commentators on regimes did not take part in public life
but remained private individuals throughout their lives, and we have spoken of almost all of these if there is something worthy of comment. And
others were lawmakers engaged in their own or also foreign political communities. Some of the politically active drafted laws, and others, such as
Lycurgus and Solon, also founded regimes, since they established both
laws and regimes.

2.   We have already spoken about the Spartan regime. And some think
that Solon was a diligent lawmaker. For he abolished a very unbalanced

oligarchy, freed an enslaved people, instituted a democratic homeland, and composed the regime well. For the regime had an oligarchic council on the Areopagus; an aristocratic element in the selection of rulers; and a democratic element in the judicial administration. And Solon seems to have left intact already existing things, namely, the council and the selection of rulers, but to have instituted a popular element, constituting the courts from all the citizens.

3. And so some find fault with him, since, by putting the courts, chosen by lot, in control of all things, he destroyed the other elements. For when he empowered the courts, they gave favors to the people as if to a tyrant and turned the regime into the current democracy. And Ephialtes and Pericles blocked the council on the Areopagus, and each successive leader of the people in this way made the regime more and more the democracy it now is.

4. But this seems to have happened by accident rather than by the intention of Solon. For the people, meeting in assembly to choose the naval command in the Persian wars, plotted craftily to assume power, and they accepted bad leaders instead of politically wise ones. And Solon seems to give to the people the most necessary power, namely, the election and supervision of rulers, without which control the people would be slaves and enemies. And he established that all the rulers were taken from nobles and the wealthy (the 500 *medimnoi*, the *zeugitai*, and a third class called knights) but none from the fourth class of hired hands.

5. And Zaleucus was the lawmaker for the western Locrians, and Charondas of Catania the lawmaker for his own citizens and other Chalcidian cities around Italy and Sicily. And some want to infer how Onomacritus was the first skillful lawmaker. Although a Locrian, he trained in Crete and skillfully ruled over the people there. Thales was his associate, Lycurgus and Zaleucus heard Thales lecture, and Charondas heard Zaleucus lecture. But they say this without considering the chronology.

6. And there was also Philolaus of Corinth, who was the lawmaker of Thebes. He was of the Bacchiad family and became the lover of Diocles, a victor at the Olympic games. The latter, mindful of the love of his mother, Alcyone, for him, left Corinth and went to Thebes. There the two ended their days. And they still show their tombs today, each of which is easily visible from the other, but only one from the Corinthian side. For people say that they planned their burial sites, Diocles so that Corinth would be invisible from his grave in order to keep the place of his suffering out of sight, Philolaus so that Corinth would be visible from his grave. Therefore, that is why they lived at Thebes.

7. And Philolaus made laws about some other things and procreation, and the Thebans called such laws prescriptive. The law about procreation

uniquely established the limit on procreation insofar as it preserved the number of estates. And regarding Charondas, there is nothing unique except criminalizing false testimony, since he was the first to consider it, and people applaud him for his precision more than even current lawmakers. Unequal property is also a particular concern of Philolaus. Common wives, children, and property, and common meals for women as well as men are unique to Plato. Moreover, there are his law about drunkenness, namely, that the sober preside at banquets, and his provision about military training, that soldiers should strive to become ambidextrous with their weapons, as is useful, instead of one hand being useless. And there are the laws of Draco, but he proposed them for an already existing regime. Nothing unique to them is noteworthy except the severity of their punishments. Pittacus was also a lawmaker but not the founder of a regime. There is a law unique to him, namely, that drunks who commit acts of violence should be punished more than sober men, since more drunks cause harm than sober people do. For he looked to utility, not to the leniency one should have for drunks. And Androdamus of Reggio Calabria was a lawmaker with the Calcidians in Thrace. His laws concerned homicides and inheritances, but one will have nothing particular to him to say about them. Therefore, we have thus considered things about the chief regimes and the regimes mentioned by some.

Comment

1. After Aristotle dealt with various regimes, he deals here with those who established regimes and laws. Regarding this, he does three things. First, he determines their difference from one another. Second, he determines about those who established regimes [2]. Third, he determines about those who were lawmakers [5–7]. Therefore, he first posits two differences between those who treated of regimes or laws. The first difference regards their lives. For some lived as private citizens, not participating at all in political activity, since they were not rulers of any political communities. Such were Plato, Phaleas, and Hippodamus, whom he has mentioned before if there was anything worthy of mention about them [chaps. 1–12]. But others lived politically active lives, establishing laws for political communities, whether their own or foreign. The second difference regards the things they handed down. For some were the authors of particular laws but not any regime. But others established regimes (i.e., constitutions for the governance of political communities) and proposed particular laws. Such were Lycurgus, who established the Spartan regime, and Solon, who established the Athenian regime.

2. Then Aristotle deals with those who established regimes. And since he has spoken before about the Spartan regime established by Lycurgus [chaps. 13–14], it remains for him to speak about the Athenian regime established by Solon. Regarding this, Aristotle does three things. First, he shows what Solon established. Second, he shows how some criticized Solon [3]. Third, he excuses Solon [4]. Therefore, he says first that some thought that Solon was a good lawmaker. Solon abolished a very excessive and immoderate Athenian oligarchy; freed the people, whom the immoderate rule of the wealthy was oppressing; established a democracy in his homeland; and composed the regime (i.e., the governance of the political community) well, giving a share in the regime to the people. He established on the Areopagus (i.e., the district of Mars that was the Athenian religious site) the council of the political community, which was oligarchic because the councilors were from the wealthy and powerful. The way rulers were chosen was aristocratic. And he established the courts (i.e., the judicial power) from the people, which was democratic (i.e., popular). And so Solon seems not to have abolished things that previously existed, namely, the oligarchic council and the popular selection of rulers, which was aristocratic. But he newly established a popular ruling power when he constituted the courts (i.e., the juror-judges) from all the citizens.

3. Then Aristotle shows how some criticized Solon. Some people accused him of abolishing another, former regime when he established the courts that later had power over all things, although this office was by lot, namely, juror-judges were chosen for it from the people by lot. And so they say that he thereby abolished the former regime because, in giving power to that office in the political community, the judges installed by the people transferred the whole governance of the political community to the people, who tyrannically oppressed the more important people. And so the regime devolved into the disordered democracy that existed in Athens. For Ephialtes and Pericles, who were the people's judges, first destroyed the council that was from antiquity on the Areopagus, and each of the people's leaders then increased the power of the people until the regime was brought to the democracy that then existed.

4. Then Aristotle excuses Solon, saying that that defect seems to have happened by accident, not by the intention of Solon. For when the king of the Persians invaded Athens, the Athenians thought that they could not defend their borders or withstand a siege of their city, since their children, wives, and property were settled in other cities of Greece. Abandoning the city, they transferred the war from the land to the sea. And so the people assembled at the time of the Persian wars to choose the naval command (i.e., the admirals) and astutely plotted to take over all power. And the result was that the people had wicked instead of good leaders, and these leaders carried out the will of the people.

But Solon gave only the most necessary power to the people, namely, the power to choose rulers and correct mistakes, and this shows that he did not intend to give all power to the people. And Aristotle says that the power of the people to choose rulers and correct mistakes is necessary, since the people would otherwise be slaves if they were to receive rulers without giving their consent and could not correct the mistakes of the rulers. And since they could not endure slavery, they would become enemies of the rulers. But Solon established all the rulers, first, from distinguished people (i.e., nobles and wealthy men).[43] Second, he established rulers from a group of 500 middle-class citizens, as it were, and he calls them *medimnoi* (moderators, as it were) and *zeugitai*, since they were the heads of associations or crafts, who united the people, as it were. Third, he established rulers from the knights, who were the third class. And the fourth class, the lowest, was that of hired hands, to whom no part of the ruling power belonged. And so it is clear that he gave the greater part of the ruling powers to more important persons rather than the people. And so it was not his intention to establish democracy. Rather, this resulted contrary to his aim.

5.   Then Aristotle determines about the framers of laws and shows first who they were and for whom they established the laws. Second, he shows what laws they drafted [7]. Regarding the first, he does two things. First, he deals with certain lawmakers in Italy, which was once called Magna Graecia. Second, he deals with certain lawmakers of Greece [6]. Therefore, he says first that there was a lawmaker named Zaleucus, who established laws for the western Locrians. (Locri is a city of Calabria opposite western Greece.) There was also a lawmaker named Charondas of Catania, who drafted laws for his own citizens and other Chalcidian cities around Italy and Sicily.

And Aristotle shows the sources from which they were instructed in lawmaking, saying that some wish to infer that a certain person named Onomacritus was the first skilled legal expert in these lands and, although a citizen of Locri, he trained in law in Crete and later ruled over the people there skillfully. And they say that a certain Thales was his associate, and that Lycurgus of Sparta and Zaleucus of Locri heard Thales lecture. And they say that Charondas of Catania heard Zaleucus lecture. But

---

43. Aquinas constitutes the nobles and wealthy as the first class, and the *medimnoi* and the *zeugitai* together as the second class. But the text of Aristotle follows Solon's division of the four classes.

they say these things without rightly considering the chronology of these events, which does not fit this account.

6.   Then Aristotle relates about the lawmakers of Greece, saying that a certain Philolaus, a citizen of Corinth, drafted laws for the Thebans. And Aristotle assigns the reason why Philolaus went from Corinth to Thebes, saying that Philolaus belonged to the Bacchiad family (i.e., those who traced their origin to Bacchus) and became the friend of a certain Diocles, who was a victor at the Olympian games. Therefore, after Diocles left Corinth, perhaps expelled for some wrong, Philolaus, conscious of the love that Diocles' mother, called Alcyone, had for him, went with Diocles to Thebes.[44] (Alcyone had perhaps nurtured Philolaus.) Both finished their lives there, and they show their tombs up to the present day. The tombs face each other, and each can be seen from the other. But the tombs were so situated across from the territory of Corinth that one tomb could be seen from there but not the other. And they relate that their tombs were arranged in this way so that Diocles would be invisible to the Corinthians, as if he wanted to keep away from them because of the things he had suffered from them. But the Corinthians could see Philolaus, who had suffered nothing from them. Therefore, this was the reason why they dwelt with the Thebans and drafted laws for them.

7.   Then Aristotle shows what in particular each lawmaker established, saying that Philolaus drafted laws for the Thebans about different things but especially about the procreation of sons, namely, that they were not to continue to beget offspring after they had a fixed number of sons. And the Thebans called these laws of Philolaus prescriptive laws. He uniquely established this rule about procreating sons in order to keep the number of estates constant. That is to say, the number of sons would always be the same as the number of citizens necessary to maintain the population, and it would be unnecessary to divide a parcel of land belonging to one man into several parcels.

And Charondas uniquely established nothing except making false testimony a crime, which he was the first to consider. People, however, applauded him because he, beyond other lawmakers, explained in detail what the laws required, rather than because of anything he particularly established. But Philolaus established something unique, namely, the abolition of inequality of property.

---

44. The text of Aristotle says that Diocles' mother had a presumably incestuous love for him, not a love for Philolaus, and that this led Diocles to leave Corinth. Aquinas suggests, without textual support, that Diocles may have been exiled for a crime, and that Alcyone may have nursed Philolaus. Note also that Aquinas calls Diocles the *friend* of Philolaus, but the text calls him the *lover* of Philolaus.

And Plato established four unique things in his laws. First, he established common wives, children, and property. Second, he established common meals for women, as there were common meals for men in other political communities. Third, he established a law against drunkenness, namely, that only the sober could preside at the banquets (i.e., the common meals). Fourth, he prescribed in military affairs that soldiers were to become ambidextrous through practice and application, so that each of the soldiers' hands would be useful for them in warfare.

Next, Aristotle says that there are certain laws of Draco, who drafted them for an already existing regime, but that there was nothing particularly noteworthy in these laws except that more severe punishment was to be given when greater harm resulted from wrongdoing.

There was also a certain lawmaker, Pittacus, who did not establish a regime, and there was a unique law of his that drunks, if they committed an act of violence, were to be punished more than sober persons, since drunks cause more injuries than sober persons do. And so he looked to utility, namely, that the injuries caused by drunks be suppressed, rather than to the leniency that one ought to have about drunks, who are not in control of their acts.

There was also another lawmaker, Androdamus, a citizen of Reggio Calabria, who established laws regarding the punishment of homicides, and inheritance rights, but one cannot call anything unique to him, as it were.

And in a final epilogue, Aristotle concludes that we have considered the things that we should consider about the best regimes (e.g., the Spartan, Cretan, and Carthaginian) and the regimes prescribed by some others.

And this is the end of Book II.

Book III

Chapter 1
Citizenship

Text (1274b32–1275b33)

1.   Whoever considers what and how each regime exists needs first to see what the political community is. For people presently hesitate, some saying that the political community acted, and others that an oligarchy or tyrant, not the political community, did. Moreover, we perceive that the whole business of the statesman and lawmaker concerns the political community, and the regime is an organization of those who dwell in the political community.

2.   And since the political community, like any other whole constituted of many parts, consists of its parts, it is clear that we should first inquire about the citizen, since the political community consists of many citizens. Therefore, we need to ask about whom we should call a citizen, and to consider who is a citizen. For people often have questions about who is a citizen, and not all interpret it in the same way. For one who is a citizen in a democracy is often not a citizen in an oligarchy.

3.   Therefore, we need to leave aside those who are in other ways allotted the name by poetic license. And merely residing in a place does not make one a citizen, since foreign residents and also slaves reside in a city. Nor does merely sharing in legal rights to sue and be sued, since this is available to those who make contracts. Therefore, foreign residents do not fully participate in many places but need to hire someone to act for them. Therefore, they do not fully participate in such communal sharing. Just so, we should call underage youths not yet enrolled because of their age, and old men retired from active duty, citizens in a qualified way, not absolutely or very much but adding *underage* or *overage* or some other such thing. (The words do not matter, since the meaning is clear.) For we are inquiring about the citizen absolutely and without added qualification, since one can then raise and answer such questions about base persons and exiles.

4. And nothing determines who is absolutely a citizen more than participation in judicial decisions and ruling. Some offices are limited to only
one term or permit another term only after a fixed period of time. Other
offices, such as juror-judges or members of the assembly, have no fixed
term. Therefore, someone will perhaps say that such persons are not officials and so do not share in the ruling power. But it should make no difference, since the argument concerns the name. For we have no name that we
ought to use for what is common to juror-judges and members of the assembly. Let us, therefore, stipulate for the sake of definition that we use
the term *unspecified office*. Thus we define as citizens those who participate in this way. Therefore, such a citizen is one who most fits all those we
call citizens.
5. But we should not ignore that, in matters in which individual things
differ specifically, one being primary, another secondary, and something
else next, there is nothing, or scarcely anything, common to all insofar as
the individual things are such things. And we perceive that regimes differ
specifically from one another, some having priority over others, and the
latter secondary to the former, since bad and deformed regimes must be
secondary to good regimes. (We shall explain later in what sense regimes
are deformed.) Therefore, the meaning of citizen will necessarily differ in
different regimes. Therefore, those called citizens in a democracy are citizens most of all. There may be citizens in other regimes but not necessarily. For there is no role for the people in some regimes, and such regimes
value only ad hoc popular meetings, not assemblies of the people. And the
rulers decide cases in divisions. For example, in Sparta, one or another of
the ephors decides contract cases at different times, the elders decide
homicide cases, and perhaps another body decides other cases. And it is
likewise regarding Carthage, since some rulers there decide all cases.
6. But our definition of citizen has an objective. For, in other regimes,
members of the assembly and juror-judges are specific, not unspecified,
rulers. To some or all of those so specified, deliberative and judicial powers are assigned, whether about all or some things. Therefore, these things
make clear who is a citizen. For when anyone has the power to share in deliberative and judicial powers, we say that he is a citizen of that political
community, and that a political community consists of enough such citizens for a self-sufficient life, absolutely speaking.
7. People also define *citizen* in a practical way as one descended from
citizen parents on both sides, not only from one citizen parent (i.e., a
father or mother). And others require descent from citizens for more
generations (e.g., two, three, or more). These things may be politically and
quickly determined, but some ask how the third or fourth generation back
will be citizens. (Therefore, Gorgias of Leontini, perhaps doubtful but

speaking ironically, said that, as mortars are what mortar makers make, so also Larissaeans are the people made by the founders of Larissa, since Larissaeans are made by Larissa.) But the answer is simple, since, if the ancestors participated according to the stated definition, they were citizens. For one cannot apply the criterion of descent from citizen mother or father to the first inhabitants or founders.

Comment

1. After Aristotle inquired in Book II about the regimes regarding what others have handed down, he begins here to deal with his own view of regimes, dividing this into two parts. In the first, he shows the different kinds of regime. In the second, he teaches how the best regime is to be established.[1] And the first part is divided into two sections. In the first, he distinguishes regimes. In the second, he determines about each of them in particular.[2] And the first section is divided into two parts. In the first, he determines what belongs to a regime in general. In the second, he distinguishes regimes [chaps. 5–6]. The first part is divided into two parts. In the first, he speaks about his aim. In the second, he deals with what he proposes [3]. Regarding the first, he does two things. First, he shows that, in order to treat of regime, one needs to reflect about political community. Second, he shows that, in order to treat of political community, one needs to reflect on what a citizen is [2].

Therefore, he says first that one who wishes to reflect on the regime that each is by its nature, and what sort it is, namely, good or bad, just or unjust, needs to consider first what a political community is. And he proves this with two arguments. The first reason is that people can have a question about this. For some question whether particular deeds (e.g., the deeds of tyrants or the wealthy of a political community) are attributable to it. And regarding such a case, some say that the deeds are attributable to the political community, and some say that the deeds are attributable to an oligarchy (i.e., the wealthy rulers) or tyrants, not the political community. And so it seems to be questionable whether there is a political community if only the wealthy rule. And since the question exists, we need to answer it. The second argument is that the whole aim of those who treat of regimes and lawmaking concerns the political community, since a regime is nothing but the organization of those who dwell in a political community.

---

1. *Politics* VII, 1 (1323a14).
2. Ibid. IV, 1 (1288b10).

2. Then he shows by two arguments that we need to determine about the citizen. The first is that, in all things composed of many parts, we need first to consider the parts. And the political community is a whole constituted of citizens as its parts, since the political community is nothing but a multitude of citizens. Therefore, in order to know the political community, we need to consider what a citizen is. The second argument is that there may also be a question about this, since not everybody agrees that the same one is a citizen. For one who is a citizen in a democracy, in which the people rule, is sometimes not so considered in an oligarchy, in which the wealthy rule, since an oligarchy is often such that the people have no share in it.

3. Then he deals with what he proposes, dividing it into two parts. In the first, he shows what a citizen is. In the second, he shows which virtue makes a good citizen [chap. 3, n. 1]. Regarding the first, he does two things. First, he determines what a citizen is. Second, he raises some questions about this [chap. 2, n. 1]. Regarding the first, he does two things. First, he shows what a citizen is regarding the truth of the matter. Second, he excludes a false definition [7]. Regarding the first, he does two things. First, he posits some ways in which some are citizens in a way but not absolutely. Second, he shows what a citizen is without qualification [4].

Therefore, he says first that we should for the moment leave aside those called citizens in a poetical way (i.e., metaphorically or analogously), since they are not truly citizens. And the first way is by residence, but we do not truly call people citizens merely because they dwell in the political community, since foreign residents and slaves dwell in the political community but are not citizens, absolutely speaking.

The second way is that some may call people citizens because they are subject to the jurisdiction of the political community. That is to say, they participate in the judicial system of the political community, sometimes gaining a favorable decision and sometimes an unfavorable decision (i.e., condemned), since this is appropriate even for those who make contracts but are not citizens of the same political community. But foreigner residents in some political communities do not fully participate as citizens in such a judicial system. Rather, if they wish to bring lawsuits, they need to hire a sponsor (i.e., one who swears to their obedience to the law). And so it is clear that foreign residents do not fully participate in the communal judicial system. And so they are not citizens in this regard, absolutely speaking, although one may call them citizens in a qualified sense.

Likewise, in a third way, we call children citizens, although they have not yet been enrolled as citizens, and we call old men citizens, although they have now been dropped from the rolls of citizens because they cannot perform the duties of citizens. For we do not call them citizens in an absolute sense but with qualification, children as underage, and old men as over the age that the status of citizen requires. Or if any other such thing should be added, it makes no difference. For it is clear what we mean to say, since we are now asking what a citizen is absolutely, without any addition being necessary to define or explain the word *citizen*.

And there is also a fourth way regarding which there is the same question and answer, namely, regarding exiles and base persons (i.e., persons of ill repute), since such persons are citizens in a way but not absolutely.

4.   Then he shows what a citizen is, absolutely speaking. And regarding this, he does three things. First, he posits a definition of citizen. Second, he shows that the definition is not common to every regime [5]. Third, he shows how the definition can be revised to fit every regime [6]. Therefore, he says first that nothing else can better define what a citizen is absolutely than the fact that one participates in the courts of the political community, namely, can decide cases about some matters, and in the ruling power of the political community, namely, has some power in its affairs.

But we should note that there are two kinds of offices. For some offices are specified for a fixed term, so that some political communities do not permit the same man to hold the same office twice, or do not permit him to hold it again for a fixed period of time (e.g., hold an office for a year and then be ineligible to hold it for three or four years). And the other kind of office is one in which there is no term limit. Rather, the individual can exercise the office at any time (e.g., juror-judges, namely, those who have the power to decide certain cases, and members of the assembly, who have the power to vote in the assembly of the political community). And some may not call such juror-judges and members of the assembly rulers and may say that they do not hold any office simply because they can vote in the assembly or judge cases. But this does not matter at all for the point at issue, since this objection is only about the name. For there is no common word for juror-judge and member of the assembly, and so we supply the term *unspecified office*. Therefore, we hold that those who share in such ruling power are citizens, and this seems to be a better definition of citizen, absolutely speaking.

5.   Then he shows that such a definition of citizen is not common to all regimes. He says that it ought to be obvious that, in all matters in which individual things differ specifically, one by nature primary, another secondary, and something else next (i.e., next sequentially), there is nothing common in them, as there is not in the case of equivocal things. Or else there is scarcely anything common in them (i.e., common to a degree). And as he will say later [chap. 6, nn. 1–4], regimes differ specifically, some primary, and others secondary. For regimes that are deformed and violate

right order are by nature secondary to good regimes, as the perfect in any genus is by nature prior to what is defective. And he will show later how some regimes violate right order [chap. 5, n. 7]. And so there needs to be a different consideration of citizen in different regimes.

And so the aforementioned definition of citizen most of all belongs to a democracy, in which anyone of the people has the power to decide cases about some matters and be a member of the assembly. But any citizen in other regimes may sometimes have this power, although this is not necessary, since the people do not have any power as citizens in some regimes. Nor do the latter regimes consider the assembly (i.e., the formal congregation of the people) important but look only to meetings called for special purposes. And only such persons, divided into groups, render particular decisions. For example, the ephors in Sparta decide cases involving contracts, but different ephors, one or another of them, decide different cases at different times. The elders decide homicide cases, and other officials decide other cases. And so also is it with the Carthaginians, since certain rulers decide all cases, and so ordinary citizens do not participate in the judicial system. And so the aforementioned definition of citizen is inappropriate in such regimes.

6.   Then he corrects the aforementioned definition of citizen, saying that it can be related to what is common in regimes, since members of the assembly and juror-judges in regimes other than democracy do not hold office for an indeterminate period of time. Rather, these two things belong only to those who hold office for a fixed period of time, since it belongs to some or even all of such persons to decide cases and deliberate in the assembly, whether about some or all things. And this can show what a citizen is. For a citizen is not one who participates in the courts and assembly but one who can be constituted in legislative or judicial office, since those who cannot be assumed into such offices seem not to participate in the regime in any way and so not to be citizens.

And finally, he infers from this that the political community is nothing but a multitude of such persons, a big enough number for self-sufficiency (i.e., a self-sufficient life), absolutely speaking. For the political community is a self-sufficient association, as he said in Book I [chap. 1, n. 1].

7.   Then he excludes a definition of citizen that some use, saying that they determine by custom that one born of citizen parents on both sides, not only on one side, namely, a father's or mother's, is a citizen. And some require something further for one to be a citizen, namely, that he be descended from citizen ancestors to the second, third, or more generations. And if one should so define citizen politically (i.e., by the custom of some political communities) and summarily (i.e., before due inquiry), the question arises regarding how the third- or fourth-generation ancestor was a

citizen. For according to the aforementioned definition, one could not be said to have been a citizen unless he should trace his ancestry back to the third or fourth citizen ancestor. And so this will be to regress endlessly.

And regarding this, he cites the saying of Gorgias, a Sicilian of Leontini, who said some wise words about the aforementioned definitions, whether because he was uncertain, or because he spoke ironically. He said that, as mortars are the things made by mortar makers, so also the citizens of Larissa are the people made (i.e., begotten) by other citizens of Larissa, who make them citizens of Larissa. But this saying is too simple and irrational, since, if some participate in the regime according to the definition we have mentioned, we need to say that they are citizens even if citizens do not beget them. Otherwise, the definition that they give cannot be applied to the original people who built or dwelt in the city, and it is obvious that the original people were not descended from citizens of that city. And so it would follow that the original people were not citizens, and so none of the others descended from them were. And this is odd.

Chapter 2
Regime Change

Text (1275b34–1276b15)

1. But those who participate after a regime change, like those Cleisthenes created at Athens after the expulsion of the tyrants, perhaps pose a bigger question. For he added many foreign residents and foreign slaves to the tribes. But the question is not whether these persons are citizens, but whether they are rightly or wrongly such.

2. And one will further question in this matter whether one who is wrongly a citizen is really a citizen, assuming that *wrong* and *false* mean the same thing. But we see that some rulers rule unjustly, and we shall indeed say that they rule, albeit unjustly. And we have defined citizen by ruling power, and those who share in such power are citizens, as we say. Therefore, it is clear that we should admit that even such persons are citizens.

3. And the question about the right or wrong way of being citizens is joined to the previously mentioned question. For some question when the

political community has acted and when not (e.g., if an oligarchy or
tyranny should become a democracy). After such a regime change, some do
not want to fulfill the agreements made by a tyrant, since he, not the political community, made them, or to honor many other such things, and they
assume that certain regimes exist for private benefit, not the benefit of the
community. Therefore, if some regimes have been transformed into such
a democracy, we should say similarly that the actions of such a regime, like
those of an oligarchy or a tyrant, belong to the political community.

4.   And this seems to be part of another question: How should we say
that a city is the same or different? Therefore, a superficial investigation of
this question concerns territory and population. For the territory and
population may be divided, some of the population in one place and some
in another. Therefore, we should consider this a less important question,
since we use the word *city* in many senses, and this somehow makes such a
question less important. Likewise, when should we consider that there is
one political community of human beings dwelling in the same territory?
It is not due to walls, since a wall will circumscribe the Peloponnese.
Perhaps Babylon and every city that includes one ethnic people rather
than one political community are like that. (People say that, two days after
the capture of Babylon, one part of the city did not know about it.) But it
will be opportune for us to consider this question later. For a statesman
should not be ignorant about the size of a political community, namely,
how many are the inhabitants, and whether one or several ethnic peoples
are beneficial.

5.   But with the same population dwelling in the same place, there remains the question whether we should say that the political community is
the same as long as the inhabitants belong to the same ethnic stock, although one generation succeeds another. Just so, we are accustomed to say
that rivers and their sources are the same although there is always an in-
flow and an outflow.

6.   Or should we say that the population is the same for such a reason,
but that the political community is different? If the political community is
an association, and an association of citizens in a regime, it will seem to be
necessary that when the regime has become specifically different and
other, the political community is also different. Just so, we say that a chorus
that sometimes sings in a comedy and other times sings in a tragedy is different in the two forms, although it often has the same members. And it is
the same with every other union and composition if a composition should
be specifically different. For example, we shall say that the harmony of the
same notes is different if it is sometimes in the Dorian mode and other
times in the Phrygian mode. And so, if the political community has the
same mode, it is clear that we, regarding the regime, should especially say

that it is the same. And we are permitted to call it by the same name or a different one, whether the population is same or altogether different. But it is another question whether it is right to honor agreements when the political community is transformed into a different regime.

Comment

1.   After Aristotle determined what a citizen is, he here makes clear some questions about the aforementioned things and answers them. He poses four successive questions. The first concerns those taken into the association of a regime after a regime change, as a certain wise man named Cleisthenes did with the Athenians after the tyrants were expelled. For Cleisthenes added many foreign residents and some foreign slaves to the associations of the political community, so that the ranks of the people were increased, and so that the wealthy could not tyrannically oppress the people. And to answer this question, Aristotle says that the question regarding such persons is not whether they are citizens, since they are because they have been made such, but whether they are rightly or wrongly such.

2.   Aristotle poses a second question. For one can question whether one who is wrongly a citizen is really one. This is as if *wrongly* should mean the same as *falsely*, since it is clear that a false citizen is no citizen. And he answers that, since we consider those who rule unjustly to be rulers nonetheless, we should by like argument also say that those who are wrongly citizens are citizens, since we call people citizens because they participate in some ruling power, as he has said before [chap. 1, n. 4].

3.   He poses a third question, saying that whether or not one is rightly a citizen seems to be linked to the preceding question that he raised at the beginning of this book [chap. 1, n. 1]. In regime changes of a political community, there is usually a question about when some deed is attributable to the political community, and when it is not. For example, the regime of a political community may sometimes be transformed from a tyranny or oligarchy into a democracy, and then the people, receiving the power of the regime, do not want to carry out agreements made by tyrants or the wealthy previously ruling. For people say that if things have been promised to a tyrant or the wealthy of the political community, the political community did not receive them. And it is thus in many such things, since those in charge of some regimes obtain things from others for their own benefit and not the common benefit of the political community.

And he answers this question as follows. Let us assume that the political community remains the same after its regime has changed. Then, as the things done by a democracy are acts of the political community, so are the things done by an oligarchy or tyranny, since, as the tyrant or wealthy formerly held power in the political community, so also do the people in a democracy.

4.   He poses a fourth question. First, he poses this question in general, saying that the proper way to answer it is to indicate how one should call a city the same or different.

Second, he divides the aforementioned question into two parts, saying that it superficially seems to be about two things, namely, the territory and the population of a city. For the population may sometimes be territorially separate in various ways (e.g., when all citizens are expelled from a city, they are transported to different places). Therefore, if other inhabitants are introduced into the territory, there can be a question about whether or not there is the same political community. And this question is less serious (i.e., easier), since we speak about a city in many senses. In one sense, it means the territory, and then the city is the same. In another sense, it means the population, and then the city is different.

But then another question remains. For if the same population always dwells in the same place, there can be a question about when it is or is not one political community. And he first excludes one concept of unity, saying that one cannot say that those dwelling in a city preserve the same political community because the city's walls are the same. For, although a wall might enclose a whole region (e.g., the Peloponnese, which is Achaia), there would not be the same political community. And such was the case of Babylon or any other very large city that includes one ethnic people rather than one political community. For example, he says that when the city of Babylon was captured, one part did not know about it for three days because of the breadth of the enclosed city.

And he interposes that he will need to consider elsewhere about the question whether it is beneficial that a political community be so large.[3] For it belongs to a statesman to know how large the size of the political community should be, and whether it should contain human beings of one or many ethnic peoples.

5.   Then he inquires about another concept of unity, namely, whether, if the population in a territory remains the same, we should call the political community the same because the inhabitants are of the same ethnic stock, namely, because one generation succeeds another, although the human beings are numerically different. Just so, we say that rivers and their

---

3. Ibid. VII, 4 (1325b33–1326b25).

sources are the same because of the constant flow of the water, although some water flows out, and other water flows in.

6.   Then, answering this question, he shows the true nature of the unity of a political community. He says that we can in some way say that there is the same population because of the aforementioned successive generation, but not that the political community is the same if the organization of a regime should be transformed. For, inasmuch as the association of citizens, which we call the regime, belongs to the nature of political community, it is clear that the political community does not remain the same after a regime change. Just so, we perceive regarding singers in a chorus that it is not the same chorus if it should sometimes perform in a comedy (i.e., sing comic songs about the deeds of ordinary persons) and other times in a tragedy (i.e., sing tragic songs about the wars of rulers). And so also we perceive in all other things consisting of a composition or union that there is a different identity whenever there is a specifically different kind of composition. For example, there is a different harmony if it should sometimes be in the Doric mode (i.e., of the seventh or eighth tone) and other times in the Phrygian mode (i.e., of the third or fourth tone).

Therefore, since all such things have this way, it is clear that we should call the political community the same in regard to the organization of its regime. And so, when the organization of the regime has been transformed, but the territory and the population remain the same, the political community is different even though materially the same. And one may then call the transformed political community by the same or a different name, whether the population be the same or different, but there will be equivocation if the same name is used. But whether or not, on account of the fact that a political community is different after a regime change, it is right that agreements of a prior regime be honored belongs to another consideration that he will consider later.[4]

---

4. Aristotle does not return to this consideration.

Chapter 3
The Virtue of a Good Man and
the Virtue of a Good Citizen

Text (1276b16–1277b32)

1. In connection with the foregoing, we need to consider whether or not the virtue of a good man and the virtue of a good citizen are the same. But if we need to decide this by inquiry, we should first understand the virtue of a citizen in a preliminary outline.

2. Therefore, as a sailor is the member of a crew, so also a citizen is the member of a community. And although sailors have different functions, one being an oarsman, another the pilot, another the lookout, and so on, it is clear that the proper nature of the virtue of each will be most precise, but also that a common virtue belongs to them all. For the business of all the sailors is a safe voyage, since each sailor desires this. Likewise, therefore, the business of all the citizens, however dissimilar they may be, is the safety of the community. But the community is a regime. Therefore, the virtue of a citizen is necessarily in relation to a regime. Therefore, if there are many kinds of regime, it is clear that there cannot be the same complete virtue of a good citizen. But we call a man good by reason of the same complete virtue. Therefore, it is clear that one may be a good citizen and not have the virtue whereby one is a good human being.

3. Moreover, in another way, our inquiry comes to the same argument about the best regime. For if it is not possible that the political community should consist entirely of good men, and if each one needs to do his proper task well, and this by his virtue, then, since all citizens cannot be alike, there will not be the same virtue of a good citizen and a good man. For the virtue of a good citizen needs to be in all citizens, since the political community is then necessarily the best. But it is impossible that all citizens have the virtue of a good man unless every citizen in a good political community is necessarily a good man.

4. Further, a political community is composed of dissimilar parts, as an animal is immediately composed of soul and body, the human soul of reason and desire, a household of a husband and wife, and estates of masters and slaves. In the same way, a political community is also composed of all these and still other dissimilar kinds of things. Therefore, there need not be one and the same virtue of all citizens, any more than the ability of a

dance master and that of an assistant need to be the same. Therefore, these things make clear that the virtue of citizens differs.

5.   But perhaps the virtue of a particular good citizen will be the same as that of a good man. And so we say that a virtuous ruler is good and practically wise, and a statesman needs to be practically wise.

6.   And some say that there is from the start a different education for rulers (i.e., the sons of kings seem to be educated in riding and war). And Euripides, as if speaking about the education of a ruler, said that there is no need to know diverse or lofty things but only things necessary for the political community. Therefore, if the goodness of a good man and that of a good ruler are the same, and a subject is also a citizen, the goodness of a good citizen and that of a good man will not be the same, absolutely speaking, but only in the case of a particular citizen, namely, one capable of ruling. For the virtue of a ruler and that of an ordinary citizen are not the same, and Jason on this account said that he went hungry when he was not a tyrant, as if not knowing how to be an ordinary person.

7.   But it is praiseworthy to be able to rule and to be ruled, and the virtue of a good citizen is to be able to rule and to be ruled well. Therefore, if we hold that the virtue of a good man is virtue in ruling, and that the virtue of a citizen is virtue in both ruling and obeying, the two virtues will not be equally praiseworthy.

8.   Therefore, it sometimes seems that the ruler and the subject need to learn the different things proper to each, and that the citizen needs to know both how to rule and how to be ruled, and how to participate in both. And we will consider the matter from this point of view.

9.   For there is despotic rule, and such a ruler needs to know how to use, not exercise, the power regarding so-called necessary tasks. Anything more is servile. By servile, I mean anything that slaves can do and do. And we speak of many kinds of servants. For there are many such activities, one of which manual workers perform, and these are, as the term indicates, those workers who earn their living by their hands, and common artisans are included among them. And it is for this reason that some say that artisans did not participate in ruling power in former times, before there was an extreme democracy. Therefore, neither a good man nor a statesman needs to learn the tasks of subjects, nor does a good citizen need to learn them, except sometimes for the opportunity the works offer him for personal benefit. For then there can no longer be a distinction between master and slave.

10.   But there is a rule in which the ruler rules over those born equal to him and free. For we say that this rule is political, and the ruler needs to learn this as a subject. Just so, one who was a junior officer in the cavalry later commands it, and one who was a junior army officer in charge of a

unit and planned attacks later commands the army. For this reason, people say, and say correctly, that one who was never subject to a ruler does not rule well.

11.   The virtue of ruling and that of being ruled differ, but the good citizen needs to know how and be able to do both, and the virtue of a citizen is to know how to rule over free men regarding both. And both belong to a good man, although there is a different kind of moderation and justice in the case of ruling. For it is clear that the virtue (e.g., justice) of a free and good subject will not be the same but take the different forms by which he will rule or be ruled. (Just so, the moderation and courage of a man and those of a woman are different. A man will seem cowardly if he should be only as brave as a brave woman, and a woman will seem loquacious if she should be as ornate in speech as a good man. For men and women have different functions even in household management, men to acquire things, and women to conserve them.) But practical wisdom is the only virtue proper to a ruler, since other virtues seem necessarily to be common to subjects and rulers. And true opinion, not the virtue of practical wisdom, belongs to subjects. For a subject is like a flute-maker, and a ruler like a flute-player using the flute. Therefore, these things make clear whether the virtue of a good man and that of a good citizen are the same or different, and how the same or different.

Comment

1.   After Aristotle showed what a citizen is, he here inquires about the virtue of a citizen, dividing the inquiry into two parts. In the first part, he shows that the virtue of a citizen and that of a good man are not absolutely the same. In the second part, he raises certain questions [chap. 4, n. 1]. Regarding the first, he does two things. First, he shows that the virtue of a good citizen and that of a good man are not absolutely the same. Second, he shows that the virtue of a particular citizen is the same as that of a good man [5]. Regarding the first, he does two things. First, he speaks about his aim, since, in connection with the aforementioned things (i.e., after them), we need to consider whether we ought to hold that the virtue of a good citizen and that of a good man are the same, and this is to ask whether we call someone a good man and a good citizen by the same consideration. For virtue makes its possessor good. And in order for this question to receive a proper investigation, we need first to show in outline (i.e., schematically and comparatively) what the virtue of a citizen is.

2.   Second, he gives three arguments to show that the virtue of a citizen and that of a good man are not the same. In the first, he offers a comparison to show what the virtue of a good citizen is, saying that, as the word

sailor signifies something common to many individuals, so also does the word *citizen*. And he demonstrates that being a sailor is common to many individuals. For we call many individuals sailors, although they are dissimilar in powers (i.e., skills and functions), one an oarsman who rows the ship, one the pilot who steers the ship, and one the lookout (i.e., the sentinel at the prow, which is the front of the ship), and others have other names and other functions. And it is clear that something as proper virtue and something as common virtue belong to each of these sailors. For it belongs to the proper virtue of each sailor to take diligent account and care of his special function (e.g., the pilot care of piloting, and so forth). And there is a common virtue that belongs to all of the sailors, since the work of all of them strives for a safe voyage. For the desire and aim of any sailor strives for this, and the common virtue of sailors (i.e., the virtue of a sailor as such) is directed to this. So also, although different citizens have different duties and positions in the political community, the common work of all is the safety of the community, and the community consists of the good order of its regime. And so it is clear that we consider the virtue of a citizen as such in relation to the regime, namely, that a good citizen is one who works for the preservation of the regime.

But there are many kinds of regime, as he will say later [chap. 6, nn. 1–4], and this is to a degree clear from things he said before [II, chap. 7, nn. 1–6, and chap. 17, nn. 2–3]. And different virtues rightly order human beings to different regimes. For example, democracies are preserved in one way, and oligarchies and tyrannies in other ways. And so it is clear that there is no one complete virtue by which we can call a citizen absolutely good. Rather, we call a man good regarding one complete virtue, namely, practical wisdom, on which all the moral virtues depend. Therefore, one may be a good citizen but not have the virtue by which one is a good man, and this is the case in regimes other than the best regime.
3.   He gives a second argument, saying that we can by inquiry or argument arrive in another way at the same conclusion, even regarding the best regime, namely, that the virtue of the good citizen and that of a good man are not the same. For, however good the regime may be, it is impossible for all citizens to be good men. Rather, each citizen needs to do well his own work pertaining to the political community, and he does this by the virtue of a citizen as such. And so I say "his own work" because all citizens cannot be so alike that the same work belongs to all of them. And so the virtue of a good citizen and that of a good man are not the same. And he then demonstrates this conclusion. For any citizen in the best regime should have the virtue of a good citizen, since the political community will be best in this way. But it is impossible that all citizens have the virtue of a good man, since not all in a political community are good men, as he has just said.

4.   And he gives a third reason, saying that every political community consists of dissimilar parts. Just so, an animal is at once composed of a soul and a body, and the human soul likewise composed of dissimilar things, namely, the powers of reason and desire. And also, the household association consists of dissimilar things, namely, men and women. And also, estates consist of masters and slaves. And the political community consists of all these differences and many others. And he has said that the virtue of the ruler and that of the subject are not the same regarding the soul and other things [I, chap. 10, nn. 7–8]. And so also he concludes that the virtue of all citizens is not one and the same. Just so, we perceive that the virtue of a dance master (i.e., the director) and that of his helper (i.e., assistant) are not the same. But it is clear that the virtue of a good man is one and the same. Therefore, he concludes that the virtue of a good citizen and that of a good man are not the same.

5.   Then he shows that that the virtue of a particular citizen is the same as that of a good man. And regarding this, he does three things. First, he shows what he proposes. Second, he infers the conclusion implicit in the foregoing [6]. Third, he raises a question about the foregoing and answers it [7]. Therefore, he says first that someone could perhaps say that a particular citizen, in order to be a good one, needs the same virtue as that of a good man. For we do not say that someone is a good ruler unless he should be good by reason of his moral virtues and practical wisdom. For he has said in the *Ethics* that politics is a part of practical wisdom.[5] And so it is necessary that a statesman (i.e., the ruler of a regime) be practically wise and consequently a good man.

6.   Then he infers from this that the virtue of a good citizen is not, absolutely speaking, the same as that of a good man. And to prove this, he first introduces the statement of some people that the education of a ruler, which should instruct him for virtue, is different from the education of a citizen, as the instruction of sons of kings in riding and warfare demonstrates. And so also Euripides, speaking in the person of a ruler, said that it was not necessary to know diverse and lofty things, namely, things that philosophers consider, but only things necessary for governing the political community. And Euripides said this to signify that there is a proper education of a ruler. And Aristotle infers from this that, if the education and virtue of a good ruler should be the same as that of a good man, and not every citizen is a ruler, subjects also being citizens, then the virtue of a citizen and that of a good man are not the same, absolutely speaking. (There may be an exception in the case of a particular citizen, namely, one

---

5. *Ethics* VI, 7 (1141b29–33).

capable of being a ruler.) And this is so because the virtue of a ruler and that of a citizen are different. And Jason said on this account that he went hungry when he was not a tyrant, as if he were not to know how to live as a simple (i.e., private) person.

7.   Then he raises a question about the foregoing. Regarding this, he does two things. First, he raises an objection against the foregoing. Second, he answers it [8]. Therefore, he says first that people sometimes praise a citizen because he can rule and be ruled well. Therefore, if the virtue of a good man is the virtue of a good ruler, and the virtue of a good citizen is disposed for both, namely, to rule and to be ruled, then both, namely, being a good citizen and being a good man, are not equally praiseworthy. Rather, being a good citizen is much better.

8.   Then he answers the aforementioned objection. First, he considers how the education of the ruler and that of the subject are the same, and how different. Second, he shows how there is the same virtue of both [11]. Regarding the first, he does three things. First, he proposes his aim. And he says that, as he said before [6–7], that each of the these propositions, namely, that ruler and subject need not learn the same things, and that a good citizen should know both, namely, how to rule and how to be ruled, sometimes seems plausible. Therefore, he says that we need to consider how each is true, as follows.

9.   Second, he lays out one kind of rule in which one of the aforementioned propositions, namely, that the education of the ruler and that of the subject are different, is verified. And he says that it is despotic (i.e., autocratic) rule, one in which the ruler is a master over his subjects. Such a ruler needs to know how to use, not how to perform, things pertaining to the services necessary for daily living. And the other element, namely, being able to perform things pertaining to the activity of servants, seems to be servile rather than proper to a ruler or master.

And there are different kinds of slaves regarding the different activities of servants, of whom manual laborers (e.g., cobblers, cooks, and the like) constitute one part. Manual laborers earn their living by the works of their hands, as the name indicates, and among such are reckoned common artisans (i.e., those who get dirty by the work of their skill), as he said before [I, chap. 9, n. 5]. And since the activities of such artisans are proper to slaves, not rulers, some of antiquity did not allow artisans to have any part in the ruling power of the political community. And I say this was the case before there was an extreme democratic, or popular, rule (i.e., before the lowest class of people assumed power in political communities).

Therefore, it is clear that neither a good statesman (i.e., the ruler of a political community) nor a good citizen needs to learn such tasks of subjects. A possible exception would be to learn such things to benefit themselves, not to serve others, since there would then not be any distinction between master and slave if masters performed such servile works.

10. Third, he lays out another kind of rule in which the other proposition, namely, that the ruler and the subjects should learn the same things, is verified. And he says that it is the kind of rule in which a ruler rules over persons free and equal to himself, not as a master over slaves. And this is political rule, in which now some, now others, in the political community are constituted rulers. And such a ruler needs to learn as a subject how he ought to rule. Just so, one learns how to command cavalry by having been a subaltern in it, and one learns how to command an army by having been a junior officer in charge of a particular unit (e.g., a company or cohort) and planning attacks at the command of a general. For a human being learns how to exercise great office by being a subordinate and carrying out lesser duties. And regarding this, the proverb says well that one who has not been subject to a ruler cannot rule well.

11. Then he shows how the virtue of a ruler and that of others are the same or different. And he says that the virtue of a ruler and that of a subject are different even in political rule, but that one who is, absolutely speaking, a good citizen needs to know both how to rule and how to be ruled, namely, according to the political rule over free men, not the despotic rule over slaves. And the virtue of such a citizen consists of being well disposed to both, namely, ruling well and being ruled well, and both also belong to a good man. And so the virtue of a good citizen insofar as he is able to rule is the same as the virtue of a good man, but insofar as a citizen is a subject, the virtue of a ruler and a good man is different from the virtue of a good citizen. For example, there are different kinds of moderation and justice in a ruler and in a subject. For a subject who is free and good does not possess only one kind of virtue (e.g., justice). Rather, he has two kinds of justice, by one of which he can rule well, and by the other of which he is a good subject. And the same is true about other virtues.

And he demonstrates this by an example. Moderation and courage are different in men and women, since we will consider a man a coward if he should be no braver than a brave woman, and a woman, to whom reticence belongs, loquacious if she should be as ornate in speech (i.e., fluent) as a good man. And this is so because, even in household management, some things belong to a man, and other things to a woman. For it belongs to the husband to acquire wealth and to the wife to conserve them. And such is also the case regarding the ruler and the subject in a political community. For the ruler's virtue in the proper sense is practical wisdom, which directs and governs human action, but other, moral virtues, which essentially consist of being governed and ruled, are common to subjects and rulers. Nonetheless, subjects share in practical wisdom to a degree, namely, to the extent that they have a true opinion about things to be done and can thereby govern themselves in their own actions according to the ruler's governance.

And he gives as an example a flute-maker, who is related to a flute-player using a flute in the same way that a subject is related to the ruler. For a flute-maker performs his work well if he should have an opinion governed by what a flute-player commands. And such is the case in the political community regarding subjects and the ruler. And he is here speaking about the virtue of a subject as a good subject, not as a good man as such, since the subject then needs to have practical wisdom. For the only requirement for being a good subject is that he have a true opinion of the things commanded of him.

And in a final epilogue, he concludes that the foregoing makes clear whether the virtue of a good man and that of a good citizen are the same or different. It also makes clear how they are the same, and how different, since they are the same insofar as a man is capable of ruling well, and different insofar as he is capable of being ruled well.

Chapter 4
The Virtue of a Good Citizen
in Different Regimes

Text (1277b33–1278b5)

1. And there still remains a question about the citizen. Is the citizen one who is allowed to participate in ruling? Or are we also to consider common artisans citizens? Therefore, if we should consider as citizens even those who do not participate in ruling, the virtue of a good citizen cannot belong to every citizen, since common artisans are citizens. But if no common artisans are citizens, in what part of the community should we include them, since they are neither foreign residents nor foreign visitors? 2. Or shall we say that nothing improper results from such reasoning, since neither slaves nor former slaves fit into any of aforementioned

classes? It is true that we need not consider all persons necessary for the existence of the political community to be citizens. For example, children and grown men are not citizens in the same way. The men are absolutely such, and the children qualifiedly such, since they are not mature. Therefore, common artisans and foreigners were slaves with some ancient peoples. And thus many are such even now, and the best political community will not make common artisans citizens. But even if the common artisan is a citizen, we need to say that the virtue of a citizen about which we are speaking does not belong to everyone or to every free man but to one who is free from necessary tasks. And common artisans and hired hands in public service, as well as personal slaves, perform such tasks.

3.   And a little further consideration shows how it stands with common artisans, since what we have said makes this clear. For, inasmuch as there are many regimes, there need to be many kinds of citizens, especially subject citizens. Therefore, common artisans and hired hands need to be citizens in one regime, but this is impossible in others. For example, it is impossible if the regime is the one people call aristocratic, in which offices are awarded on the basis of virtue and merit, since it is impossible for one living the life of a common artisan or hired hand to produce things proper to virtue. And in oligarchies, a hired hand cannot be a citizen, since only those of long-standing rank share in ruling, although a common artisan can be, since many artisans are wealthy. Moreover, there was a law in Thebes that only one who had refrained from business for ten years shared in power. And in many regimes, a law also admits foreigners to citizenship. For in some democracies, those born of a citizen mother are citizens. And many peoples apply this principle to illegitimate sons. But they make such persons citizens because they lack enough legitimate citizens, for, not having a large population, they employ these laws to remedy the shortage. Therefore, little by little, they at first elect to citizenship those born of a citizen and a slave father or mother, then only those born of a citizen mother, and finally only those born of citizens on both sides. Therefore, these things make clear that there are many kinds of citizens.

4.   And we say that a citizen is most of all one who shares in offices. (Just so, Homer said poetically that a certain person rising to speak after others is like one disenfranchised.) And when this is concealed, it is to mislead cohabitants. For one who has no share in offices is like a resident foreigner.

5.   Therefore, whether we should hold that the virtue by which one is a good man is the same as, or different from, the virtue by which one is a good citizen, it is clear that a good man and a good citizen are the same in one political community and different in another. And where they are the

same, not every citizen is such but only the one who is a statesman and master, or one capable of being a master, in care of the community's affairs, whether alone or with others.

Comment

1.   After Aristotle showed what the virtue of a citizen is, and whether it is the same as the virtue of a good man, he here raises a question about what he has determined before. And regarding this, he does three things. First, he raises the question. Second, he answers it [2]. Third, he clarifies the answer [3].

Therefore, he says first that there still remains a question about the citizen, namely, whether we should consider as citizens only those who can share in the ruling power, or also common (i.e., the lowest) artisans, who cannot. And he raises an objection to each position. For if we should call common artisans, to whom nothing concerning political communities belongs, citizens, then the virtue that we said belongs to a good citizen, namely, to be able to rule and be ruled well, does not belong to every citizen, since we thereby consider as a citizen one who cannot rule. But if we should say that none such is a citizen, there will remain a question about the class in which we should include common artisans. For we cannot say that they are foreign residents, as if they come from abroad to dwell in the city. Nor can we call them foreign visitors, who come to the city for the sake of some business, not for the sake of permanently residing. For such artisans reside in the city and, having been born there, do not come from abroad.

2.   Then he answers the aforementioned question, saying that nothing ill fitting results from the foregoing argument raising a question about the class in which we should include artisans if they were not citizens. For there are many noncitizens who are not foreign residents or foreign visitors, as is clear in the case of slaves and freedmen emancipated from slavery.

Truly, not all those necessary for the perfection of the political community, without whom the political community cannot exist, are citizens, since we perceive that slaves and youths are not citizens as completely as adult men. For adult men are citizens absolutely, capable of doing the things that belong to citizens, as it were. But youths are citizens conditionally (i.e., with a limiting specification), since they are not mature. And as slaves and youths are citizens in a way but not completely, so also this is the case regarding artisans. And so, in ancient times, common (i.e., the lowest) artisans, who get dirty from the work of their skills, and foreigners were slaves in some political communities,[6] as many are even now. But common artisans even now cannot be citizens in the best organized political community.

And if we should say that a common artisan is a citizen in a way, then we need to say that the virtue of a citizen that we have specified [chap. 3, nn. 2 and 11], namely, the capacity to rule and be ruled well, does not belong to each citizen in whatsoever way we call persons citizens. Rather, in order that such a virtue belong to citizens, they need to be both free men and free (i.e., relieved) of the tasks necessary for daily life. For if those assigned to such necessary tasks should serve only one individual, this belongs properly to slaves, since slaves customarily performed such services for their masters. But if they should perform these services for anybody in general, this belongs to common artisans and hired hands. For example, cobblers and bakers serve anybody for money.

3.   Then he clarifies the proposed answer, doing three things in this regard. First, he shows how one is a citizen in different ways in different regimes. Second, he shows that one who participates in ruling is most a citizen in any regime [4]. Third, he sums up in an epilogue the things he has said about the virtue of a citizen [5]. Therefore, he says first that the truth about the foregoing will be clarified by briefly considering the things that follow. For if one should completely perceive what will be said, what has been said will become clear to the person.

Since there are indeed many specifically different regimes, and we speak of citizens in relation to regimes, as he has said [chap. 1, n. 2], it is also necessary that there be many kinds of citizens. And we most consider this difference regarding citizen subjects, who are related to ruling in different ways in different regimes, and those in charge in any regime are its rulers. And so, because of different regimes, and so different kinds of citizens, common artisans and hired hands are necessarily citizens in a particular regime, namely, a democracy, in which liberty is the sole end, since they could be promoted to office because they are free. But in other regimes, this is impossible, as is especially the case in an aristocracy, in which offices are awarded to those worthy by reason of their virtue. On the other hand, those who live the life of common artisans or hired hands

---

6. Aquinas reads the Latin text of Aristotle to mean that common artisans and foreigners were slaves in some political communities. His reading is possible, but an alternate reading consistent with the extant Greek text, namely, that common artisans were slaves or foreigners, seems more probable, as the context favors the latter reading. I translated the text of Aristotle to accommodate Aquinas' reading.

cannot, in ruling, produce for the political community things proper to virtue, since they are not experienced in such things.

And in an oligarchy, hired hands cannot be citizens, since persons are raised to office because of past long-standing honors. And so it cannot happen that hired hands, who can hardly accumulate in their lifetime enough money to become wealthy, are easily raised to offices. But common artisans (i.e., lowly skilled workers) in such regimes can be citizens and rulers in such regimes, since many artisans quickly become wealthy and so can because of their wealth be raised to offices. For, having abstained from their occupation for a period of time after they became wealthy, they have led honorable lives. And so the Thebans had a law that only those who had refrained from commercial affairs for ten years could share in power, namely, the power to rule.

But although foreign visitors, foreign residents, and persons of the lowest class could not be citizens capable of ruling, as it were, in rightly ordered political communities, the law in many regimes, namely, democracies, against foreign visitors and foreign residents being citizens is relaxed. For some democracies consider a person born of a citizen mother to be a citizen, although his father is a foreign resident or a foreign visitor. And so also the law of many peoples regarding illegitimate offspring is relaxed, namely, allows them to be citizens. But they do this because they are short of good citizens. And because of the shortage of citizens, they lack a sufficient population, in which the strength of a democracy consists, and employ such laws at first to admit as citizens those who are the offspring of a male or female slave, provided that the other parent is free. Then, with the population increasing, they exclude all the sons of slaves but consider as citizens those who are born of citizen mothers and foreign-resident fathers.[7] Finally, they come to consider as citizens only those born of both a free citizen mother and a free citizen father. Therefore, it is clear that there are different kinds of citizens according to the different kinds of regime.

4.   Then he shows what a citizen is especially, saying that he is most of all a citizen in any regime who participates in the offices of a political community. And so Homer said poetically of a certain person that he arose after others (e.g., to speak) as one dishonored (i.e., like a resident foreigner

---

7. Aquinas here distinguishes between all sons of slaves (even with citizen mothers) and the sons of resident foreigners with citizen mothers. But the Latin text of Aristotle distinguishes the sons of a citizen mother and a slave father from the sons of a citizen father and a slave mother, with the former no longer admitted to citizenship.

who was not a citizen). But where this aspect of citizen is hidden in order to deceive, citizenship belongs to a city's cohabitants, namely, so that people call all who inhabit the city citizens. But this is improper, since those who do not share in the offices of a political community are like foreign residents in it.

5. Then he sums up in an epilogue what he has said. Regarding the question that he asked, whether the virtue of a good man and that of a good citizen are the same, he says that he has shown that in one political community, namely, the aristocratic one, a good man and a good citizen are the same. That is to say, offices are awarded according to the virtue that belongs to a good man. But in other political communities, namely, corrupt regimes in which offices are not awarded according to virtue, the good citizen and the good man are different. Moreover, not every citizen is the same as a good man. Rather, the citizen who is a statesman (i.e., the ruler of a political community) and master, or one capable of being master, of things belonging to care of the community, whether alone or with others, is the same as a good man. For he has said before that the virtue of a ruler and that of a good man are the same [chap. 3, nn. 5 and 11]. And so, if we should understand citizen to mean the ruler or one capable of being ruler, the virtue of a citizen is the same as the virtue of a good man. But if we should understand citizen to mean one incompletely such (i.e., one incapable of being ruler), the virtue of a good citizen and that of a good man differ, as what he has said makes clear.

Chapter 5
The End of the Political Community

Text (1278a6–1279b21)

1. Since we have determined these things, we need next to consider whether we should posit one or many regimes, and if many, what kind and how many, and their differences.

2. And the regime is an organization of various offices of the political community, especially the one that controls all the others. For the governing body of the political community is everywhere supreme, and the governing body is the regime. And I say, for example, that the people control

in democracies, but the few control in oligarchies. And we also say that these regimes are different, and the same about other regimes.

3.   Therefore, we should first posit the purpose for which a political community is established and the kind and number of rule over its members and their common life.

4.   And at the beginning of this work, when I determined about household management and despotic rule, I said that human beings are by nature political animals. Therefore, they desire to live together even when they have no need of help from one another. Nonetheless, common benefit unites it insofar as the benefit contributes something to living well. Therefore, this is most of all the end of a political community both collectively and distributively. But people also form and maintain the political community for the sake of life itself. For there is perhaps some portion of good even in life itself, provided that life is not too beset with hardships. And it is clear that many people persevere in bearing many evils, absorbed in their desire to live, finding some solace and natural comfort in it, as it were.

5.   But it is easy to distinguish the said ways of ruling, and we indeed often determine about them in public discourses. For despotic rule, although only one thing, in fact benefits the one who is by nature a slave and the one who is by nature a master. A master rules for his own benefit but incidentally for the benefit of his slave, since there can be no rule of a master if his slave has died. And there is the rule over children, women, and the whole household that we call domestic, whether for the sake of the dependents or something common to both the one ruling the household and the dependents. This is intrinsically for the benefit of the dependents, just as we perceive that other skills (e.g., of doctors and physical trainers) benefit clients. But the skills will incidentally benefit the doctors and trainers, since nothing prevents a trainer from sometimes being a member of the team training, as a pilot is always part of a ship's crew. Therefore, a trainer or pilot considers the good of his subjects. But when he himself is also one of these, he shares incidentally in the benefit, the one as a sailor and the other as a member of the team while he is training it.

6.   So also citizens deem it right to hold political offices in turn when equal and like citizens constitute a regime. This was natural and suitable in former times. Citizens thought it right that they in turn perform public service, and that others in turn consider their good just as they, when ruling earlier, considered the others' benefit. But now, because of the benefits accruing from common goods and office, citizens want to rule continuously, as if those always ruling would be restored to health if they were to become ill. And they would indeed perhaps seek offices in this way.

7.   Therefore, it is clear that any regimes aiming to benefit the community are just, being in accord with absolute justice, but any regimes

benefiting only the rulers are unjust, and all of the latter are deviations from just regimes. For they are despotic, but the political community is an association of free men.

Comment

1.   After Aristotle determined about a citizen, from the knowledge of which one can know what a political community is, he here next aims to distinguish the kinds of regime, dividing this question into three parts. First, he distinguishes regimes. Second, he shows what is just in each.[8] Third, he shows which regime is better.[9] Regarding the first, he does three things. First, he speaks about his aim. Second, he shows what a regime is [2]. Third, he distinguishes regimes [3]. Therefore, he says first that, with the aforementioned things determined, it remains to consider whether there is only one regime or many, and if there are many, how many and what kind, and how they differ from one another.
2.   Then he shows what a regime is, saying that it is simply the organization of a political community regarding all its offices but especially its highest office, which controls all the other offices. And this is so because the whole governing body of the political community (i.e., its established order) rests in the ruler in control of the political community, and such an established order is the regime itself. And so the regime most consists of the organization of the supreme ruling power, different kinds of which distinguish regimes. For example, the people control in democracies, and the wealthy few control in oligarchies, and this distinguishes these regimes. And we should speak of other regimes in the same way.
3.   Then he distinguishes regimes. First, he shows how just regimes are distinguished from unjust ones. Second, he explains how both kinds of regimes are distinguished in themselves [chap. 6]. Regarding the first, he does three things. First, he shows toward what end the political community is directed. Second, he shows how the ruling powers are distinguished from one another [5]. Third, he infers the difference between just and unjust regimes [7]. Regarding the first, he does two things. First, he speaks of his aim. Second, he begins to carry out his aim [4].

Therefore, he says first that, since we need to distinguish regimes from one another, we need first to articulate two things: the reason why the political community is established and the number of different kinds of

---

8. *Politics* III, 9 (1280a7).
9. Ibid. III, 10 (1281a11).